The Influence of Mysticism
on 20th Century British
and American Literature

The Influence of Mysticism on 20th Century British and American Literature

DAVID GARRETT IZZO

McFarland & Company, Inc., Publishers
Jefferson, North Carolina, and London

ALSO OF INTEREST AND FROM MCFARLAND
Christopher Isherwood Encyclopedia, by David Garrett Izzo (2005)
W.H. Auden Encyclopedia, by David Garrett Izzo (2004)
The Writings of Richard Stern: The Education of an Intellectual Everyman, by David Garrett Izzo (2002)
Charles Chesnutt Reappraised: Essays on the First Major African American Ficiton Writer, edited by David Garrett Izzo and Maria Orban (2009)
Huxley's Brave New World: *Essays*, edited by David Garrett Izzo and Kim Kirkpatrick (2008)
Henry James Against the Aesthetic Movement: Essays on the Middle and Late Fiction, edited by David Garrett Izzo and Daniel T. O'Hara (2006)
Stephen Vincent Benét: Essays on His Life and Work, edited by David Garrett Izzo and Lincoln Konkle (2003)

LIBRARY OF CONGRESS CATALOGUING-IN-PUBLICATION DATA

Izzo, David Garrett.
 The influence of mysticism on 20th century British and American literature / David Garrett Izzo.
  p.   cm.
 Includes bibliographical references and index.

 ISBN 978-0-7864-4106-8
 softcover : 50# alkaline paper ∞

  1. English literature — 20th century — History and criticism.
  2. American literature — 20th century — History and criticism.
  3. Mysticism and literature — Great Britain. 4. Mysticism and literature — United States. 5. Mysticism in literature. I. Title.
 II. Title: Influence of mysticism on twentieth century British and American literature.
 PR478.M94I99   2009
 820.9'38 — dc22   2009009753

British Library cataloguing data are available

©2009 David Garrett Izzo. All rights reserved

No part of this book may be reproduced or transmitted in any form or by any means, electronic or mechanical, including photocopying or recording, or by any information storage and retrieval system, without permission in writing from the publisher.

Cover image: ©2009 Shutterstock

Manufactured in the United States of America

McFarland & Company, Inc., Publishers
 Box 611, Jefferson, North Carolina 28640
 www.mcfarlandpub.com

Contents

Preface: The Man of Steel as Mystic — 1
Introduction: The Comet That Changed the World — 5

1. Vedanta and Theosophy: Preludes to a New Literature — 13
2. Aldous Huxley and W.H. Auden: Mysticism as a Literary Theory — 23
3. Mystical Philosophy as Applied to Philosophers and Literary Theorists — 63
4. Mystical Theory Applied to 20th Century British Literature — 93
5. Mystical Theory as Applied to 20th Century American Literature — 129

Chapter Notes — 163
Bibliography — 167
Index — 181

To Carol Ann Carrody,
Laura Archera Huxley and Aldous Huxley

Preface:
The Man of Steel as Mystic

IN 1969 (AGE 19) I ATTENDED the annual National Comics Convention in New York City. Nineteen sixty-nine was the 30th anniversary of the first Superman comic. Kirk Alyn was an honored guest, as he was the first film Superman in serials of the mid-to-late forties. He was a member of the Vedanta Society of Southern California. At that time I had some vague mystical inclinations of an immature variety. Mr. Alyn talked to me very kindly — and in retrospect — very patiently about Vedanta. We corresponded briefly afterwards. I did not sustain a serious interest in Vedanta for many years after, although the idea of telling and writing stories did seem to me an "otherworldly" vocation.

By 1989, however, after years as a commercial writer and then as a high school teacher, I saw that in writing and teaching there was an ineffable "something" between readers, and then students. I renewed a now very serious interest in mysticism and Vedanta, which led me to Aldous Huxley and Christopher Isherwood as philosophers before I turned to their literary art. I was a philosopher first and came to literature somewhat through a side door. I have always believed that this is an important distinction that helped me to see literary art and then literary theory from a different perspective. This philosophical perspective also made it very difficult for me to see the modern literary theories as any more than derivative of the Perennial Philosophy. This is not necessarily to see fault with modern literary theory, but rather to see that these more recent theories are derivations with self-derived nomenclatures that only seem to give new importance to what had already been done before. T.S. Eliot said that once one had read the East, the West seemed to need to catch up with the East. In the perpetual continuum, every theory is a graduating event in the process of evolving consciousness. Each new generation finds a new way to say what has been said before. This is inevitable. One must learn the world through the influences of others, and the medium for learning is language. One cannot create in a vacuum. One responds to the known (past knowledge) before one can create new derivations from the previously known and add new knowledge (understanding) to the old knowledge. Even if one responds to the known in diametrically opposed rebelliousness, this is a reaction, an opposition that needs to be reconciled.

As for comic books, at age twelve (1962) I began reading Marvel Comics with the new breed of sensitive, angst-ridden superheroes who had frailties as a price to pay for their supernatural powers—Spider-man most of all. I loved them for I was certainly a sensitive adolescent with frailties. I saw myself in them in a pattern that began with the primitive storyteller. We want to see ourselves through a commiseration with others whether real or fictional. Heroism and goodness were and remain key components of an inner quest for a *Great Yearning*, a desire for some form of transcendence that stories can provide. Over time stories evolve into philosophies that try to tell us intellectually what we have already learned from the stories intuitively. Stories as food for the mind are as necessary to life as food for the body. Today, as I write this on 21 July 2007, I have just returned from seeing *Spider-man 3*, a fairytale of heroes, goodness, loyalty, devotion, and villains redeemed with their dying wishes. The audience loved it and so did this 57 year-old child who feels no differently than he did in 1962. (Spider-man is a version of the earliest primitive parables that were often spiritual in their intentions. On 9 July 2004 Jeffrey Weiss's article "Spider-man's Theme Appears in Many Faiths" was syndicated in U.S. newspapers.) I have known since I was 12 that I yearned for something more than an earthbound existence and that stories were a vicarious medium in trying to understand this. With comics I began. The comics caused the later encounter with Superman. I never was able to thank Mr. Alyn for his gift, as he left his body before his gift fully took hold of me. I thank him now.

A Bit about This Book's Organization

The work that follows intends to explicate the nature and background of mystical philosophy as the impetus for the creative impulse, and thus the *raison d'être* underlying all art, consciously or unconsciously.

The Introduction, "The Comet That Changed the World," explains the precepts and concepts that inform the following chapters and how a comet was an impetus for new influences on 20th century art and philosophy.

Chapter 1, "Vedanta and Theosophy: Preludes to a New Literature," examines these two late 19th century mystical movements that attracted artists and intellectuals, and will also elucidate the governing principles of each movement as a foundation for correlating the principles of mysticism so as to inform the subsequent chapters.

Chapter 2, "Aldous Huxley and W.H. Auden: Mysticism as a Literary Theory," compares these writers, not as literary artists but as essayists that wrote copiously on philosophy and aesthetics to a degree that could only have been reached by their relative co-existence —1919 to 1973 — as writers who were exposed to the same *Zeitgeist*, particularly the years between the wars. Both authors believed in mysticism and that art is a vehicle for mystical transcendence, such that their essays can be organized as a literary theory.

Chapter 3, "Mystical Philosophy as Applied to Philosophers and Literary Theorists," examines how mysticism (the Perennial Philosophy) as described in the ancient Hindu texts is the world's first recorded philosophy and traveled from India to the Orient, to the Middle East, to the Greco-Roman Empires and Europe, influencing subsequent thought systems with parallels to theorists and philosophers going back 400 years. The Perennial Philosophy is the precursor that later philosophies derive from.

Chapters 4 and 5 put mystical literary theory into practice as applied to 20th century British and American authors and each writer's *Weltanschauung*. A literary theory only works when it can be applied to all literary art. For example, one can apply a literary theory based on Jungian psychoanalysis retroactively to the Greek tragedies, and one can apply Jameson's neo–Marxian dialectic retroactively to Greek tragedies; mystical philosophy can also be applied retroactively to Greek tragedies. Jung, in fact, was influenced by the Vedas and said so; consequently, a Jungian analysis is a mystical analysis. Jameson was influenced by Hegel's dialectics (reconciliation of opposites), also from the Vedas. Actually, since mystical philosophy preceded the Greek tragedies, perhaps it is not retroactive but the forerunner of how these tragedies evolved.

A purpose of the present work is to demonstrate that the wisdom of mysticism underlies and precedes all wisdom in any discipline. Mystical philosophy as a literary theory applies to *all* literary artists beginning with the first stories told by the primitive storyteller. All literary artists are writing art as an outcome of a process of living in their era. The art is one outcome in the process of evolving consciousness. Art demonstrates that the creative impulse and the art created are the representational reflections of an era's essence, its moment of "*is*ness," its *Zeitgeist*. The writer's attitude towards his moment of "*is*ness" cannot exist without the emotional effusions that result from the influence of the *Zeitgeist* that forms him. The artist and art are outcomes of the metaphysical process that were derived from the discoveries occurring earlier in the process. The artist and the art become the influences in the process leading to the next generation's outcomes.

Introduction: The Comet That Changed the World

MYSTICISM *IS* LITERATURE; literature is the means to an end and that end *is* mysticism.

On May 17, 1910, Halley's Comet shatters the peace of Europe's skies. "On or about December, 1910," claims Virginia Woolf, "human character changed." In truth, however, what changed was not character itself but the way it was viewed. At the end of King Edward's reign, as Woolf argues in [an] essay from the twenties, people suddenly became conscious of needs they never knew that they had. Up until 1910, artists had considered the needs of human nature to be adequately reflected by the material and historical conditions in which it was rooted. But at the end of the first decade external situations appeared to have lost their revelatory power, their complicity, as it were, with inner intention. Scientists and philosophers began to wonder whether the most well-established truths were nothing more than matters of impression and mood, of perspective and judgment. Positivism, realism, and naturalism appeared to have forsaken the subject they first intended to serve, but of which they had never really spoken: the human subject, the psyche, self, or however one wished to call it — the innermost truth of subjective experience — which was improperly reflected by historical events [Thomas J. Harrison, *1910: The Emancipation of Dissonance*].

An end of dissonance signifies a renewed beginning for consonance. When Harrison notes that "the innermost truth ... was improperly reflected by historical events," this is exactly what mystics have elucidated for centuries: that reality is not the material world and that history is a byproduct, not the end of human endeavor — which is evolving consciousness. Halley's Comet was a wake-up call that man is not the center of the universe, nor is he likely made in God's image, which has always been one of the most egotistical manifestations of a very egotistical species. Rather, the universe works in a way described by Aldous Huxley: "Any given event in any part of the universe has as its predetermining conditions all previous events in all parts of the universe" (*Grey Eminence*, 16). This axiom summarizes the nature of what mysticism means: there is a whole in which all parts are unified in an ascending spiral of evolving consciousness. Halley's Comet and the transcendent mystical feelings derived from seeing it became a profound influence on 20th century thought and literature. Earth and humanity are events in a contiguous and continuous perpetual continuum; the impetus for both began after the "big bang" banged.

Human beings have always had —consciously or unconsciously— an intuition that there is *something* going on that we don't understand and that whatever it is unifies rather than separates. Artists are intuitively compelled to turn a creative impulse into a medium that can be understood by the many and not just themselves.

The Perennial Philosophy[1] (the philosophy of mysticism) has its seminal beginnings in the ancient Hindu sacred texts that are the first enunciations and elucidations of mysticism as an integral, continuous, contiguous, atomized essence within and without all of existence, physically and psychically. Atoms move but we can't see them; yet, they exist. We take their reality on faith. Consciousness evolves but we can't see it; yet, mystical philosophers believe it—beginning with the ancient texts. These texts—the Vedas—made their way from India to inform the East, then the West, through the derivatively evolving disciplines of Buddhism, Confucianism, Taoism, Platonism, Zen, Christian Mysticism, German Transcendentalism, British Romanticism, American Transcendentalism, Theosophy, and on the eve of the 20th century they came full circle in the revitalization and dissemination of the Vedas through the worldwide Vedanta Society. The Greeks may have been the cradle of Western civilization, but the Vedas are the womb of world civilization. The links in the chain are definitive and strong; yet, for many in the West, Hegel, Emerson, and Fredric Jameson are read as originals when they are merely—if creatively—derivative. Hegel, with his dialectic, was one of the first Western philosophers to lecture extensively on Eastern Religion. Emerson was a devoted Vedantist who freely credited the Vedas as the source of his "Oversoul." Jameson's dialectics, his "combinatoire" (synthesis), is Hegelian, hence, Vedantic. This, however, is to the credit of these writers since the wisdom of the Vedas is not proprietary but meant to be revisited in different epochs and geographical locations. This wisdom is perennial from some amorphous, indefinable beginning to some future, as yet indefinable end—and then it will start all over again in an endless cyclical regeneration. The Vedas' impetus of creation is exactly the "Big Bang" theory of an initial first cause that evolves as an ascending, widening spiral of the expanding universe, which scientists see as a physical process. The Vedas see it as both physical and metaphysical, believing that there is a corresponding psychical expansion and evolution concurrently.

According to mystical philosophy there are immutable constructs that change constantly in appearance but remain constant in their essence; still, the changes are distinct and recognizable to non-mystically inclined perceivers, which cause these perceivers to see only flux as defined by the five senses. These senses and the individuals using them feel a separateness devised by eye and ear that assumes that one is never part of a whole because one cannot see one's self included with others without aid of still water, a picture, photograph or mirror — relatively recent methods that have not yet quite caught up with the thousands of years of "I am I, you are not I." Indeed, the revelation of a primal group standing over their reflection in still water must have been as astounding as thunder and lightning. Separateness is man's physical condition; alienation his assumption inculcated from his inability to see himself with others. Thus, Vico's theory that humans created language to explain the disturbances to their senses (thunder, lightning), and from which they developed fables about natural events, was initially inspired by their awe and fear of the natural world. Language is a creation that attempts to overcome both the awe and fear of nature and human separateness, but in its development further separated individuals, as no two people interpret language in exactly the same way. Vico believed that these *awe*-sociations that were derived from natural events became fables, then became poetic wisdom, then became esoteric wisdom (philosophy) in an ever-ascending and widening spiral of complexity that became so far removed from the initial feelings of awe-sociation that individuals can no longer intimate feelings of awe solely from the natural world as did their child-like primitive ancestors.

Feelings of awe are transcendent; concentration upon the feeling of awe is systematic transcendence. Mystics meditate; artists create — both are intuitive concentrations that hope — and often succeed — in evoking awesome transcendent feelings. The *Katha Upanishad* (1.2.22–24) explains the importance of intuiting the undifferentiated unity of the Self: "The wise who knows the Self as bodiless within the bodies, as unchanging among changing things, as great and omnipresent, does never grieve. That self cannot be gained by the Veda, nor by understanding, nor by much learning. He whom the Self chooses, by him the Self can be gained. The Self chooses him [his body] as his own. But he who has not first turned away from his wickedness, who is not tranquil, and subdued, or whose mind is not at rest, he can never obtain the Self [even] by knowledge."

Intuition is paramount; however, spiritual intuition is less likely for the many that do not have any clue about achieving some form of inner self-understanding. Mystics and artists pursue self-understanding by design.

Disciples or audiences wish to share in the awe-sociations of the mystic and artist. This desire has not changed since the earliest fable-makers created Viconian "fabula." The essence of awe has not changed either; the wise artist knows he is reflecting new images that are updated versions derived from the same long-evolving spiral begun by his ancestors. Artists are wise. A creator knew that the artist reaches into the primary world of the separating, utilitarian language of particularities to create a secondary world of essential universality that transcends individuality to move audiences as a unity. Poets take the earliest Viconian awe and the passion that awe inspires to claim literary art (and all art) to be the true bearer of the continuing, moment by moment, integral essence begun with the first people and the first awe. Fables to poetry to philosophy — all the same. Sankara was right; Heraclites was right; Plato was right; Kant was right; Vico was right; Hegel was right; Emerson was right; Nietzsche was right; Jung was right; Aldous Huxley was right; Michael Polanyi was right; Iris Murdoch was right; Fredric Jameson is right. Flux is a process, not the chaos that is seen in the material world; dialectics is a process, not an end. Consciousness evolves from the reconciliation of opposites as described in the Isha Upanishad and in the sixth chapter of the Bhagavad-Gita:

The Isha Upanishad "teaches that evolving consciousness comes through the reconciliation of opposites through the perception of an essential Unity of the apparently incompatible opposites, God and the World, Renunciation and Enjoyment, Action and internal Freedom, the One and the Many, Being and its Becomings, the passive divine Impersonality and the active divine Personality, the Knowledge and the Ignorance, the Becoming and the Not-Becoming" (Pandit, *Online*).

The Gita teaches that only the discerning man who chooses to be a calm center within life's hurricane and understands the reconciliation of opposites can hope to see the undifferentiated unity of the Ultimate Reality.

> He who regards
> With an eye that is equal
> Friends and comrades,
> The foe and the kinsman,
> The vile, the wicked,
> The men who judge him,
> And those who belong
> To neither faction:
> He is the greatest [81–82].

Through the fission of the reconciliation of opposites, activity creates graduated resolutions that proceed to another moment of the *eternal now* of "*is*ness," which is described by the Vedanta-influenced T.S. Eliot in "Burnt Norton." Eliot echoes the Vedas and concludes: "And all is always now" (www.allspirit. co.uk/norton.html). The resolutions that graduate from the reconciliation of opposites exist in the *eternal now* and move fluidly without interruption to become the next sources of opposites needing to be reconciled while consciousness continues to move up the ascending spiral. The movement is fluid and imperceptible. The senses may see, hear, feel, touch, or taste the outcomes of these resolutions, but these physical outcomes are static. The outcomes are the residue of a movement after a particular movement is over. One drinks water, eats food, touches silk only after the process of their becoming reaches its material end; one is rarely conscious of the process and becomes focused only on the results. For the many, awareness of process, whether of an apple or consciousness, is rarely and barely thought about unless an aspect of process becomes an expedient necessity such as drought or famine. Necessity may be the mother of invention, but for the many, "mother" often doesn't speak until necessity is expedient and mandatory. Throughout history farsightedness has been in short supply and the barn door has been closed after the animals escaped. (Or a need to cut oil consumption is not seen as a necessity until chaos is recognized.) The many cannot grasp the hidden *all*ness of the bigger picture. What is misperceived to be linear, to be before and after, cause and effect, is finite and confined to an expedient present disconnected from the process of evolution. To the misperceiving majority, events are dots on a line and the majority cannot see the continuity and contiguity of the present dots and how they are related to previous dots. The previous dots are forgotten or they are only memories or histories. The majority also cannot see the future that is ahead and too far off to consider or imagine. Conversely, to artists and mystics time is only a man-made construct to which we adhere slavishly and detrimentally.

Thornton Wilder wrote, "It is only in appearance that time is a river. It is a vast landscape, and it is only the eye of the beholder that moves" (*The Eighth Day*, 395). If one throws a rock into a pond, one can watch the process from the initial splash to the expanding circular ripples. If one could stand back far enough and see the "big bang," one could see the first cause and follow the oval expansion of the universe moment-to-moment, *istgeist* to *istgeist* (*is*ness to *is*ness), and see the cause and effect of how each *is*ness ripples into the next *is*ness. From the expanding ripples in the pond to an expanding universe, these images — one real, based on visible nature, one "metaphorized" as an extrapolation of invisible nature — help one's actual eyes to "see" an idea, like atoms, that the mind's eye can understand only by a leap of the imagination, even though atoms *are* real, not imagined. To imagine connotes "seeing" what isn't there; but atoms *are* there, spinning in a circle that is the ultimate microcosm of the larger microcosm of the pond, and both the atom and the pond are within the ultimate macrocosm of the expanding universe. All the sense-perceived microcosms seem differentiated, but if one sees as the mystic sees, then Ultimate Reality is both *is*ness and process. One sees a cloud that is made up of condensed water, from which drops of rain merge into an ocean. The drops are a process, a moment of *is*ness that flows from one *is*ness (cloud) to another *is*ness (ocean).

From the eye of the beholder who sees the vast landscape, one can see both the *is*ness and the process simultaneously and one can again refer to Huxley: "Any given event in any part of the universe has as its determining conditions all previous and contemporary events in all parts of the universe."

Imagination (intuition) can allow us to see the timeless interrelations. But imagination is not just about seeing what isn't real; it is equally about "seeing" what *is* real — an atom. Imagination leads to the discovery of what is physically real and can be measured (science). Imagination also leads to the discovery of what is metaphysically real and can be "metaphorized" (art). Science and art are about seeing what previously was not seen but was imagined (intuited). Michael Polanyi said: *We know much more than we can tell* (*Tacit Dimension*, 5).[2] *Telling* is an outcome of what is already known, even when that telling might be imagining what is not yet known. (A science-fiction writer takes the known to imagine what an unknown future might be like. He wishes to transcend the known through the creative impulse.) Art is one vehicle for transcendence. Humans have a compelling desire for transcendence, which for most is an unconscious need without a cognitive, let alone a philosophical, basis. There are forms of upward transcendence and downward transcendence.[3] Upward transcendence is more conscious of its own ambitions; downward transcendence is often crudely unconscious. Upward: Mysticism, art, spirituality, love (mystic love as *Eros*, then transformed to the transcendently awesome love of *Agape*—the love for all existence); Downward: addictions (drugs, alcohol, sex, religious dogma and fanaticism, nationalistic fanaticism).

Transcendence, conscious or unconscious, is the desire of humanity; transcendence is the design of mystical philosophy, as first recorded in the Vedas. Still, long before the 3,000 year-old Vedas, awe-sociations were recorded by the primitive fabulists described in Vico's *New Science*. The creative impulse of art and literature is the reflective dialectical synthesis of moments in space. These moments re-create awe and evoke a sense of unity that seeks to overcome feelings of separation. Unity with the Ultimate Reality is the goal of mystical philosophy.

The continuum of the statement above starting "Any given event" includes the evolution of man's consciousness. Within this philosophy is the concept of an Ultimate Reality or Ground of Being (perhaps Divine) that is both the first cause of the continuum and the continuum itself. An artistic perspective that is grounded in mystical philosophy is just now becoming a view that some critics, particularly in Europe and Russia — and Satya Mohanty in America — have begun to apply to literature, seeing certain writers as exponents who have consciously or unconsciously incorporated this philosophy into their art. While the idea of a "Divine Ground" concerns a spiritual basis, mystical philosophy can still be a paradigm for literature with or without a belief in divinity. Vico's Science asserts that man "created" stories to explain his sensory experiences as having a spiritual basis. (Where else could the awesomely scary thunder and lightning be coming from but a spiritual source?) All wisdom evolved from these initial "fabula." Consequently, even if Vico did or did not believe in spirit, he believed that his primitive constituents *did* believe in spirit and that rightly or wrongly this belief is the integral and dominating aspect of man's psychological and philosophical evolution.

As for form, the vast literature of mysticism has been given an encapsulated form by Huxley. Referring again to the "Any given event" statement, this aphorism is a good basis for understanding what Huxley called "The Minimum

Working Hypothesis," which summarizes the common denominators of mysticism into four basic tenets that were first stated in his introduction to the 1944 Isherwood/Prabhavananda translation of the *Bhagavad-Gita* (7). To consider these tenets as a prelude to this study's views on language (and life) is to make the same metaphysical leap that artists and philosophers have made since there have been artists and philosophers. If the reader is also able to make this leap even temporarily, then what this study describes will fit into a much clearer context.

Minimum Working Hypothesis

1. The phenomenal world of matter and of individualized consciousness—the world of things and animals and even gods—is the manifestation of a Divine Ground within which all partial realities have their being, and apart from which they would be non-existent.

2. Human beings are capable not merely of knowing about the Divine Ground by inference [intimating the awe-sociations]; they can also realize its existence by a direct intuition [e.g., meditation, art] superior to discursive reasoning. This immediate knowledge unites the knower with that which is known.

3. Man possesses a double nature, a phenomenal ego and an eternal self, which is the inner man, the spirit, the spark of divinity within the soul. It is possible for a man, if he so desires, to identify himself with this spirit and therefore with the Divine Ground which is of the same or like nature with the spirit.

4. Man's life on earth has only one end and purpose: to identify himself with his eternal self and so come to unitive knowledge of the Divine Ground of all existence.

The key to Huxley's axioms is the role of intuition as a guide to knowledge not to be found empirically:

> It is the task of philosophy to try to translate and understand analytically in terms of thought or conceptual thinking what has been presented in the living experience of intuition. It must start from experience and it must recognize experience to be the goal of all philosophy. Philosophy cannot give us an experience of the actual—it attempts to show what is possible, not what *is* but what *may be*. The merely possible demands verification or rather an actualization in concrete experience. This is supplied by intuition. A philosophy that does not base itself on this solid footing of perfect experience is a merely barren speculation that moves in the sphere of ideas alone, detached from Reality. This is what distinguishes Hegel's Idea from Sankara's Brahman. The latter is a concrete experience in ecstatic intuition, while the former is only the highest achievement of reason [Brahma, 167].

Intuition drives the inspiration of the creative impulse even if hard work follows to see that impulse through to the art's completion. Art is a means to the end for the artist and his audience to intimate the *awe*-sociations that are harbored in the unconscious in order to identify with and come to "unitive knowledge of the Divine Ground of all existence." The poet or artist does so by using language that he has learned from the common, profane speech of the people in such a unique way that these words intimate the numinous and sacred. For both artists and audiences the goal of their reciprocity is ultimately to explain how, through art, both the artist and his readers might ask themselves the two paramount questions of individual existence: *Who am I? Whom ought I to become?*

CHAPTER 1

Vedanta and Theosophy: Preludes to a New Literature

THE 20TH CENTURY RESURGENCE of interest in Vedanta in the West and the factors that fostered this interest began in the late 19th century with the founding of the Theosophical Society in 1875 and Swami Vivekananda's speech at the Parliament of Religions in Chicago on September 11, 1893. Both galvanized new interest in the Vedas, although an attraction to these ancient Hindu sacred texts had always existed since they were first written 3,000 years before, with certain periods having more explicit study than others. Implicitly, the Vedas have suffused the mystical aspects of all spiritual thought under an umbrella designated The Perennial Philosophy. The Theosophical movement in the West began the modern era of interest and, in fact, made it possible for Vivekananda to have his successful Western debut in 1893.

The Theosophical Society was founded by Helena Petrovna Blavatsky, Col. Henry Olcott, and W.Q. Judge, among others. Blavatsky was a Russian noblewoman; Olcott was an American attorney and judge. Blavatsky presented ideas and concepts that unified science, religion and philosophy — ideas showing a spiritual purpose and design behind the facts of science, as well as giving a spiritual depth to religion and philosophy.

With its strong resemblance to Eastern mysticism and spirituality, Theosophy has an intertwining relationship with Hinduism — especially the Upanishads and Advaita Vedanta, and also Buddhism. While Theosophists added their own nuances, Theosophy, like every other spiritual system, was extrapolated from the Vedas. Indeed, some of theosophy's original adherents soon understood that the Vedas were behind the Theosophical ideas and chose to go to the original sources directly, among them William Butler Yeats and his friend Æ (George William Russell).

Nonetheless, Theosophy is to be fully credited with reviving interest in Vedanta. Mysticism also played a large part in Theosophy. Blavatsky worked to introduce into the West the philosophical and religious ideas of the East, with the aim of showing their mutual and interdependent values. She and her colleagues met with a great deal of opposition, but they also attracted much interest through their writings, lectures, and personal contacts with many influential artists and intellectuals.

Blavatsky wrote many books, with *The Secret Doctrine*, published in 1885, her most well known and a bible of Theosophy. In essence, however, the "secret" of the doctrine was how much it took from Vedanta. She had traveled to India and entered Tibet via Kashmir and Ladakh. The *Secret Doctrine* contains quotations and in-depth knowledge of the Upanishads, Smritis, as well as other Hindu shastras. Much of Blavatsky's learning was intuitive. (Intuition, or the ability for one to discover one's own inner spirituality independently from organized religion, is a foundation of the Perennial Philosophy.)

Her philosophy was altruistic, as dictated by the Vedantic principle of unity that is the same as the unity that Theosophy talks about, a unity to be used for the good of humanity. Since Theosophy and Vedanta teach that all existence is an undifferentiated unity — that each is part of all — then when one would harm another being, one would be harming one's self.

In England Annie Besant became a founder of Britain's Theosophical Society. Besant first came to know about Theosophy in 1889 when she was asked to review *The Secret Doctrine*. She was so impressed that she was drawn into the Theosophical Society. She had made a name for herself as a journalist, prolific writer and publisher, and was actively involved in many movements. She first went to India in 1893 in connection with the Theosophical work. Besant made India her home and saw the Vedas as the source of Theosophy. She translated several Upanishads with commentaries in English. She contributed significantly to the cause of Vedanta as well as Theosophy.

Besant was an advocate for Indian home rule. She saw in India that through British influence the Vedas had been pushed aside by the occupier in a pattern that colonization has always followed — the repression of the colonized people's singular identity. Besant and Vivekananda revived Vedanta in India and directly influenced Mahatma Gandhi, Jawaharlal Nehru, Sarojini Naidu, C.P. Ramaswami Aiyer and more. Besant's advocacy for home rule led to her arrest by the British in 1916. There was an unexpected and worldwide backlash against her arrest, which resulted in many more coming forward to fight for India's freedom.

Besant became the international president of the Theosophical Society after the deaths of Madame Blavatsky and Colonel Olcott. Charles Webster Leadbeater became a colleague of Annie Besant. He is credited to have "discovered" Krishnamurti in 1908 when the boy was 13. Claiming clairvoyance, Leadbeater said he saw a luminous aura, without a trace of selfishness, around Krishnamurti. He declared him an incarnation of Lord Maitreya and the future Messiah. In 1929 Krishnamurti renounced his messiah designation and left the Theosophical Society to become a spiritual philosopher with worldwide influence.

Theosophy and Vedanta are intertwined together. What continues to make Theosophy and Vedanta appealing is that both give people access to a self-discovery of an intuitive spirituality that is more satisfying than lockstepping in a dogmatic religion.

Theosophy's Western Impact

After 1875 many influential people were attracted to Theosophy and Vedanta: playwright Oscar Wilde; Irish poets W.B. Yeats and Æ, who added Celtic nuances; author George Bernard Shaw; architect Frank Lloyd Wright; and inventor Thomas Edison; among others. The key point is that Theosophy revived Vedanta.

In the 1960s the translations by Swami Prabhavananda and Christopher Isherwood of The Upanishads, Bhagavad-Gita, Shankara's *Crest Jewel of Discrimination*, and Patanjali's Yoga Aphorisms in *How to Know God* were singularly successful in clearly conveying Hindu thought to the West, with millions of copies sold and these books still in print. Aldous Huxley's 1954 book, *Doors of Perception*, and his novel, *Island*, a manual for enlightened living that sold over a million copies in 1968–69, promoted mystical experience, also leading directly to the explosion of interest in the East in the 1960s.

The Influence of Vedanta on Theosophy

Theosophy deals with that which is hidden, not obvious, and must be discovered through a non-discursive intuition. Blavatsky's *The Secret Doctrine* quoted from Plato, Confucius, Jesus, and Buddhism (which all followed the Vedas), and borrowed heavily from the Hindu Upanishads.

According to Theosophy, the root cause of the entire universe, inclusive of all its animate and inanimate creation, is an entity that is boundless, and an immutable principle, which is an Ultimate Reality that antecedes all manifested, conditioned being — a divine ground of being.

Theosophy further describes the three aspects of this ultimate reality as Absolute Abstract Motion, and Absolute Abstract Space and Duration. The Absolute Abstract Motion is pre-cosmic ideation. It is the impetus of the source that makes creativity possible, and it is also the cause of individual consciousness.

Absolute Abstract Space gives shapes or forms to the different things in the universe. Duration is the root of time, from which the principle springs into manifestation. This aspect makes "action" possible. Thus, Theosophy states that from this Ultimate Reality, we derive consciousness, minds, thoughts, and our impulse to create. Absolute Abstract Space and Absolute Abstract Motion are Theosophical terms for Vedic concepts. In Chapter 2, see the discussion of *Nama-Rupa* for a more detailed account.

This Theosophical concept of the Ultimate Reality is akin to the Brahman principle propounded by the Advaita Vedanta, the only subtle difference being that while the Upanishadic sages and the commentators of Brahmasutras like Shankara described the nature of Brahman as Sat, Chit and Ananda, or existence, consciousness and bliss, Theosophy delineates its aspects in the same way but with a different nomenclature.

Humanism

Theosophy looks upon the love for all existence as an inescapable law, as inevitable as the law of gravity, or any other natural law. It connotes an implied respect for all human beings as well as for the entire realm of living things. The law is independent of the individuals who act for the law (upward transcendence) or against the law (downward transcendence). The concept of an Ultimate Reality behind all existence is a benevolent declaration with applications in daily, practical life.

Maya and Cycles

The second proposition of Theosophy states the absolute universality of the law of regeneration through which the One Life operates, the flux and reflux, the ebb and flow of activity. Blavatsky states that the alternations of day and night, life and death, sleeping and waking are so common that it is easy to realize that the rule of regeneration is one of the fundamental laws of nature. The sixth chapter of the Bhagavad-Gita similarly talks about the pairs (and reconciliation) of opposites such as pleasure and pain, light and darkness, night and day that follow each other, with the effort of these reconciliations creating the energy and design for evolving consciousness. All opposites are within nature and to be discovered intuitively by the mind, which is part and parcel of nature. This idea is one that is also found subsequent to the Vedas in Heraclites, Plato, Hegel, et al., and up to the present.

Blavatsky refers to the universe itself as the periodic manifestation of the Ultimate Reality. The universe is *Maya*—an idea directly from Vedanta—in the sense that it is temporary. There will be many phases of creation through millennia upon millennia. Creations and appearances change; the only constant factor is the Ultimate Reality from which creation emerges. *Maya*, for Blavatsky, is not illusion, but the power of creation. The root interpretation of the word *Maya* signifies a magic creation or display. This translation has been misinterpreted in the West to signify that physical reality—trees, rocks, creatures, chairs, tables, and so on are not in actuality physically real, that they are an illusion of the senses. This interpretation is incorrect. The illusion is not about whether the trees and rocks exist, but rather about a person's perception that these are the only reality and there is no conjoining, essential Ultimate Reality of spirit within and without these physical entities.

Spirit within all of existence is the same as atoms within all physical matter.

Soul and Oversoul

The third basic proposition of Theosophy affirms the fundamental identity of every soul with the universal Oversoul (Emerson's term for the Vedas' Brahman within which are Vedantic archetypes that Jung incorporated into his own philosophy of archetypes) and the obligatory pilgrimage of every soul through the cycle of incarnation or necessity, as Blavatsky comments on the cycle of births and deaths that each soul undergoes. Each soul is responsible for its own actions, but it should travel in the company of other pilgrims in mutual affection and helpfulness rather than away from affection and helpfulness—or as Huxley called this, upward or downward transcendence.

Because of an individual's identity with the Oversoul human beings are integral with the antecedent Ultimate Reality that initiated and maintains the complex universe within its set of natural laws that keeps it in perfect balance through the fission that is derived from the reconciliation of opposites.

Fundamentals of Vedanta

- Spirituality of the soul as integral to a divine ground of all existence
- Unity of Existence: oneness of matter and energy or the ultimate oneness of God, man and nature
- Harmony of all spiritual systems as manifestations of an essential Perennial Philosophy
- Immanence and Transcendence of Spirit that is both the material and the efficient cause of the universe Cyclic Theory of Creation through the Reconciliation of Opposites
- *Mukti,* or total freedom from the weakness for temptations and desires that interfere with the spiritual union with the Ultimate Reality[1]

Duality is a misperception of the senses. Duality exists only in appearance, not in actuality. The Reconciliation of Opposites does not signify that there is any essential duality in actuality but that there are poles of integral forces that are undifferentiated but require a more effective balance on the path of evolving consciousness. In the sciences, mathematical, chemical and physical equations relate matter that already exists in a manner that allows the scientist to "see" what is not readily visible. In effect, the Reconciliation of Opposites is more about balancing an essence than it is about a true opposition of separate entities. $E=MC^2$ does not describe separation but an equation of balance.

Shankara (c. 788–820)[2] systemized the Vedic texts and with his commentaries on the Vedas established the vision of Vedanta's non-duality that still predominates. Shankara developed a complex, "neither/nor" dialectic from the Upanishads. The term *neti, neti* (not this, not that) of the *Brihadaranyaka Upanishad* (4.5.15) and verse seven of the *Mandukya Upanishad* are the basis of Shankara's neither/nor dialectic. P. T. Raju has shown that Shankara uses dialectical negation in order to ultimately affirm a doctrine of an absolute Ultimate Reality. *Neti, neti* (not this, not that), signifies that if spirit is not in any particular physical or metaphysical entity then spirit can only exist in every physical and metaphysical entity.

R.C. Zaehner recognizes a "both-and" dialectic, as well as the "neither/nor" dialectic in the *Bhagavad-Gita*: "Arjuna, like most Europeans, thinks in either/or categories: he has not yet realized that Krishna's [God's] categories and those of the religion he inherits and further develops are not either/or but both-and. Opposites do not exclude each other but complement each other" (200). Arjuna is deeply puzzled about the apparent exclusion of a life of renunciation (which he now desires) and the life of action (which he now abhors). In Chapter 5 of the *Gita* Krishna's answer is a dialectical union of both renunciation and action.

Hegel called the Reconciliation of Opposites, "dialectics." Hegel tells us that he is indebted to the pre–Socratic Greeks, especially Heraclites' idea of logos reconciling all opposites into a unitary process. Aristotle's criticisms of the pre–Socratics prevailed, however, and the law of contradiction and traditional logic won out in the West. Until Hegel, a both-and dialectic survived in the Western mystical tradition, most notably in Nicholas of Cusa and his doctrine of *coincidentia oppositorum*.

In Hegel's introduction to his lectures on religion he writes:

> In the relation in which religion, even in its immediacy, stands to the other forms of the consciousness of man, there already lie germs of division, since both sides are conceived of as in a condition of separation relatively to each other. In their simple relation they already constitute two kinds of pursuits, two different regions of consciousness, and we pass to and from the one to the other alternately only. Thus man has in his actual worldly life a number of working days during which he occupies himself with his own special interests, with worldly aims in general, and with the satisfaction of his needs; and then he has a Sunday, when he lays all this aside, collects his thoughts, and, released from absorption in finite occupations, lives to himself and to the higher nature which is in him, to his true essential being.
>
> Thus the spirit has entered into the condition of opposition — as yet, it is true, artlessly, and without at first knowing it — but the opposition comes to be a conscious one, for the spirit now moves between two sides, of which the distinction has actually developed itself. The one side is that in which the spirit knows itself to be its own, where it lives in its own aims and interests, and determines itself on its own authority as independent and self-sustaining. The other side is that where the spirit recognises a higher Power — absolute duties, duties without rights belonging to them, and what the spirit receives for the accomplishment of its duties is always regarded as grace alone. In the first instance it is the independence of the spirit which is the

foundation; here its attitude is that of humility and dependence. Its religion is accordingly distinguished from what we have in that region of independence by this, that it restricts knowledge, science, to the worldly *side,* and leaves for the sphere of religion, feeling and faith [www.marxists.org/reference/archive/hegel/works/re/parta.htm].

The key to a reconciliation of opposites or a synthetic dialectic is the rejection of the law of contradiction and the belief that opposites coincide or are reconciled (Hegel's *aufgehoben*) in the higher synthesis. Indeed, Hegel's thoughts on "feeling and faith" (intuition), dialectics (reconciliation of opposites) and his "absolute idea/mind" (Ultimate Reality) are Vedantic:

Thesis	Antithesis	Synthesis
Logic	Nature	Mind / Spirit
Idea in itself	*Idea for itself*	*Idea in and for itself*
Triad of Logic	Triad of Nature	Triad of Mind
Thesis: *Being*	Thesis: *Mechanics*	Thesis: *Subjective Mind*
Antithesis: *Essence*	Antithesis: *Physics*	Antithesis: *Objective Mind*
Synthesis: *Notion or Conception*	Synthesis: *Organics*	Synthesis: *Absolute Mind*

Logic, also known as ideas or essences, precedes the phenomenal world — nature. This theory was later described as "Essence precedes existence" by Jean-Paul Sartre. Understanding logic, the thesis of the Absolute Truth, is the goal of the Hegelian Dialectic.

Nature is the phenomenal form of a concept. According to Hegel, nature was the physical expression of God's ideas. The Creator had to develop a plan before creating. The creations are nature; the plan is logic.

Mind or Spirit is the synthesis of logic and nature. By measuring and understanding the phenomenal world, we can hypothesize about the underlying logic of creation. It is this synthesis of individual and group necessity that produces the Absolute Mind, which is a goal of a process, and this process is more important than reaching the goal, as the goal of Absolute Mind is an end of an infinite not within the current grasp of comprehension.

Hegel's dialectic process moves from the thesis to the antithesis. When considering a concept, Hegel's model requires the philosopher to determine the opposite concept. The final step is the determination of a synthesis between or derived from the two conflicting concepts. It would be simple if the synthesis represented an ending point, but Hegel's triad is a continuum. A synthesis becomes the thesis in a new triad. According to T.Z. Lavine, the three functions of synthesis are:

1. Cancel the conflict between thesis and antithesis.
2. Preserve the element of truth within the thesis and antithesis.
3. Transcend the opposition and sublimate the conflict into a higher truth [41].

Fredric Jameson, to follow, calls step three a *Combinatoire*.

It was Hegel's contention that the Absolute Truth was a collection of all possible triads in the universe. Mankind could discover truth only if mankind could recognize every phenomenal triad that existed. Since this was not possible, Hegel concluded that mankind could never attain knowledge of Absolute Truth. It was the quest for this Absolute Truth (the *Welt Giest*, the World Spirit, the guiding reason behind the evolutionary progress of the universe and mankind) that Hegel considered essential to the evolution of mankind.

In Hegel's lifetime few Vedic texts had been translated and certainly fewer analyzed. Hegel lectured extensively on world religions over a number of years. His understanding of the Vedas evolved from misconceptions (he believed Buddhism preceded the Vedas) to a better if not complete understanding. His dialectic is Eastern but not necessarily from the original source, rather from that source's subsequent derivations. Shortly after Hegel, Schopenhauer would translate and analyze the Vedas and become devoted to them. His philosophy is Vedanta philosophy directly, not indirectly. Through Schopenhauer, Vedanta was available to inspire Theosophy. Over time, with the knowledge that Vedanta had so much influence on Theosophy, interested adherents left Theosophy to study Vedanta directly. The Theosophical Society sharply declined in number while Vedanta-inspired organizations grew, particularly the Vedanta Society. It then became an enormous influence through the efforts of the Vedanta Society of Southern California, begun by Swami Prabhavananda in the late 1920s and which then found its voice beginning in 1939 when Aldous Huxley, Gerald Heard, and Christopher Isherwood became members and began writing about the nature of Vedanta in copious essays and in their fiction in a manner much more accessible to Western readers.

Methodology of the Upanishads and the Bhagavad-Gita

Their exposition is in four different modes:

1. Dialogue with questions and answers.
2. Narration and episodes.
3. Similes, metaphors and illustrations.
4. Symbolism, such as "pure light," sattva, and so on.

Number one is in the nature of Platonic Dialogues, but earlier. Plato's dialogues are Vedantic. Indeed, in Plato's *Phaedrus*, his famous metaphor of the chariot and horses was used first in the Katha Upanishad, and then extensively in the Bhagavad-Gita. Much of Western thought evolves from Plato without consideration of the likely Vedic influence. A certain amount of Western collective subjectivity has resisted seeing the Vedic antecedent and until relatively recently much Western philosophy and commentary about Plato or Hegel blindly omits Eastern influence. Yet, even though, for example, Emerson freely said his philosophy was from the Vedas (and in fact, supplanted his previously Platonic influence), often in Emerson studies there is scant interrelating of Emerson to Vedanta. There is, in fact, an irony in that the Indian-born Krishnamurti became famous for his philosophy, which sounded much like Emerson's derivations from the Vedas.

The symbol of "pure light" is sattva in Vedanta and the causal world is the level where sattva predominates. In Plato's cave analogy, it is "seeing the Forms in the light of the Sun, but not yet the Sun itself." In Patanjali's Yoga Aphorisms, it is called *ritam bhara pragya*, or truth-bearing wisdom. What the "fixed realities" are cannot be put into words (Plato uses the poetic image of Forms). The "fixed realities" are the unfolding of the internal dynamics of "pure awareness" (the real meaning of *Veda*) in an illumined mind whereas subtle, conscious individuals experience this as the subtle world, and ordinary people experience this same unfolding in the gross mind as the gross world, where only the "shadows" of the Forms (the material outcomes) are visible.

CHAPTER 2

Aldous Huxley and W.H. Auden: Mysticism as a Literary Theory

It is only for strictly human purposes that the Idea can be considered truer than the appearance. Subtracted from a mass of the most diverse sensations, the Idea is a sort of Lowest Common Measure of appearances. For the purposes of Man the remembering and foreseeing animal, of Man the exerciser of persistent and conscious action on the external world, the Idea or abstraction is truer than the immediate sensation. It is because we are predominantly purposeful beings that we are perpetually correcting our immediate sensations. But men are free not to be utilitarianly purposeful. They can sometimes be artists for example. — Aldous Huxley ["One and Many," 9]

POETS PAST AND PRESENT SENSE intuitively and choose to articulate with words what the rest of the tribe, group, or community passively or unconsciously knows within the instinctive group mind: that there are *awe*-sociations intimating an Ultimate Reality to be found between these words that connote ineffable meanings over and beyond the language of common speech. The poet's choice is self-imposed, motivated by some personal and gratuitous necessity that is different from the necessity that is required for physical survival. Primitive tribe members, acting intuitively rather than articulately, will avoid waking sleeping dogs for fear of being chased by the dogs. If the dogs, however, attack a little boy who is saved by the tribe's hunter-warrior, a witness is moved by the warrior's courage and retains this memory, which he shapes with sound-symbols: this is the first poet in the manner Vico describes in his *New Science*. The first poet emerges as the recorder and teller. This poet soon becomes a focal point of the tribe's collective identity as a historical entity. The story as a whole has an integral purpose greater than the individual tribe members and the individual tales and legends, indeed, even greater than the tribe itself. This first poet is a reporter, gossip, philosopher, and historian. He selects the words he will use to explain, exhort, and dramatize the past and present. With his power to embellish the stories creatively the poet gratuitously adds to the telling, from which he discovers that he has some control over the ineffability between and behind the words that has a life and spirit of its own. There is a developing intuition of an underlying Ultimate Reality that is a transpersonal supraconsciousness permeating the lives of the tribe. The teller's understanding of his power, and the satisfaction he derives from his ability to "mythify" the tribe's story and give his audience pleasure, are proof to the poet that his skill earns him a status he would like to keep. Yet, this wish fulfillment also comes with a temptation to taint the words with nuances derived from personal motive. The poet knows he can, if he chooses, encourage the tribe not just to listen, but to follow. Not many poets have chosen the latter, and perhaps even less have succeeded; however, the power of words is not just a temptation for the poet. The propagandist learns to use words for more nefarious purposes. This chapter will concern the poet as a poet only — albeit one who teaches through parable, for all literary art is parable. Some artists see this more acutely than others.

The poet, driven by sympathy and empathy, needs to witness, record, and tell, to explain, justify, and immortalize himself. The poet does so by intimating for himself and his audience the intuitive desire for awe-sociations that touch the Ultimate Reality residing in a Jungian (Gerald Heardian) collective unconscious (more on Heard in a following section). Art is the poet's vehicle for transcendence, and there is a willing audience that vicariously shares in this transcendence. The artist and audience represent their time and zeitgeist, their moment of *is*ness. Yet, which comes first — the artist or the zeitgeist?

> Does art hold up the mirror to its period? Or does every period hold up the mirror to its art? Does the artist follow or lead? Or does he walk alone, heeding only the categorical imperatives of his talent and the inner logic of the tradition within which he works? Is he the representative of his epoch?
> All these questions can be answered now in the affirmative, now in the negative, now with simultaneous yes and no. There are no general rules; there are only particular cases [Huxley "Man and Religion," 161].

Each particular case, new man or new woman, whether as artist or audience member, uniquely re-evaluates the world again for the first time, as did the very first storyteller and his listeners. Each person notes his birthday, which measures life but also measures the coming death of the body. Life and death — the artist, as any man or woman, has two compelling drives: for his life to be acknowledged through communication with others, and to cheat death by leaving something identifiable for posterity, in the poet's case, a verbal artifact. To communicate one's life as a self-validation and to challenge the fear of death and nullity are universally identifiable human traits — they are understood by all, consciously and unconsciously, meaning they are among the many shared, common experiences integrating humanity's collective unconscious. For the poet, this is the mine where he digs for subject matter. No poet will succeed with readers if he attempts to convey in a poem that which is beyond any possible recognition by a potential audience. An audience must be able to recognize in the artist's art some identifiable context that relates to their own life experiences. If the audience is unable to share some common experience with the artist, the art will engender no empathy or sympathy, possibly leaving it to be thereafter ignored and unpreserved for posterity. Readers cannot empathize or sympathize with another's emotive evocations of previous experiences if they cannot find something in those evocations relevant to their own common experiences. (Sometimes, however, an audience is simply not ready to understand a work of art that will later be appreciated by a future audience: Melville, Samuel Beckett, Stravinsky.)

Readers *do* want to learn about the writer's individual and intellectually abstracted and amphibious existences; and though the writer uses *his* words, these words will be read, learned, interpreted, and enjoyed in the reader's terms, meaning generally accepted conventional language. While the poet may intimate to listeners and readers *awe*-sociations that he hopes will imply the numinous, sacred, and highbrow to them, these intimations will reach only the smallest audience if not written in common language that is the vulgar, profane, and lowbrow language of everyday speech. "Common" herein does not imply "simple." The words are carriers of messages that are to be gathered between the words. Words come from common usage, even if they seem to be literary words. The message is more important and the message can be a very profound message told with any words, even non-literary or non-high-falutin' words. It is the message, not the words, that can turn the knowledge of the lowbrow words into a highbrow understanding.

This is a tall order, one that requires that the *awe*-sociations the poet is intimating be framed in relatively common language. Consequently, even when the subject matter is decidedly mature and the poet's metaphors complex, the audience wants to be told in words that are commonly known, rather than esoterically unknown but to a few. (This is not to say a writer can't write a work of literary art that requires erudition and a dictionary but this writer and his words will reach a smaller audience.)

For the most part any audience also wants the poet to add a childlike freshness of insight to the poem so that the poet and, subsequently, his readers can temporarily pretend, as Huxley said, to "see with the eyes of children [so that the language used to recall the poet's] immediate impressions of actuality seem to have a supernaturalness" (*Texts and Pretexts*, 22).

All art, even when it is dealing in vulgar, profane reality, is supernatural by definition because it is the translation of, ruminations upon, and recollections of what were once — even if only a second before — immediate experiences, never the actuality of them. (To describe how the hunter-warrior saved the child cannot be re-actualized, only retold.) And since it is impossible for any other person to get inside the artist and become the artist, art, to be the most evocative for the audience, works best when it becomes a mirror in which an audience may become conscious of what their own feelings really are. In July 2002, Bruce Springsteen's album *The Rising* treated 9/11 and its aftermath with impressionistic songs that were not narratives of events but emotional outcomes of what the events meant to people. Springsteen spoke with survivors and family members of non-survivors. He synthesized their emotions rather than tell their stories. Each listener forms his or her own individual impressions based on one's individual memories that are prompted by Springsteen's words. (Springsteen's career depictions of the working class have found their way to academia with a course taught at Duke University.)

The poet-reader translation, while analogous to previous knowledge each references generally, is a new, specific, virgin communication between a particular poet and a particular reader. Each poet and reader become metaphorically a new Adam or Eve, seeing everything again for the first time.

What people want to appreciate in art is its function to intimate and arouse awe, and no artist, whether he wants to or not, as far as an audience is concerned, can prevent his work being used as magic, for that is what an audience secretly wants art to be.

And, more specifically, what is it about poetry that readers "secretly want"? The poet W.H. Auden's answer was that, "What the child, and the child-in-the-adult, most enjoys in poetry ... is the manipulation of language for its own sake, the sound and rhythm of words" ("The Good Life," 342). And what do readers secretly want from a particular poem? "We want a poem," Auden said, "to be a beautiful object, a verbal Garden of Eden which by its formal perfection, keeps alive in us the hope that there exists a state of joy without evil or suffering which it can be our destiny to attain. At the same time, we look to a poem for some kind of illumination about our present wandering condition, since, without self-insight and knowledge of the world we must err blindly" ("Walter de la Mare," 385).

And "err blindly" we will anyway, for in our uniqueness and the ego-derived separateness that our uniqueness entails, we struggle in the amphibious realms of within and without, inner and outer, mind and body, just as did every single one of our unique ancestors. Each new birth is a unique opportunity for an individual to exercise free will and make choices that ultimately help mankind's collective unconscious progress toward the Ultimate Reality. We are all makers — as is the artist — making choices that influence our individual and collective destiny. If we merely followed dogmatically the directions of our parents, teachers, media, there'd be no choices based on independent thought and no progress, either as individuals or for mankind. The progress looked for is toward what Gerald Heard — a great friend of both Huxley and Auden — called the "unified consciousness." Heard believed that "All men's work is to express a need. But the work does not necessarily relieve the need." This is because the many haven't as yet figured out what the need is. Man works and makes history, of which, Heard said, "history is, *au fond* [at bottom] the history of man finding himself. All his physical achievements, constructive or destructive, can be co-coordinated, and only so if we view them as the symptom of his realization, first of what he really needs, and then what he is, what he has been, and *what he may be*" (*Emergence*, 21). (The idea of a psychic evolution is not today so rare in a New Age milieu, but was rather *outré* when Heard wrote this in 1931. As H.F. Heard, he wrote fiction, mysteries, and bizarre tales in a mode that one might have imagined Jung trying, if he had been so inclined.)

For Heard, what man needs is to reunify with the unified consciousness which his assertive ego separated him from; what man *is*, is a part of a collective psyche learning how to reunify; what he has been, is lost; what he may become, if he makes the right choices, is a spirit independent of body or ego, permanently realigned with the Ultimate Reality. Mystical philosophy sees this as humanity's true and only purpose, one which man intuitively senses from intimating awe-sociations, but one his ego often confuses with selfish ends rather than selfless ends. In effect, history has been made, in many cases, by people looking in the wrong direction for their salvation, searching without, instead of within. But through these experiences and conflicts that reconcile opposites, civilization learns slowly — very slowly, measured in eons— to turn towards the right path which is expressed in tenet four of the Minimum Working Hypothesis: *Man's life on earth has only one end and purpose: to identify himself with his eternal self and so come to unitive knowledge of the Divine Ground of all existence.*

Heard believed that much of history was made by men seeking *something,* but not realizing that their ego-driven efforts in the material world were misdirected distractions from the metaphysical world. Nonetheless, these misguided efforts still had some benefit.

> What we now can see in history, the clue to the sequence and process is, then, this: *The Emergence of Man.* All his acts and achievements, however extravagant and even contradictory they must appear when only viewed by themselves, can be co-ordinated and understood if we realize that they are shadows cast on the outer world by the changing shape of his spirit, projections and symptoms of a slow inner evolution of mind whereby it has stage by stage taken its present form. As in the Paleontological record of the rocks we have learnt to recognize as stages toward our present form, types which, till the idea of evolution was grasped, were thought wholly distinct, so now we can see the stable "superstitious," Magical Aeon, the Heroic Age of violent strife, and our present individualised age as all connected, successive, inevitable phases of a single evolutionary process— evolution being carried on now in the mind as it was once carried on in the body [*Emergence*, 23].

Man works or makes in order to find out what he is about, but his alienated, yet malleable ego often misdirects him from the right path and what he makes is a mess. The artists, poets, and their audience unconsciously want to be led back to a "psychical" Eden, which resides in their hidden wishes and dreams. This Eden, to Heard, is actually the intuitive sense of the metaphysical First Cause (or synonym) that is the origin of the universe, a spark of which is retained in the unconscious, and merely waiting to be ignited and awakened by self-realization. This spark is a gift of heredity, according to Heard, passed on through genes just as physical traits are. Thus, what the makers or artists make or intimate is a continuance of the ritualized *awe*-sociations first recreated by the storyteller for his tribe as a form of communal reconciliation reminding them of the "mystery" of initial existence — whatever it was or is.

The public, through art, subconsciously wishes to have a transcending moment, however fleeting, in their inner Eden that has been intimated for them by the art's *awe*-sociations. The effect provides temporary escape from their earth-bound existence.

Poems are mainly aesthetic, but can also be functional, by serving as parables, which is of major importance.

Knowledge gives people perspective, artists or otherwise. Hence, that old saying: "If I knew then, what I know now." Maturity takes the past and sees in it knowledge and lessons unrecognized when that past actually was the present. Writers mull knowledge prodigiously before that mulling will bubble over into integrated correlations. Often, one needs psychoanalysis, or at least self-introspection, to help make the correlations. Knowledge and understanding only come after experience — if they come at all.

That life influences art is essential to understanding artists, and this includes childhood ruminations that lay a foundation for the artist's future. Auden elaborates:

> Most of what I know about writing poetry, or at least the kind I am interested in writing I discovered long before I took an interest in poetry itself.
>
> Between the ages of six and twelve I spent a great many of my waking hours in the fabrication of a private secondary *sacred* world, the basic elements of which were (a) limestone landscape, mainly derived from the Pennine Moors in the North of England and (b) an industry — lead mining.

Auden continues to explain that even in a secondary world, one must constitute it from what can be referenced in the existing primary world:

> Even the purest poem, in the French sense, is made up of words, which are not the poet's private property, but the communal creation of the linguistic group to which he belongs, so that the meaning can be looked up in the dictionary.
>
> A secondary world must be as much a world of law as the primary. I instinctively felt that I must impose two restrictions upon my freedom of fantasy. I was free to select this and reject that, on one condition, that both were real objects in the primary world.
>
> When, later, I began to write poetry, I found that, for me at least, the same obligation was binding. That is to say, I cannot accept the doctrine that in poetry there is a "suspension of belief." A poet must never make a statement simply because it sounds exciting; he must also believe it to be true.

> What the poet has to convey is not "self-expression," but a view of reality common to us all, seen from a unique perspective, which it is his duty, as well as his pleasure to share with others ["Writing," *A Certain World*, 423–25].

Auden wrote this at age 64, two years before his death, as the last item in his Commonplace anthology, *A Certain World*. It is a succinct, eloquent, and poignant summation of his artistic *raison d'être*, which, for Auden, meant it was his philosophy of life. It is also, in large part, the critical framework of this chapter.

Without truth, beauty in a poem is without soul, admirable, but engendering no reverence or sympathy; it is not sacred; it does not intimate the awesociations that are both desired and needed by its readers. Awe should be the end of art; beauty, the means to that end, which is to say that truth, once established, becomes the sacred foundation, the framework upon which the embellishments of beauty are overlaid, for it is the beauty that attracts one to the truth underneath, even if it is the bitter truth. The hidden strength of truth within reinforces and enhances the beauty without. A desire for some form of metaphysical truth has existed in the psyche since the origins of consciousness. Human beings recognize the beauty-truth dialectic — and seek it — because it harkens back to the ritualized tribe or group where unspoken communication of mutual need and endeavor had not as yet been disturbed by assertive, separating egos. The truth, even when it hurts, is the end of art, and beauty, the means. For the poet the means of art is language, which is the collective representation of the society it represents. Experiences are carried forward by memory and words.

An initial experience creates an urge for another, then another, and so on. The sensations felt from these immediate experiences are translated into the symbology of language, stored in the memory as knowledge, and called forth as needed in response to new urges, like the one to make a poem for example. This urge may or may not come in a moment of tranquility but, in fact, may be more of an itch that must be scratched or a rage or guilt that must be expiated. Emotional urges drive the creative impulse so that art can have some control over these emotions by better understanding them. The emotions and feelings of the primitive tribe are not so different from the present tribe. The first thoughts initiated all subsequent thought in every successive generation. Different nuances change for successive generations but not the core emotions.

> Human nature does not change, or, at any rate, history is too short for any changes to be perceptible. The earliest known specimens of art and literature are still comprehensible. The fact that we can understand them all and can recognize in some of them an unsurpassed artistic excellence is proof enough that not only men's feelings and instincts, but their intellectual and imaginative powers, were in remotest times precisely what they are now. In the fine arts, it is only the convention, the form, the incidentals that change: the fundamentals of passion, of intellect and imagination remain unaltered.

> It is the same with the arts of life as with the fine arts. Conventions and traditions, prejudices and ideals and religious beliefs, moral systems, and codes of good manners, varying according to the geographical and historical circumstances, mould into different forms the unchanging material of human instinct, passion, and desire.
> At any given moment human behaviour is a compromise (enforced from without by law and custom, from within by belief in religious or philosophical myths) between the raw instinct on the one hand and the unattainable ideal on the other [Huxley, "Do What You Will," 130].

"Raw instinct" without ideals to modify the raw instinct is not a pretty picture. The raw is downward transcendence into possible anarchy. Instinct (intuition) shaped by ideals is upward transcendence. In all respects, as per Heard, if one seeks to satisfy the ego only, work and desires will not necessarily relieve man's unconscious needs. If work and achievement of material gain cannot do it, one turns to escapism, Huxley said, of either upward, but more often, downward, transcendence, for relief of the itch. Upward transcendence is selfless movement towards the unified consciousness, via mystical philosophy; downward transcendence is selfish movement away from unity through various means such as mind-dulling, passive entertainments: junk reading, television, "B" movies, pornography, or active, yet still mind-numbing, alcohol, narcotics, sexual obsession, and aggression. All of these negative escapes are used by the future totalitarian government to control constituents in Huxley's *Brave New World* (1932). The idea is to pacify and brainwash the society to be "happy," cooperative slaves. This is a bread-and-circuses pacification. One could argue that there are aspects of this type of mindless pacification present in modern American society.

The distance between the downward raw instinct and the upward unattainable idea can seem insurmountable, and it is the gap between what *is* and what *could be* that stimulates desires which cannot ultimately be satisfied, as these desires mask a latent, and for the majority, inexplicable dissatisfaction with life. This, however, has never stopped anyone, particularly artists and mystics, from trying to find the "ineffable" meaning that would at least narrow the gap between the instinct and the idea. The very effort to escape or transcend, in all its positive or negative modes, is proof enough that we require more from life than we are getting — if only we knew what we wanted. The poet tries to find out what he or we want, and in so doing he builds bridges from his separate self to the separate selves of his readers; he attempts to scratch at the door to the ineffable. Many in the poet's audience — not the junk readers — also seek to see more clearly through the doors of perception and choose "serious art" that will help them with the challenge to be found from seeking *awe*-sociations through the beauty-truth dialectic. What people hope to find is that elusive more satisfying *something* that hints at the ineffable *other self* that they, like the poet, are consciously or unconsciously looking for.

The poet wants to be appreciated and is compelled, not just to make something of what he observes and perceives, but to share it with others whether this means the one, the few of the tribe or group, or the many reached through mass media. Numbers are incidental to the poet's motivation, which is to gain approval for his choosing to play the game of poetry, resulting in the *acte gratuite* of a poem created from desire, not as a necessity for survival. What becomes a necessity for all tribe members, the poet included, is the sharing aspect of human relations which is motivated by both the need of companionship and the protection the tribe, group, or community provides. The poet, through his gift, has something to offer the others, and he can be satisfied of his need by telling even just one listener. A larger number of listeners or readers may increase the poet's final degree of satisfaction with duplicate validation, but that initial urge to be appreciated needs just that one initial listener if that listener is a good one and returns the emotional reciprocity the teller-listener interchange is meant to achieve.

The poet, prompted by a particular muse, is motivated from personal pride or ego to play his game. He begins by rummaging into his memory bank of archetypal images to select from his inventory of raw materials (experience and knowledge) those he feels will work. Then he gives order to his choices and makes a poem. The poet's degree of proficiency in making his aesthetic choices depends on the depth of his perception. A poet perceives, rather than just observes; although, of course, he does both. Not all people do. Everyone that observes can see but not all perceive, which is to both see and understand. Artists and scientists (*Eureka!*) mutually share this asset, and then they just have to tell others what they've made or discovered (science measures nature; art "metaphorizes" nature). Artists and scientists, as all individuals, are virtually driven to share their news and signify the achievement of knowing something others don't. New news gives a person a reason or excuse to communicate with others; it can be something to barter in order to get more attention and approval. The "show and tell" of youth, where student becomes teacher, always remains within the actual child or the adult's inner child. The relationship of the good listener and the good teller is a perpetuation of the teacher-student dichotomy. Auden said: "We respond and obey before we can summon and command." He also said: "Since we are not born with instinctive modes of behavior, the teacher-pupil [teller-listener] relationship is of essential importance to our lives" ("A Novel by Goethe," 12). Huxley added: "Artists are eminently teachable and also eminently teachers. They receive from events much more than most men receive, and they can transmit what they received with particular penetrative force, which drives their communication deep into the reader's mind. One of our most ordinary reactions to a good piece of literary art is expressed in the formula: 'This is what I have always felt and thought, but have never been able to put clearly into words, even for myself'" ("Tragedy and the Whole Truth," 5).

To retain readers or listeners the poet maintains a delicate balance between his own needs, desires and wishes, and the needs, desires, and wishes of a potential audience. In general, these needs are the same. Yet, what becomes different is how each particular poet and reader wishes to fulfill these needs. This is what ultimately will link certain poets with certain readers: the degree of mutual sympathy on their terms, which may be of different shadings and nuances than another poet and his particular contingent of readers.

This also raises the issue of who a poet's readers are. Can a poet write for any and every possible person who might happen to read a certain poem? Can he determine who will possibly even see his poem? A poet, unless he reacts to the lowest common denominator of potential readership, cannot write something for everyone, no more than any single individual can be liked by everyone. (If everyone likes you, you must be lying to somebody.) The poet's best bet is the one Polonius made: "To thine own self be true!" A sincere poet (or novelist, or essayist, or dramatist) should write as "play," for self-satisfaction that he hopes will also please others. But if the poet (etc.) writes to fit what will, so to speak, sell, if not actually for his personal approval, he may please an audience, but not himself; in effect, *play* is no longer play, but work. Auden, Eliot, Aiken , et al. did not, and could not, write for everyone, each choosing to strive for a personal message and letting those readers who got the message choose themselves to be recipients.

For example, Auden, when asked if he thought about whom he was writing for, said: "No, I just try to put the thing out and hope somebody will read it. Someone says: 'Whom do you write for?' I reply: 'Do you read me?' If they say, 'Yes,' I say, 'Do you like it?' If they say, 'No,' then I say, 'I don't write for you'" ("Interview with W.H. Auden," 269).

In all cases, however, poets are still obliged to consider intuitively the four basic tenets of his craft that will help result in his successful intervention and connection with potential readers:

1. To convey the "thoughts of the wise man in the speech of the common people."

2. To "see with the eyes of children" and bring a freshness of insight that seems to have been rendered with a seemingly effortless naturalness (rather than sounding in any way artificial).

3. To tell the truth, to the best of one's ability as one sees it, but not to compromise one's inner truth or sincerity by manipulating the message and pandering to what one thinks readers want to hear in order to get their approval instead of having readers hear what one really thinks.

4. To spread some relevant news that also intimates *awe*-sociations and seems to do so as if they've been transmitted from the muse of inspiration directly to the writing hand in a trance. (The hard work is supposed to be a secret, although this author once had the "trance" experience in completing a novel.)

Number four concerns the public's perception of how art gets to be that way. The artist or poet knows too well that the old adage of ten-percent inspiration, ninety-percent perspiration, is true.

Poetry and magic are equally a question of illusion and, even more so, of fantasy as escapism. Says Auden, "The identification of fantasy is always an attempt to avoid one's own suffering: the identification of art is the *sharing* in the suffering of another" ("The Guilty Vicarage," 158). "Suffering" herein is in the sense of mutual commiseration, whether good or bad.

Individuals fantasize as a means to escape, however briefly, from the routine of daily existence into some other world of either upward or downward transcendence. (Or to escape from some situation that is more painful: illness, injury, bereavement, war, prison, etc.)

For a poet, the avoidance of his own suffering becomes an itch to be scratched by creative activity, and this is so whether the suffering is contemporaneous or being recalled from memory. The poet chooses avoidance through the escape mechanism of fantasy-as-poetry with the intention of sharing it with others who will likewise escape into the poems by way of the empathy and sympathy of mutual commiseration.

Fantasy, although motivated by a need for avoidance or escape, is not just a matter of what one escapes from, but more importantly, concerns the question of choosing where one escapes to. The poet knows that his fantasy is an *escape-by-yearning* for a temporarily autistic Secondary World of the imagination created as an alternative to the Primary World. The poet also knows that both his impulse to make poetry and the audience's desire to be given it is correspondingly a by-product of mankind's collective yearning for, and fantasizing upon, the psychic Eden.

The poetry of music also satisfies yearning: "I'm talking about the energy, the wistful yearning, the inexplicable exhilaration, the sporadic sense of invincibility, the hope that stings like chlorine. When I was younger, rock music articulated these feelings, and now that I'm older it stimulates them, but either way, rock 'n' roll was and remains necessary because: who doesn't need exhilaration and a sense of invincibility, even if it's only now and again?" (Hornby, "Rock of Ages," *New York Times*, www.nytimes.com/2004/05/21/opinion/21 HORN.html).

The sincere poet (or musician) wants to help himself and his audience by temporarily displacing the disorder of daily reality and reaching for the ordered realm of that psychic Eden latently residing in the unified consciousness. The poet wishes to imagine being there, even fleetingly, in a temporary return to that subliminal world of tranquil order that unifies egos instead of separating them.

> Both in life and art the human task is to create a necessary order out of an arbitrary chaos. A necessary order implies that the process of its creation is not itself arbitrary; one is not free to create *any* order one chooses. The order realized must, in

> fact, have been already latent in the chaos, so that successful creation is a process of discovery. As long as this remains latent and unconscious, conscious life must appear arbitrary; one grows up in the degree to which this unconscious order becomes conscious and its potentialities developed, to the degree that one's life ceases to be arbitrary, to the degree that one becomes conscious of and true to one's fate. An artist is someone who is able to express human development in a public medium [Auden, "Review of *Open House*," 30].

Both the artist and the audience wish to make some order out of the chaos of daily life not only as a model for the future, but equally as a recall of the order within the unified consciousness that already exists in that psychic region of the brain where it has been carried along, evolving through the generations. For mystics, order exists in the psychic continuum as a matter of course; it only needs to be recognized by the humans who lost it when they asserted their separate and collective egos. The scientist also seeks order, but does so in the physical realm. The artist, in contrast, seeks it in the metaphysical realm. The scientist wishes for an external order in physical nature; the artist wishes for internal order in metaphysical nature. Combined, this is the Ultimate Reality of Brahman in which both cause and effect, idea and form, are an undifferentiated unity seeking perpetually to find balance through the reconciliation of opposites.

> To use a phrase originally used by Clive Bell, the artist gives order to the world in terms of: "significant form." What he does is try and perceive forms inherent in nature and to find a symbolic equivalence for these forms which he then imposes upon the world in order to produce the order which he feels to be so supremely important, and which, indeed, we all feel to be supremely important.
>
> The artist seeks to impose this order of beauty and significant form upon both the external reality and the internal reality within him. He wants always to see himself in relation to the world and to create symbolically a harmony in which both fit. In this respect—in that it consciously takes into account the internal world as well as the external—art differs markedly from most types of science [Huxley, "Art," 83].

What is also supremely important, besides the external order in nature, is the internal order of man reconciling his living in nature while also living within himself.

Art and science approach nature differently, but they are not mutually exclusive; each confronts nature from opposite poles. Ideally, one can serve the other to synthesize outer order in nature and inner order in man. Ultimately, however, it is not the scientist, but the poet who preserves the spirit of an era as per Huxley, "And yet it is only by poets that the life of any epoch can be synthesized. Encyclopedias and guides to knowledge cannot do it, for the good reason that they affect only the intellectual surface of a man's life. The lower layers, the core of his being, they leave untouched" ("Introduction," *Texts and Pretexts*, 4).

Reason and imagination: by reconciling these two seemingly opposite poles of man's conscious existence, man is also making a statement about the fallacy of two-ness, the mistaken assumption by individuals that each is separate not only from other individuals—"I am I and you are not I"—but from the rest of the universe. A person's sense of separateness and duality—inner and outer, public and private, mind and body—are all ego-generated, illusory perceptions exacerbated by the artificial man-made construct of time. It is man's stressful allegiance to time that fuels his ego-driven separateness and his mistaken self-image of inner-outer duality.

Time is man's artificial construct, which he created in order to meet external demands that require his attention. He implemented and referenced arbitrary terms—seconds, minutes, hours—as a way to be able to respond to necessary situations beyond his control. Necessity herein means a self-generated or societally imposed need to be somewhere or do something which entails some form of response to external obligations such as planting or harvesting, or to the tribe, group, state, nation, all of which are always accounting for "time" as that which urgently needs to be responded to in this lifetime. (Necessity simply means "work" as opposed to gratuitous "play.") Hence, man's ego-driven, compulsive-obsessive rush is to change the world right now—or at least before he dies. One result of this clock-bound urgency is that the individual and collective mind are perpetually juxtaposing their "present" with what has come before or what will lie ahead. (For the mystic, "past," "future" and "present" are a single entity.) At best this constant referencing of past and future is nostalgia for the past or pleasant anticipation of the future. More likely, however, the mental referencing about past and future entails debilitating guilt, regret, and remorse or even more debilitating anxiety or fear about what's coming ahead. And in the name of this fear about the future, many individual and collective traumas, including wars, have been perpetrated.

Awareness of "time" adds to the inherent fear humans have concerning the death of the body, since reminders of advancing time (like an appointment with the dentist Thursday) also remind them that time is running out. Man sees death as the "end" of his ego-bound existence; but the death of the body—and the body is, from the mystic's perspective, just a finite suitcase containing an infinite spirit—is not an end, but a release into a different form of being, one that is both a reflection of, and indistinguishably integral to, the *eternal now* of the unified consciousness.

For each individual, the illusion of time exists along with the stress of being responsible for adhering to it. Man then seeks ways to relieve his stress. One way to suspend time is through the relief of seeing or hearing timeless art, within which man senses intimations of the timelessness within the psychic Eden that he intuitively yearns to return to. Another way is mystical contemplation or meditation. For 3,000 years mystics have intuitively known that man-made time is an obstacle to be overcome. Writes Meister Eckhart: "Time is what keeps the light from reaching us. There is no greater obstacle to God [unified consciousness] than time. And not only time but temporalities, not only temporal things but temporal affections; not only temporal affections but the very taint and smell of time" (as quoted in Huxley, *The Perennial Philosophy,* 189). Additionally, man-made time is progressive. Natural "time" is not. Or as Thornton Wilder said: "It is only in appearance that time is a river. It is a vast landscape, and it is the eye of the beholder that moves" (*The Eighth Day,* 395).

The ego-bound beholder's eye mistakenly creates the sense of a progressive time that does not actually exist. When Shakespeare and Huxley said that "time must have a stop," they were directly confronting the fear of time and the fear of death. When time stops, and existence reasserts its status as a continuum of an *eternal now,* then the fear of disorder and the fear of death stop as well. For the time being, however, masses of still-separate egos are in a rather disorderly arrangement so that when arbitrariness and the pressure of time reign externally, the retreat into one's inner self is very tempting. The only problem with this psychic retreat is that the noise and chatter of the outer world eventually call one back, and to it one must go, however reluctantly. (Autistics retreat permanently and refuse to be called back.)

Man seeks, by whatever means of upward or downward transcendence, to get away from this seemingly endless noise and chatter. Therein is a paradox: The inner world is a retreat; however, if the withdrawal is made without a conscious, positive relation to the whole of existence, as in the upward transcendence of meditation or art, but as merely negative escapism, the temporary separation from the outer world just adds to a person's alienation from it, and the eventual recall to external existence becomes even more painful with each re-entry, or "coming-down" from the inner world.

Amphibious man's often conflicted existence is caused by his ability to live in, if not always well, the two-ness or duality of his inner and outer worlds. The struggle is such that Huxley described the inherent negativeness of two-ness as being factored within the very nature of language itself: "How significant is it that in Indo-European languages ... the root meaning of 'two' should connote badness. The Greek prefix dys- (as in dyspepsia) and the Latin dis- (as in dishonorable) are both derived from the 'duo.' The cognate bis- gives a pejorative sense to modern French words as *bevue* ('blunder,' literally 'two-sight'). Traces of that second which leads you astray can be found in 'dubious,' 'doubt,' and *Zweifel*—for to doubt is to be double-minded. Bunyan has his Mr. Facing-both-ways, and modern American slang its 'two-timers.' Obscurely and unconsciously wise, our language confirms the findings of the mystics and proclaims the essential badness of division — a word incidentally, in which our old enemy 'two' makes another decisive appearance" (*The Perennial Philosophy,* 10). The effort to give order to that which seems arbitrary is the mind's way of expressing the need to lend some comprehensible connection and relevance to a world that can otherwise make individuals feel disconnected and irrelevant. Disconnection — or twoness— has been the fate of hundreds of generations with self-assertive egos that alienate individuals into separate islands with their drawbridges mostly raised; the "moats" of division thus prevent man's re-integration back into the unified consciousness that makes inner and outer worlds integral.

It is man's ego-bound duality that fosters his false perception of separateness and prevents his re-integration or synthesis into the unified consciousness. "For the doctrine of [unified consciousness] to be illustrated belongs to the science, not of the personal ego, but of the eternal Self in the depth of particular, individualized selves, and identical with the Divine Ground.... This teaching is expressed most succinctly in the Sanskrit, *tat twam asi* ('Thou art that; that art thou.'); the absolute principle of all existence" (Huxley, *Perennial Philosophy*, 3).

The term *tat twam asi* signifies that there is no separation of body and mind or one and many; separation is an illusion of the ego in deceitful collaboration with the senses. To say, as Vedantists do, "*Thou* art that / *That* art thou" means: you are integral to *that*, and, *that*, which is anything or everything else, is integral to you. *Thou art That* describes humanity's intuitive sense of its underlying unity within the Divine Ground of the *eternal now*, an *eternal now* that is considered by mystics (and T.S. Eliot) to be the normal state of being. What's not normal is the illusion of differentiation that promulgates man's misperception of separateness. There is no real distinction between inner and outer. There are continual distractions of a mistaken perception of an inner or outer duality. These distractions impede the truth of the underlying unity of the divine ground and they are magnified in importance by the ego, which is the mind's defense mechanism activated by the insecurity engendered from this illusion of separateness. This is not to say that man isn't an amphibian capable of being in more than one world simultaneously; he is however, if he so chooses, capable of not just bouncing between the two worlds but of seeing them as just aspects of his being in one world, which, in fact, is the case as per Auden:

> Man's *consciousness* of himself exists as a unity-in tension of three modes of *awareness*:
> (a) The consciousness of the self as self-contained; as embracing all of which it is aware in a unity of experiencing....
> (b) The consciousness of beyondness, of the ego standing as a spectator over against both itself and the external world....
> (c) The ego's consciousness of self as striving towards, as desiring to transform the self to realize its potentialities ["Nature, History, and Poetry, 416].

In the third step, the poet and reader wish that poetry be written and read, thus implying that they hope the process can teach and help readers and listeners to fulfill their positive potential and unicity. Taking words and "purifying" them is how the poet converts a "crowd" of words into the "community" of a poem. The poem is a verbal system derived from the poet's feelings. The nature of the final order is the outcome of a dialectical struggle between those feelings and the verbal system.

Consequently, this reconciliation between the feelings and the verbal system is the art of finding a balance between recalled emotions and the choice of language to evoke these memories for a reader. A poem is not about what we know, but how we *feel* about what we know. The key to this balancing act of emotive evocation is to strive for telling the news with a pleasing aesthetic framework. A poem's beauty is a symbolic evocation of the natural world as derived from memories of immediate experience that are recorded for posterity:

> [A poem's] Beauty arises when the parts of a whole are related to one another and to the totality in a manner which we apprehend as orderly and significant. The beatific vision of divine beauty [which the poem evokes] is the knowledge, so to say, of Pure Interval, of a harmonious relationship apart from the things related. A material figure of beauty-in-itself is the cloudless evening sky, which we find inexpressibly lovely, although it possesses no orderliness of arrangement, since there are no distinguishable parts to be harmonized. We find it beautiful because it is an emblem of the infinite Clear Light of The Void [Huxley, "Seven Meditations," 164].

The beauty of art reflects a society's degree of interest in and yearning for a greater role in relating itself to the potentialities of total existence in a unified consciousness. Historians recording the progress of metaphysics can look back and measure a society's yearning for inner progress by the level of its interest in art. The goal of the synthesis of inner and outer worlds into one harmonious world is also a measure of man's yearning for an ideal man, or the man Gerald Heard labeled the Priest/Seer who could be equally adept in either world, inner or outer. This is not necessarily to say that the poet is himself the ideal man (or woman), but that he may describe and define an ideal man for his readers to recognize as an emblem for emulation. An ideal man is, nonetheless, not a perfect one; he is, however, a person who strives for perfection as a goal, and it is in the striving for perfection that he is lionized, more so than the reaching of it which is not possible in life, but waits for realization on some other plane of awareness. The poet intimates perfection for himself and his readers, but this can only remain intimation. While the poet and his poem will not induce a permanent euphoria, the poem's supernatural power to evoke upward transcendence can be repeated when it is being read and reread by readers present and future.

All artists actively perceive the external world of the vulgar, profane, and lowbrow in a new way in order to create art that intimates the inner world of the numinous, sacred, and highbrow. The poet takes conventional language and uses it to bridge the gap from the tangible, primary world of daily reality, to the ineffable, secondary world of the imagination. As children emerging from the safe cocoon of "wombland," we overcome our initial terror by learning language that frees us from the psychological umbilical cord and weans us off dependency on others by teaching independence through self-sufficiency. We learn to imitate, listen, respond, and obey before we learn to initiate, speak, summon, and command by absorbing enough language to survive and even thrive. While absorbing language we also learn habits, customs, traditions, dogma, and prejudices about which, if they are distorted, we will have those distortions transferred to us. Consequently, unlearning language — and the accumulative influences carried with it — is much more difficult than learning it.

Mystics and artists are among those who consciously attempt to overcome these impediments and share what they've learned with their disciples and audiences, all of whom seek and yearn for those momentary intimations of *awe-*sociations that fleetingly free them from routine existence. The literary artist, as an initiative-taking highbrow, challenges himself to find these moments by remaking a new language in order to free himself from his old language and share the new *news* with readers. "A good writer," said Huxley (from Mallarme, quoted in "Knowledge and Understanding," 57) "is one who knows how to *donner un plus sens pur aux mots de la tribu* (to give a purer sense to the words of the tribe)." Thanks to this purer sense, his readers will react to his words with a degree of understanding much greater than they would have if they had reacted in their ordinary self-conditioned and culture-conditioned way to the events to which the words refer. "A great poet ... knows how to express himself in words which can cause other people to understand [what he has understood]. Time lost can never be regained; but in search for it, he may reveal to his readers glimpses of timeless reality" (Huxley, "Knowledge and Understanding," 57).

As Nietzsche asserted in his *Genealogy of Morals* we must strip our minds of the previous influences of others who, in effect, have mediated our interpretation of life. The Vedas call this "discrimination." This view is the same as Emerson's *Self-Reliance* of the nineteenth century, and the *Freedom from the Known* of Krishnamurti — Huxley's friend — in the twentieth. It was Huxley who encouraged Krishnamurti to write down his philosophy and put it in a book for public consumption. This was *The First and Last Freedom* (1954) for which Huxley wrote an introduction. Those who can empty their minds of clutter leave the mind open as *no-mind* where revelation of awe-sociations might fill the now more usable space.

The wish for writers and readers to intimate timeless *awe-*sociations springs from the desire to momentarily fulfill two wishes: to better understand their relation to the world of immediate experience and to sometimes escape into the "womblike" world of the psychic Eden. For Auden, these desires seek dual paths to the same goal. "Present in every human being are two desires, a desire to know the truth about the Primary world, the given world outside ourselves in which we are born, live, love, hate, and die, and the desire to make new secondary worlds of our own or, if we cannot make them ourselves, to share in the secondary worlds of those who can" ("The World of the Sagas," 49). All human beings want to partake of a secondary world in order to temporarily (or permanently for autistics) gain relief from the everyday routine of the primary world. In simple daydreams, everyone imagines being the smart one, or the heroic one, or the one who saves the day and is loved and approved of by all. Unlike most other men who observe passively, the poet sees and also perceives actively with the intuitiveness of his highbrow muse, and chooses with his highbrow initiative to write about it. He takes what he sees and correlates it with his mind's mental inventory of stored raw materials as retained in memory. Combining the new experience with the old, the poet transforms both, attempting to make better sense of what he has previously learned, not merely as particulars in isolation, but to remake these particulars so they are more clearly integrated with the whole of existence. "Indeed," Auden said, "every set of verses, whatever their subject matter may be, are by their formal nature a hymn to Natural Law and a gesture of astonishment at the greatest of all mysteries, the order of the universe" ("Today's Poet," 187).

Vico in his *New Science* explained that the initially inexplicable feelings of *Awe* felt by the primitive tribe about natural phenomena evolved into theological explanations to soothe the frightened tribe. The tribe then ritualized these feelings into their own form of the spiritual manifestation they called God (or a synonym). "He [the artist] gives meaning and order to something which, when it is not ordered, is apt to seem terrifying—the movement toward an inevitable darkness in the future. Man has to make these patterns to give a kind of sense and coherence and meaning to the flux of time; he derives them from elements in nature, strengthens them in his system of symbols, and then re-imposes them upon nature so as to make nature more coherent in his own mind (Huxley, "Art,"189).

The feelings of awe were immediately experienced first and they were experienced viscerally by seeing and/or hearing natural phenomena: rainbows, mountains, waterfalls, lightning, thunder, the lion's roar. If the tribe survives all of the preceding, these phenomena, after the fear subsides, are then pondered upon in a state akin to the awesome wonder of the wide-eyed child. This wonder is a temporary suspension of the primary and routine everyday world of dutiful and responsible work, in favor of the secondary world of play that exists in the psychic Eden of innocent, child-like purity and goodness. For Auden, by way of Gerald Heard, these *wonder*-full intimations of *awe*-sociations were a yearning to rediscover the spiritually motivated need to become one again with a unified consciousness.

> Goodness is rooted in wonder ... [although] wonder itself is not goodness ... but it is the only, or the most favorable, soil in which goodness can grow ... a sense of wonder is not something we have to learn, for we are born with it. Those who lose the capacity for wonder may be clever but not intelligent, they may lead moral lives themselves, but they will become insensitive and moralistic towards others. It is only with the help of wonder, then, that we can develop a virtue which we are certainly not born with, compassion, not to be confused with its conceit-created counterfeit,

pity. Only from wonder, too, can we learn a style of behaviour and speech which is no less precious in art than in life; for want of a better word we call it good manners or breeding, though it has little to do with ancestry, school or income ["Walter de la Mare," 393-94].

Attempts to understand the feelings of wonder aroused in the tribe by an awesome event, whatever it was, naturally followed the event, and, in order to rationalize these events, the tribe gave to those feelings some kind of supernatural explanation. (To speak or write of a natural phenomenon no longer present is always supernatural.) By speaking of it, new language was created after the event to cope with the residual awe stored in memory and for the tribe to share the awesome memory with others who had been likewise present and equally awed. What is inexplicable can be fearsome; new language ameliorates the fear through a process of mythifying. The event, now mythologized, comes under that unique human power that's derived from naming, just as Adam named the beasts to have dominion over them. The naming reduces fear by giving some control to the event's newly created meaning, if not control over the event itself. (The god of thunder didn't stop coming; he was just given a more friendly face.) In time, with repetition of the event — the next thunderstorm — and repeated telling of it, the residual awe coheres, at first, into a crude story; then, over more time, the telling of the story evolves into a simple ritual to be shared by the tribe — the Thunder-God brings rain — then complex ritual to be shared by society — planting or harvesting. Rituals follow awesome experiences and convey how one feels about what one knows or imagines he knows. Eventually, the catalyzing experiences become history; the initial, genuine awe once felt by the tribe is de-mythifed into the dogmatic *faux*-awe of a ritual turned static by habitual compliance. Passed on through the generations, the cumulative effect of this process of awe-into-myth-into-theology-into-dogma adds up to: *Awe first, ask questions later.* Still, no matter how distanced, dogmatized, or complicated a mythologized theology evolves into, Huxley observed that "The elaborate constructions of theology are [still] based on ... the rationalizations of numinous feelings first felt by the tribe generations before" (*Texts and Pretexts*, 308).

Consequently, these "elaborate constructions of theology" subliminally influence society long after their intricacies have become dogmatic habit or forgotten completely. Subsequently, when man encounters in the primary world either directly, or through art indirectly, intimations of *awe*-sociations that induce a trip to his secondary world, he evaluates them, consciously or unconsciously, based on his society's theologically based, previously accumulated influences even if these influences are not acted upon, but are subliminally and collectively subjective. For example, the Puritan ethic's influence in America still strongly exists in many people who have never heard of it. When man is newly and viscerally awed in the present, he simultaneously recalls previous feelings of awe felt in the past for comparison. In doing so, his mind almost concurrently converts his immediate emotional response to fit the residue of whatever mythical or theological schematic for which his societally acculturated brain has been pre-programmed. In effect, Awe *and* God (or synonym) are always correlatives when man reacts to his primary and secondary worlds. These emotional and intellectual co-responses may be accessing separate memory files but the mind skips conscious awareness of the integrating process and concerns itself only with the now indistinguishably merged co-response that is thus described by Huxley:

> Direct or remembered experiences [are] conditioned, as to mode and quality, by a theological hypothesis. For it is obvious, emotional experience, and intellectual interpretation of that experience cannot be kept permanently separated in alternating [primary and secondary] strata. Crudely and schematically, what happens is this: something is directly experienced [primary emotion]; this experience is intellectually interpreted, generally in terms of some existing system of metaphysics or mythology; the myth, [and/or] the philosophical system are regarded as true and become in their turn the source of new experiences and the channels through which the old emotions must pass ["Pascal," 252–53].

The mind engages in a constant process of "re-mythifying" and is aided and abetted through the medium of a language that is constantly reinventing and reinterpreting itself to suit man's changing needs. Moreover, by the poet's remaking of words, he can give certain words numinous and sacred mystical significance. People rarely forsake the need for secondary worlds that are evoked by awe-sociations; they just change the nomenclature. These *awe*-sociations can only be felt, never duplicated in words. The best that words can do is to evoke memories of the awe and mimic distantly the original feelings. All literary artists try to intimate the inexpressible ineffable of the God-Awe correlatives through deft presentation of the expressible. Somewhere between the writer and his audience there is the bridge of unconscious meaning:

> The ambition of the literary artist is to speak about the ineffable, to communicate in words what words were never intended to convey. Every literary artist must therefore invent or borrow some kind of uncommon language capable of expressing, at least partially, those experiences which the vocabulary and syntax of ordinary speech so manifestly fail to convey. *Donner un sens plus pur aux mots de la tribu* — that is the task confronting every serious writer; for it is only by an unusual combination of purified words that our more private experiences in all their subtlety, their many-faceted richness, their unrepeatable uniqueness can be, in some sort, re-created on the symbolic level and so made public and communicable....
>
> Every concrete particular, public or private, is a window opening to the universal....
>
> Literature's concern is not with regularities and explanatory laws, but with descriptions of appearances and the discerned qualities of objects perceived as wholes with judgments, comparisons and discriminations, with "inscapes" and essences, and finally with the *Istikgeit* ("isness") of things, the Not-thought in thoughts.... Every human being is aware of the multifarious world and knows (rather confusedly in most cases) where he stands in relation to it. Moreover, by analogy with himself, he

can guess where other people stand, what they feel and how they are likely to behave [Huxley, *Literature and Science*, 10, 117, 8].

To say, "every concrete particular, public or private, is a window opening to the universal," is a succinct, aphoristic summary of the role language plays in the perpetual continuum.

When a mystic is metaphysically integrated with the undifferentiated unity, it is because he has looked into the face of the "immensities" and feels not apart from them, but one with them, unseparated, unified indistinguishably with a similar comprehension to that of the God-Awe correlative, but considered more through meditative contemplation than visceral emotionalism. In contemplation, he becomes the calm center of life's hurricane, observing the storm's spin, but not being caught up in it and dizzied by it. Vedantists, three thousand years ago, understood this detached unity and later disseminated it in the Bhagavad-Gita and the Upanishads. In Huxley's essay collection *Tomorrow and Tomorrow and Tomorrow*, there are two essays, "Education of an Amphibian," and "Adonis and the Alphabet," in which he relates the development of language to seminal Indian Vedantism, which is the original basis for mystical philosophy:

> Every existing language is an implied theory of man and his universe, a virtual philosophy. Without exception, all languages are stupendous works of genius. One is almost forced to believe in the existence, within each one of us, of *something* other and much more intelligent than the conscious self ["Education of an Amphibian," 3].

In every system of Hindu philosophy the phenomenal world is called *nama-rupa*, "name and form." "The totality of this is called (to quote Heinrich Zimmer [*The Philosophies of India*, New York: Pantheon, 1951, 23]) in Indian philosophy, *naman* (Latin *nomen*, our word 'name'). *Naman* is the internal realm of concepts, which corresponds to the external realm of perceived 'forms,' the Sanskrit term for the latter being *rupa*.... *Rupa* is the outer counterpart of *naman*; *naman* the interior of *rupa*. *Nama-rupa* therefore denotes, on the one hand, man, the experiencing and thinking individual, man as endowed with mind and senses; and on the other, all the means and objects of thought and perception. *Nama-rupa* is the whole world subjective and objective, as observed and known.

But no language is perfect, no vocabulary is adequate to the wealth of the given universe.... Consequently the phenomenal forms of our name-conditioned universe are by nature delusory and fallacious.... [M]ost of the interconnections within the general Gestalt are, and will always be, unrecognized. For us, the world is full of a number of things which we tend to see as so many independent entities. The *what* we think we know is never only *what*. There is a togetherness of all things in an endless hierarchy of living and interacting patterns ("Adonis and the Alphabet," 199–200).

This realization is the *isness* of the Divine Ground's simultaneous existence, which the poet intimates to his readers by making particulars universal.

> The concern of the primary imagination is with sacred beings and sacred objects....
> The impulse to create a work of art is felt when, in certain persons the passive awe provoked by sacred beings or events is transformed into a desire to express that awe in a rite of worship or homage, and to be homage, this rite must be beautiful. In poetry the rite is verbal, it pays homage by naming.... *Every poem he writes* involves the whole past.... every poem is rooted in imaginative awe.... there is only one thing that all poetry must do; it must praise all it can for being and for happening [Auden, "Making, Knowing, and Judging," 34–62].

The creative impulse is a desire for transcendence by intimating awe-sociations. In Vico's account, art came first as "Poetic Wisdom," which evolved into the "Esoteric Wisdom" of science, philosophy, and history. The tribal poet came first and the modern poet comes after as the synthesizer of his era's zeitgeist: The poet finds

> a truth, finally, about creatures, in whose minds far deeply interfused than any scientific hypothesis or even archetypal myth, is the *Something* whose dwelling is everywhere, the essential suchness of the world, which is at once immanent and transcendent—"in here" as the profoundest and most ineffable of private experiences and at the same time "out there," as the mental aspect of the material universe, as the emergence into cosmic mind of the organization of an infinity of organizations, perpetually renewed [Huxley, *Literature and Science*, 117–18].

Advancing together into the unknown, Huxley and Auden metaphorically envisioned individual poems as decentralized verbal communities within the larger verbal society of language. Poems are driven by their past, which asserts that their formations are dependent on previous knowledge, particularly as predicated on underlying God-Awe correlations residing in the collective consciousness. There are words, poems, and language; and there are people, communities, societies. In an ideal world the ideal formation of a poem, and the ideal formation of a society, would be the same:

> The subject matter of a poem is comprised of a crowd of recollected occasions of feeling, among which the most important are recollections of encounters with *sacred beings or events*. This crowd the poet attempts to transform into a community by embodying it in a verbal society.
> The nature of the final poetic order is the outcome of a dialectical struggle between the recollected occasions of feeling and the verbal system. In a successful poem, society and community are one order and the system may love itself because the feelings which it embodies are all members of the same community, loving each other and it [Auden, "The Virgin and the Dynamo," 68].

Art should stimulate thought, not substitute for it. Genuine sacred beings and events are derived from the tribe's initial catalyzing experiences with natural phenomena, which are then mythified and perpetuated into the continuum of evolving consciousness. True God-Awe correlatives are thus an unbroken continuance of original feelings and emotions, regardless of how those original feelings and emotions have been extrapolated over time.

> The new is the given on every level of experience — given perceptions, given emotions and thoughts, given states of unstructured awareness, given relationships with things and persons. The old is our home-made system of ideas and word patterns. Knowledge is primarily a knowledge of these finished articles. Understanding is primarily direct awareness of the raw material.
> Knowledge is always in terms of concepts and can be passed on by means of words or other symbols. Understanding is not conceptual, and therefore cannot be passed on. It is an immediate experience, and immediate experience can only be talked about (very inadequately), never shared. Nobody can actually feel another's pain or grief, another's love, joy or hunger [Huxley, "Knowledge and Understanding, 33–34].

Within the above assertion, there are three *modis operandi* coalescing systemically: (1) A distinction is made between knowledge and understanding. (2) There is an implication of man needing a *new* state of being in order to see everything *anew*. This new state, however, is not really new, but the oldest state of mind, the primeval tribe's state of "wombland" existence, before too much knowledge, and the language symbolizing that knowledge, diffused the wholeness of the intuitively together tribe-community into very "un-womblike" separate egos. (3) Understanding, in the sense herein to be elucidated, is not, like knowledge, calculatedly analytical of previous data, but rather is intuitively and *awe*-somely epiphanous in the manner of a *Zen Koan* realization. The result is an epiphany that results in the "Ah" effect, such as Stephen Daedalus has in Joyce's *Portrait of the Artist as a Young Man*, which is Joyce's Viconian — and Vico was an influence on Joyce — elucidation of how dogma is overturned to arrive at an awesome epiphany. (See discussion of Vico and Joyce to follow.)

This interpretation of understanding as being different from knowledge implies that understanding is also preferable to knowledge, though, of course, there can be no understanding without knowledge. This, in itself, seems like a Zen Koan contradiction. The message is that we must free ourselves from the old (previous knowledge) so that we can make unmediated contact with the new freed from societally influenced dogma. Does this imply that we abandon all that we have learned and start over again? Not exactly, but what Emerson, Nietzsche, Huxley, and Krishnamurti advocated is stripping knowledge of its accompanying societally acculturated dogmatic influences and see it for itself, dissociated from and "unmediated" by preconceptions. Within and between the mind's endless chatter of random thoughts and data there are intervals of the Zen, *No-Mind* of virgin silence, which is akin to the prenatal state of "wombland," the period before sensory and cognitive knowledge begins. Krishnamurti describes this silence:

> If you watch very carefully, you will see that though the response, the movement of thoughts seems so swift, there are gaps, there are intervals between thoughts. Between two thoughts there is a period of silence which is not related to the thought process.

> If you observe you will see that the period of silence, that interval, is not of time, and the discovery of that interval, the full experiencing of that interval, liberates you from conditioning.... We are now not only discussing the structure and the process of thought, which is the background of memory, of experience, of knowledge, but we are also trying to find out if the mind can liberate itself from the background. It is only when the mind is not giving continuity to thought, when it is still within a stillness that is not induced, that is without any causation — it is only then that there can be freedom from the background [*The First and Last Freedom*, 225–26].

Krishnamurti later called this liberating process the freedom from the known.

A century before, Emerson said: "We live in succession, in division, in particles. Meantime within man is the soul of the whole; the wise silence; the universal beauty" (as quoted in Ando, 49). It is from the integrated "wise silence" that understanding derives, not the divisions within our fragmented minds or from the divisions of separated egos. The difference between knowledge and understanding correlates to this: The lowbrow observes knowledge; the highbrow perceives understanding. The mystics, despite any misconceptions about what the term "mystic" implies, sought nothing more than to quiet the endless chatter of the mind, still the ceaseless distractions of "knowledge" and allow the "wise silence" to assert itself through contemplation and meditation. Artists do it through art by having "Zen" moments (or God-Awe moments) during their own intervals, however brief, of silence, and then intimate these moments analogously in their work.

The "new" state of mind yearned for is not new, but the oldest state of mind as it existed with the primeval non-verbal tribe. This is the *no-mind* — or the *non-ego* of the unified unconscious, the spark of which has been retained by present minds in a dormancy that has been pushed to the back of the distracted brain's cluttered garage to be superseded by both useful and useless stuff in front of, surrounding, and covering it. The junk in the garage prevents us from getting a clear look at the core of the Ultimate Reality. And more knowledge in itself will not clarify perception, as it just means more stuff blocking the view to the truth. "No amount of theorizing," Huxley said, "about such hints as may be darkly glimpsed within the ordinary, unregenerate experience of the manifold world can tell us much about divine Reality as can be apprehended by a mind in a state of detachment, charity, and humility" (Knowledge and Understanding," 19). The latent power residing in the psychic Eden or the *spirit* in man is a force about which each individual can say to himself that it is one known to his unconscious mind, and that this force or power latent in the mind is just waiting for self-realization.

Man is a creature of free will; he can choose to become the detached center within the hurricane of his ego-bound life. To be detached, however, does not imply disaffection, far from it. Mystically motivated detachment doesn't exclude the world, but filters the extraneous distractions, separates the wheat from the chaff, calms the mind, and lets that mind be a witness that calmly, rather than frantically, participates in the well-being of the world.

Artists and scientists are re-discoverers, not discoverers, of what already exists, and these are the mysteries inherent to nature that the artist and scientist attempt to make manifest to the world. (Just as there are no "mute and inglorious Miltons," there are no mute and inglorious Einsteins. See Michael Polanyi's *Personal Knowledge*.) The artist and scientist differ only in their means and ends, but not in their motivation. Each is equally inspired by an awe of nature that includes the workings of that most unique creature in his most unique environment: man and society. The artist or scientist both start from the premise of: *Awe first, ask questions later.* Each has an awesome inspiration, and then each figures out how to embody that inspiration in an outcome. These inspirations and their outcomes differ in that the awe-inspired scientist may already foresee the outcome and merely needs to prove it, while the awe-inspired artist only sees what his outcome has proven after he is done. Every poem is a self-contained psychic Eden. Hereafter, ontological paradises and the God-awe correlative may be considered as a wish for the psychic Eden to be engendered by a poem.

> One of the principal functions of poetry — of all the arts ... is the preservation and renewal of natural piety toward every kind of created excellence, toward the great creatures like sun, moon, and earth on which our lives depend, toward the brave warrior, the wise man, the beautiful woman. Sometimes poetry regards the excellence of its subjects as self-derived, at other times as an outward and visible sign of an invisible uncreated God, but in either case it is with the outward, concrete and visible that it is concerned [Auden, "Introduction," *An Armada of Thirty Whales*, i–ii].

When the poet reinvents and thus purifies the words of the tribe, he is also attempting to remake and purify his perceptions of the routine everyday world of the vulgar, profane, and lowbrow so he might intimate the numinous, sacred, and highbrow. Quite simply, why else would he make the effort? Even if writing about hell, the artist is choosing to exercise his free will and do something that is play as opposed to work. Art is a rebellion against the mundane; a gesture of liberation made by exerting independence through doing something that is purely gratuitous and eminently self-gratifying for its very non-essentialness. (This is in terms of physical survival; psychological survival is another matter.) In effect, art is a wish to take back some control over one's own actions by doing what one likes, not what one must, and to feel momentarily an autonomous existence. Autonomy is the ultimate paradise on earth. It means control over one's own sense of having some degree of independence without obligation or responsibility; it is also rarely more than a fantasy for most people. Art is an autonomy of an upward transcendence as it has lasting value and by its material outcome exists to reiterate a vicarious sense of the autonomous status of its maker. These feelings of Awe are a hint of the mystical state called variously, *nirvana,* or *samadhi,* or *satori,* when the mind empties itself of the distracting clutter and reunifies with the undifferentiated, unified consciousness of the tribal *no-mind*. Or, perhaps it should be called the *one-mind* that is unencumbered of dogmatic pre-knowledge, or "background." *Satori*, in particular, is the term for the awesome epiphany following a Zen Koan realization:

> In Zen lore, there was a Chinese Bodhidarma [guru] who was approached by a disciple who asked of him:
> "My mind is always wavy and disturbed. Please make it peaceful."
> The master answered:
> "Bring your mind to me. Then I will make it peaceful."
> The disciple, reflecting on himself a moment, said:
> "I have sought it within, but I can find *no mind*."
> The master said:
> "I have set your mind at rest" [as quoted by Ando, 4].

At this point the disciple felt the Zen state of *Satori*, which was the electric surge of Awe that followed his self-discovery. This feeling of spontaneous Awe, achieved in Zen, art, or any other way, constitutes the "Ah" effect. The "Ah" effect is the goal of the mystic's, artist's, and scientist's autonomous game, the purpose of which is to feel awe, which then inspires discoveries. To let the Awe in, the mind needs to be momentarily empty, or of *no-mind*, and does so by suspending dogmatic knowledge in favor of *understanding*. Whitman sums up this "Ah" effect of the God-Awe correlative:

> When I Heard the learn'd astronomer,
> When the proofs, the figures were ranged in columns before me,
> When I was shown the charts and diagrams, to add, divide, and measure them,
> When I sitting heard the astronomer where he lectured with much applause in the lecture-room,
> How soon unaccountable I became tired and sick,
> Till rising and gliding out I wander'd off by myself,
> In the mystical moist night-air, and from time to time,
> Look'd up in perfect silence at the stars [*The Anthology of American Poetry*, 264].

"Perfect Silence" allowed the Awe into the uncluttered mind and Whitman, motivated by the "Ah" effect, wrote a poem.

When the artist or scientist feels the "Ah" effect, he then applies it to making or discovering. This effect is shared with peers and the public. All people can vicariously enjoy a distillation of the awe that originally motivated the artist's art or the scientist's discovery. All people can be directly awed by the same natural phenomena the artist was motivated by. For example, a beautiful full moon becomes a numinous, sacred being to artist and non-artist alike, especially if viewed in auspicious circumstances, such as by two people who are feeling "romantic love." To such a couple, sharing in the awesome sight doubles the awe and the moon becomes a symbol of their romance. Romantic love itself is awesome and its importance to the collective psyche is such that it is the primary "mythified" motivation of the ego's individual existence. For many, finding romantic love is a lifelong quest; losing it is lifelong distress. The evidence that this is the case surrounds us ubiquitously. Evidence also abounds throughout world history. Is it love itself that drives people? Or is it the awesome feeling that accompanies romantic love's first stirrings that people actually want while chasing romance as a vehicle for getting it?

The present consumer culture propagates the myths of romantic love as a can't-miss-moneymaker and does so by enlisting people to use *white magic* on a public that craves "love" or reasonable substitutes. Pop culture loves love stories, in song, or in the mass-consumed pop fiction such as the phenomenon of the "romance" novel, or in TV and cinema. *White magic* is employed to arouse superficial feelings of *faux* awe with *faux*-awe versions of romantic love by idealizing it in a way people wish it could be permanently, but seldom is. This vicarious need is a multi-billion-dollar industry. Most of the white magic produced is not art, as the producer is making it not from genuine feelings of his own sincerity and sympathy, but to arouse the emotions of a public primed, even compelled, to be manipulated by preconceived notions inured from the generational inculcation of the societal images of what romantic love is imagined to mean.

If, then, romantic love is more of a creation passed on to the public to fill their need for an awesome sensation, what are people seeking for which romantic love is a substitute? Perhaps romantic love is like art, an outlet for something else.

Auden believed there was another kind of awe that is meant to flow from the stirrings of romantic love, and before he states it, to prepare us, he explains the difference between physical and spiritual beauty. For physical beauty, he said:

> Moral approval is not involved. It is perfectly possible ... to say: "Elizabeth has a beautiful figure, but she is a monster."
>
> If, on the other hand, I say: "Elizabeth has a beautiful ... expression," ... I am speaking of something which is personal.... Nature has nothing to do with it. This kind of beauty is always associated with the notion of moral goodness. And it is this kind of beauty which arouses in the beholder feelings [not of admiration or lust], but of personal love. [This love is] intended to lead the lover towards the love of the uncreated [unmediated] source of all beauty [or the awe that such beauty evokes] ["Introduction," *Shakespeare: The Sonnets*, xxx–xxxii].

In his Introduction to *Shakespeare: The Sonnets*, Auden discusses this other kind of love that romantic love leads to. He explains what the Bard was really writing about to that mysterious person who has never been positively identified.

> The subject was, indeed, love, but not of just a romantic, or even sexual love, but a mystical love — known as the *Vision of Eros*, which, is concerned with a single person, who is revealed to the subject as being of infinite sacred importance [xxxv].

Simone Weil wrote of the vision of Eros in mystical experience that, "The Ontological Proof is mysterious because it does not address itself to intelligence, but to love" (quoted in Murdoch, 504). Love here is not knowledge but intuition.

Moreover, Iris Murdoch equated love with goodness: "I want now to speak of what is perhaps the most obvious as well as the most ancient and traditional claimant, though one which is rarely mentioned by our contemporary philosophers, and that is Love. Of course Good is sovereign over Love as it is sovereign over other concepts, because Love can name something bad. But is there not nevertheless something about the conception of a refined love, which is practically identical with goodness? Will not 'Act lovingly' translate 'Act perfectly,' whereas 'Act rationally' will not? It is tempting to say so" (Murdoch, 384).

Finally, Theresa Morris in an abstract of a paper titled, "How Word Relates to the Other, Through Love," writes: "What does language mean when we use it to speak to another? How does the idea of language relate to the idea of the other? ... What happens when we move outside ourselves into relation with another human, and how language contributes to the exploration of that relation ... [and also to] the definition of love, self, soul, and desire. Specifically ... what happens to the self in its relation to the other and how does language complicate or facilitate this process? Working off references by Plato, Emmanuel Levinas, and Iris Murdoch, [the] conclusion points to the possibility that consciousness in both language and love may enable us to better grasp what at first seems essentially unknowable (paper given by Theresa Morris, SUNY New Paltz, at the SUNY Oneonta Philosophy Conference on 3/31/2000; online at //organizations.oneonta.edu/philosc/abstracts01.html).

In supporting Auden, Weil, and Murdoch, Morris suggests that goodness and love as the *Vision of Eros* seem interrelated.

Auden also defines how one can determine if he/she has had the mystical *Vision of Eros*:

> a) the experience is a genuine revelation, not a delusion; (b) the erotic mode of the vision prefigures a kind of love in which the sexual element is transformed and transcended; (c) he who has once seen the glory of the Uncreated revealed indirectly in the glory of a creature [beloved one] can henceforth never be fully satisfied with anything less than a direct encounter with the former ["The Protestant Mystics," 65].

Art and romantic love are rivers to the ocean from which all Awe really derives: the Vedantic Ocean of mystical consciousness. (Existence is a metaphorical ocean into which individual drops of water merge indistinguishably.) Awe, however it chooses to manifest itself, intimates the unified unconscious of the psychic Eden. Artists and lovers are attempting to feel the vicarious God-Awe correlative; consequently, they are seeking to do unconsciously what the mystics are trying to do consciously — which is to *un*-separate themselves and *re*-unify with the *all* of mankind, the *all* of the universe.

Huxley: "And in point of fact, artists and mystics do succeed from time to time and for a brief moment, in cleansing their perception" (*Texts and Pre-*

texts, 55). "For those who have actually *felt* the supernatural quality of nature, dogmatic atheism seems absurd" (*Texts and Pretexts*, 27).

Huxley emphatically dismisses those who would dismiss mysticism because there have been centuries of written accounts of it as documented around the world by hundreds of learned spiritual scholars. There were and are skeptics who refute mysticism, as there were once skeptics who refuted evidence that the earth was neither flat, nor the center of the universe. What one cannot materially grasp does not make it non-existent.

> Mankind [lives] their daily lives with the intimate conviction that molecules not only don't move, but don't exist. The *all* feeling is brief and occasional; but this is not to say that a metaphysical system based upon it must necessarily be untrue, nor does the great pre-dominance in our lives of *not-all* feelings necessarily invalidate an *all*-theory, by our almost constant [and false] sense of the solidity ... of matter [Huxley, *Texts and Pretexts*, 34].

"Religion and, in its widest, mistiest sense, mysticism, have an important place in human life" (Huxley, *Vulgarity in Literature*, 58). In the "widest, mistiest sense," one could imply mysticism to include the various viable substitutes. Throughout history, too many humans, highbrow or lowbrow, artists, scientists, mystics or lovers, have expended a great deal of energy trying to feel awesome, to escape worldliness for unworldliness. All people are trying to have mystical experiences, although nearly all of them have no idea that this is what they are trying to do. This includes the skeptics who discount mysticism proper while in fierce pursuit of mystical feelings through vicarious substitutes. The compulsion to intimate awe-sociations must have a basis. Those with separated egos—virtually everyone—are intuitively wanting to feel connected to something greater than themselves, a *something* in a state without need of language, which is the state of either wombland, or the pre-language archetypal tribe in their primeval unified consciousness, or a mystical experience. In the primordial past mystery was normal, and awe a regular symptom of perceiving nature before man got overly habituated to nature and to nature's second-hand descriptions via language.

Hence, if utilitarian language demystifies nature's existence, the poet's intuitive role is to remystify nature and recapture the rapture of unmediated awe by purifying the words of the tribe, and in so doing analogously intimate the God-Awe correlative. It is the poet who, by purifying language, gives words back their magic, signifies their *all*-ness, over their *thing*-ness. Thought of as things, words separate; purified as "essence," they unify.

"Our ordinary day-to-day existence," Huxley said, "is that of a separate being having contact with his own abstractions from, and generalizations about, the world revealed to him by his sensations and intuitions. At certain moments this separate being goes behind the abstractions and generalizations and becomes directly conscious of his sensations and intuitions—an apocalyptic process, which Keats describes, 'as the forming of a fellowship of *essence*.' The *not-self* [meaning the unseparated collective *Self*] is the very core and marrow of our beings" (*Texts and Pretexts*, 41). Many poets, of course, not only write poetry, but also like Keats theorized on the poetic process equating it with — in whatever theoretical terms they preferred — some kind of "otherworldy" aesthetic. There has long been a belief in purified words as signifying something more than themselves. The something more is the God-Awe correlative. Poetry is a vehicle to this correlative; mysticism *is* the correlative.

Consequently, the theories of poetry often sound like theories of mysticism because, in effect, they are; both are trying to explain the inexplicable and ineffable:

> For the literature of mysticism, which is a literature about the inexpressible, is for the most part misty indeed.... It is only in works of the very best mystical writers that the fog lifts—to reveal what? A strange alternation of light and darkness: light to the limits of the possibly illuminable and after that, the darkness of paradox and incomprehensibility, or yet deeper, the absolute night of silence.... Mystical religion is the ideal religion for doubters—those ultimate schismatics who have separated themselves from all belief. For the mystic is dispensed from intellectually *believing* in God; he *feels* God. Or to put it more accurately, he has a "numinous" emotion [Huxley, *Vulgarity in Literature*, 43].

(A "tearing-down" of all belief can either be a nihilistic vacuum or an emptying that will allow a "building up" of "new belief" antithetically.)

Huxley here refers to "doubt" in the sense of the mystic's spiritual recalcitrance regarding blind adherence to religious dogma. The "numinous" emotion for the mystic is the same numinous emotion for the poet; each merely writes about it in a different way, or, perhaps, not so differently. For example, Huxley thought "Perhaps the best accounts of physical passion are to be found in poems which are not about profane [earth-bound] love at all. The writings of the mystics contain amazingly precise renderings of experiences which are, at any rate superficially, indistinguishable from the erotic experience" (*Texts and Pretexts*, 107). This statement also suggests that erotic, physical passion may be, as has been already suggested, one of the viable substitute vehicles people try in seeking, if not always consciously, the mystical God-Awe correlative. To extend this metaphor of erotic or physical passion and mystical passion further, erotic passion also relates to the "Ah" effect of the mystical experience. The post-release from the passionate or mystical experience could be called "the grin factor," that self-contented awareness of having just returned from an "other-worldly" experience. (For those who practice meditation, the grin factor is as palpable to them during and after meditation as it is to others during and after erotic passion.) In effect, the *Vision of Eros* and the *Vision of God* are remarkably alike. The God-Awe correlative is an attribute of passion, period—divine or erotic. Discovery, art, beauty, love, religion, and mysticism are all paths to the same goal, the intimation of Awe-sociations that make themselves manifest by [our] circumventing or temporarily abolishing the psychological obstacles which normally prevent us from becoming blissfully conscious of our solidarity with the universe. It is only exceptionally, when we are free from distractions, in the silence and darkness of the night, or of night's psychological equivalent, that we become aware of our own souls and, along with them, of what seems the soul of the world.... While it lasts it is felt to be a supernatural state; it provides us with otherwise inaccessible knowledge about ourselves and, according to the theory, the world [Huxley, *Texts and Pretexts*, 15, 19–20].

Humanity's goal, individually and collectively, is to tap into that psychic region of the brain that is just as much an inherited trait as are the more visible physical traits. For Heard the compelling urge to be "otherworldly" is part of man's natural evolution, and this psychical goal is just as immanent in the mind as the gene for red hair is in the body. Nonetheless, unlike the gene for red hair, which is static, the immanent spark directing the path of consciousness is progressive individually and also for all of humanity, but it is so in an eternal time frame that most finite individuals cannot fathom. Each person, whether having awareness or not, is a microcosm of the macrocosm, reproducing individually, what humanity, over a longer period, does collectively. Of this dichotomy, an idea originating with Heard, Huxley said:

> Spiritual progress is always in an ascending spiral. Animal instinct gives place to human will and then to grace, guidance, inspiration, which are all simply instinct on a higher level. Or consider the progress of consciousness. First there is the infant's undifferentiated awareness, next comes discrimination and discursive reasoning, and finally (if the individual wishes to transcend himself) there is a rise which is also a return towards an obscure knowledge of the whole, of the realization of the timeless, the non-dual in time and multiplicity ["Adonis and the Alphabet," 192].

It is pertinent that Huxley would say that a "rise" in consciousness is not a discovery, but a rediscovery, and "a return towards an obscure knowledge." We seek not what will be, but what has always been. Of course, only the person who is mystically inclined chooses "to transcend himself" more or less deliberately. The majority does the upward transcending vicariously through the awe-stimulating substitutes of love, art, discovery, or non-dogmatic religion. The important element here is that the urge for transcendence through *awe*-sociations, whether recognized as such or not, seems to be an intuitively dominating human trait. Hence, whether vicarious or intentional, man seeks instinctively some form of mystical experience. This established, Huxley asks, rhetorically, what that means, and why it is not only important, but intrinsically valuable:

> I take it that the mystical experience is essentially the being aware of ... a form of pure consciousness, of unstructured transpersonal consciousness which lies, so to speak, upstream from the ordinary discursive consciousness of everyday.
> Why should this sort of consciousness be regarded as valuable? First, it is regarded as valuable because of the self-evident sensibility of values.... It is intrinsically valuable, just as the experience of beauty is intrinsically valuable, but much more so.

Second, it is valuable because ... it does bring about changes in thought and character and feeling which the experiencer and those about him regard in him as manifestly desirable. It makes possible a sense of unicity and solidarity with the world. It brings about the possibility of that kind of unjudging love and compassion which is stressed so much [in scripture]. The mystic ... is able to understand organically such portentous phrases, which for the ordinary person are extremely difficult to understand — phrases such as "God is love" ... the sense being that the deepest part of the soul is identical with the Divine nature.... It is the idea of the inner light, the scintilla animae (spark of the soul); the scholastics had a technical phrase for it, the "synderesis" ["Man and Religion," 212–13].

Auden further interprets mystical experience by telling how a person can identify that one has taken place. Auden does so in his introduction to *Shakespeare: The Sonnets*. Auden believed that Shakespeare's principal motivation in writing the sonnets was mystical more than romantic: "the *primary* experience — complicated as it became later — out of which the sonnets to the friend spring — was a mystical one" (xxiv). Auden then followed by explaining what "mystical experience" means:

All experiences which may be called mystical have certain characteristics in common.
(1) The experience is "given." That is to say, it cannot be induced or prolonged by an effort of will, though the openness of any individual to receive it is partly determined by his age, his psychological make-up, and his cultural milieu.
(2) Whatever the contents of the experience, the subject is absolutely convinced that it is a revelation of [ultimate] reality. When it is over, he does not say, as one says when one awakes from a dream: "Now I am awake and conscious of the real world." He says, rather: "For a while the veil was lifted and a reality revealed which in my 'normal' state is hidden from me."
(3) With whatever the vision is concerned, things, human beings, or God, they are experienced as numinous, clothed in glory, charged with an intense being-there-ness.
(4) Confronted by the vision, the attention of the subject, in awe, joy, dread, is absolutely absorbed in contemplation and, while the vision lasts, his self, its desires and needs, are completely forgotten [xxix–xxx].

(Mystics would disagree with Auden that the experience can't be induced by an effort of will.)

Further, there are four different types of mystic visions: *The Vision of Dame Kind* is the mystical state catalyzed by an awesome experience in nature, which induces a state of oneness with nature; the aforementioned *Vision of Eros* is the mystical state aroused by the awesome experience inspired by love for another individual. By extension, if it is possible, through the *Vision of Eros*, to feel "mystical" about one person, then, as the *Vision of Agape,* one can feel mystical about not just the one, but the many. Auden recounts a personal experience as evidence:

One fine summer night in June 1933 I was sitting on a lawn after dinner with three colleagues, two women and one man. We liked each other well enough but we were certainly not intimate friends, nor had any of us a sexual interest in another. Incidentally, we had not drunk any alcohol. We were talking quite casually about everyday matters when, quite suddenly and unexpectedly, something happened. I felt myself invaded with a power which, though I consented to it, was irresistible and certainly not mine. For the first time in my life I knew exactly—because, thanks to the power, I was doing it—what it means to love one's neighbor as oneself. I was also certain, though my conversation continued to be perfectly ordinary, that my three colleagues were having the same experience. (In the case of one of them, I was later able to confirm this.) My personal feelings towards them were unchanged— they were still colleagues, not intimate friends—but I felt their existence as themselves to be of infinite value and rejoiced in it.

I recalled with shame the many occasions on which I had been spiteful, snobbish, selfish, but the immediate joy was greater than the shame, for I knew that, so long as I was possessed by this spirit, it would be literally impossible for me deliberately to injure another human being ["The Protestant Mystics," 69–70].

The feeling Auden describes is one that, as Huxley already said, "is valuable because as a matter of empirical experience it does bring about changes in thought and character and feeling which the experiencer and those about him regard in him as manifestly desirable. It makes possible a sense of unicity and solidarity with the world." Did the experience influence Auden? Shortly after it, in October of 1933, Auden wrote this: "the first criterion of success of any human activity, the necessary preliminary, whether to scientific discovery, or to artistic vision, is intensity of attention or ... love" ("Review of the *Book of Talbot*," 319). (Later, Iris Murdoch would agree.) After one achieves the *Vision of Agape*, the fourth vision is the *Vision of God* directly, which is very rare and beyond possible expression even analogously. This vision is *felt;* and there are no words that will suffice to remotely intimate the feeling. Mystics of all persuasions have said and would ultimately say—there's nothing to be said about it.

In equating the poet's motivation and writing experience to being the same as or reasonably similar to the mystic's, it follows that just as the mystic may get therapeutic benefit from his process, the poet may also. And just as those who know the mystic may be able to see and receive these character-enhancing benefits, so may those who know and read the poet. The mystic, however, unless he is also a writer, cannot reach and influence as many people as the poet can. The poet's poetry, a product of his efforts to intimate the *Awe*-sociations of the unified consciousness, can and will communicate to, and provide therapy for, certain readers just as it did for the poet when writing it. Poems unify by identifying, purifying, and embodying human feelings that are universal. The reader, by sharing with another person, the poet, feelings he has also known, no longer feels so separated from others. Poetry makes us more human by including us in the all of the unified consciousness. The degree of the reader's understanding is a reflection of the poet's sympathy and empathy. As Huxley said, "The greatness of the great artist depends precisely on the width and depth of his sympathy.... the artists whom the world has always recognized as the greatest are those with the widest sympathy" ("Art," 184). Huxley then quotes Walt Whitman: "The messages of the great poets to each man and woman are, Come to us on equal terms, Only then can you understand us, We are no better than you, What we enclose you enclose, What we enjoy you may enjoy. Did you suppose there could be only one Supreme? We affirm there can be unnumbered Supremes, and that one does not countervail another any more than one eyesight countervails another" ("Art," 185).

The same thought was earlier conveyed in the Gita:

> Who burns with the bliss
> And suffers the sorrow
> Of every creature
> Within his own heart,
> Making his own
> Each bliss and each sorrow:
> Him I hold highest
> Of all the yogis.

Sympathy is a paramount ingredient that can only be felt by a reader when a writer provides recognizable characters and circumstances for the reader to identify with.

> When we read a book, it is as if we were with a person.... When we say a book is good or bad, we mean that we feel toward it as we feel towards what we all feel toward a good or bad person.... Actually we know we cannot divide people into good and bad like that; everyone is a mixture.... The same is true of books....
>
> Reading is valuable just because books are like people, and make the same demands on us to understand and like them.... You must use your knowledge of people to guide you when reading books, and your knowledge of books to guide you when living with people.
>
> Reading is valuable when it improves our technique of living.... It fails when we can't understand or feel what we read, either because of ignorance of our own or obscurity in the writing.
>
> It is a danger when we only read what encourages us in lax and crude ways of feeling and thinking.... It is also dangerous when it becomes a substitute for living, when we get frightened of real people and find books safer company; they are a rehearsal for living, not living itself.... The underlying reason for writing [and reading] is to bridge the gulf between one person and another [Auden, "An Outline..." 310–312].

Language can be a bridge between people. Language is always analogously supernatural as it describes what has already happened, what may happen, or what is no longer there. When the poet attempts to inform and enlighten, he will be least successful as a didacticist and much more successful as a parabolist. "Often," Huxley said, "the best way of expressing one thing is by talking about another" (*Texts and Pretexts*, 216). He explains this further by comparing the scientist and literary artist:

The scientist's aim ... is to say one thing, and only one thing, at a time. This, most emphatically is not the aim of the literary artist. Human life is lived simultaneously on many levels and has many meanings. Literature is a device for reporting the multifarious facts and expressing their various significances. When the literary artist undertakes to give a purer sense to the words of the tribe, he does so with the express purpose of creating a language capable of conveying, not the single meaning of some particular science, but the multiple significance of human experience, on its most private as well as on its more public levels. He purifies, not by simplifying and jargonizing, but by deepening and extending, by enriching with allusive harmonics, with overtones of association and undertones of sonorous magic [*Literature and Science*, 13].

The key words above are *allusive*, *overtones*, and *undertones*. Each intimates that the literary artist takes the particular and turns it into the universal by an indirect parabolic process rather than a didactic one. Aesop's Fables are the prototype of this intent of indirect teaching. "Didacticism," Thornton Wilder said, "is an attempt at the coercion of another's free mind, even though one knows that in these matters beyond logic, beauty is the only persuasion" ("Foreword," *The Angel*, vii).

Auden agreed. "You cannot tell people what to do, you can only tell them parables; and that is what art really is, particular stories of particular people and experiences, from which each according to his immediate and peculiar needs may draw his own conclusions. There must be two kinds of art, escape-art, for man needs to escape as he needs food and sleep, and parable-art, that art which shall teach man to unlearn hatred and learn love" ("Psychology and Art Today," 341). And as the reader learns these parabolic lessons, he learns who he is and who he can be.

Human nature as conjectured upon by the ancient poet-philosopher or philosopher-poet was not too far off the future studies of man by men of science. Today's nomenclature is more sophisticated, but the general predilections are still what they have always been. The essentials remain unchanged; only the nuances change to fit current fashions. Consequently, with literature as a teacher through parable, the lessons of Professors Homer, Sophocles, Dante, Milton, Shakespeare, Pope, Hawthorne, Melville, Whitman, et al. still stand up in comparison and often exceed modern clinical dissertations on human behavior.

Who is particularly inclined to read the latest Harvard Medical School Study of Criminal Pathology as compared to *Macbeth*, *Hamlet*, or *Richard III*? Or, as this author learned from teaching college English in a federal prison, inmates learn more concerning their own behavior from reading about Christopher Isherwood's notorious and amoral Berlin con man, the "fictional" Mr. Norris, than what they would learn from their own clinical psychiatric reports.

When literary philosopher-poets philosophize and teach in their God-Awe correlated parables, then, indeed, school is in session. A reader is a student, consciously or not. When he reads, he absorbs and correlates intuitively and, sometimes, intentionally. Auden said that there are two "questions which interest me most when reading a poem or two. The first is technical: 'Here is a verbal contraption. How does it work?' The second is, in the broadest sense, moral: 'What kind of a guy inhabits this poem? What is his notion of the good life or the good place? His notion of the evil one? What does he conceal from the reader? What does he conceal even from himself?'" ("Making, Knowing, and Judging," 51). Auden also wrote, "that the primary intention of poetry, as of all the arts, is to affirm personal being and becoming and to defeat their enemies, the accidental and the fantastic" ("The Dyer's Hand," *Anchor Review*, 271). Man needs to believe he is not an arbitrary number of either science or history, randomly dropped into existence by a fluke he has no control over. Man wishes, through his vicarious *modus operandi* of upward transcendence, to intimate the *awe*-sociations of the God-Awe correlative that will give his being and becoming a significance that is more than just the whim of chance or the predictability of a calculus.

Man wants to know that other men also feel as he feels, that they are also not arbitrary happenstances, that there must be a plan, and a continuum perpetuating that plan, and that his existence has meaning beyond the end of his finite corporeal suitcase. These are the subjects of literature. Poetry seems always to ask readers to find the "other" meaning that resides between the lines, and while readers are doing so they also re-evaluate their own "otherness." We, as sentient beings, are much like poems because, just as a poem is a medium for analogous comparison, so does each person constantly, if not always consciously, compare his existence with the rest of existence, particularly the existences of other individuals. This comparing is often a reconciliation of opposites. Life, begun as the child who responds and obeys in order to win approval, becomes a perpetual juxtaposition of what one is and what one thinks one should be. We determine who we are as compared to who others are. We may want to be accepted by some of those "others" by imitating them, and reject a different set of "others" that we do not wish to be like. Every time one meets a person, a process of juxtaposition instinctively takes place. Every time one "meets" a poem, this is also like encountering an "other."

> Reading a poem is an experience analogous to that of encountering a person. Just as one can think and speak separately of a person's physical appearance, his mind, and his character, so can one consider the formal aspects of a poem, its contents, and its spirit while knowing that in the latter case no less than in the former, these different aspects are not really separate but an indissoluble trinity-in-unity. We would rather that our friends were handsome than plain, intelligent than stupid, but in the last analysis it is on account of their character as persons that we accept or reject them [Auden, "Introduction," *A Change of World*, 7].

It is a person's character, his "*is*ness," that we accept or reject. His appearance or material circumstances may attract attention, but those alone cannot retain it. Ultimately, we accept or reject a poem or a person's character by tacitly asking of the poem or person: "Who are you? What do you represent? What do you want to become?" These intuitive questions are explicit or implicit during human contacts and represent one person's reflexive juxtaposition of comparing one's self to the other's "self." The automatic comparison-by-juxtaposition which these questions entail has an equally automatic flip side because by asking them, we are simultaneously asking ourselves, according to Auden, "Who am I? Whom ought I to become?"

> (1) *Who am I?* What is the difference between man and all other creatures? What relations are possible between them? What is man's status in the universe? What are the conditions of his existence which he must accept as his fate which no wishing can alter?
>
> (2) *Whom ought I to become?* What are the characteristics of the hero, the authentic man whom everybody should admire and try to become? Vice versa, what are the characteristics of the churl, the unauthentic man whom everybody should try to avoid becoming?
>
> We all seek answers to these questions which shall be universally valid under all circumstances, but the experiences to which we put them are always local both in time and place. What any poet has to say about man's status in nature, for example, depends in part on the landscape and climate he happens to live in and in part upon reactions to it of his personal temperament ["Robert Frost, 344–45].

In addition to environment, there are societal influences that one reacts to by either accepting or rejecting them. For each person who asks the above two critical questions, history is entirely responsible for what the reactor reacts to, but history is tangential as to why and how the reactor reacts. This is personal. Even when seeming to be in concert with the many, the reaction is based on the decision of the one. The artist knows this is true; the historian wishes it weren't true. The artist knows because he himself cannot be transformed by his own art, which is symptomatic of thought processes he has already experienced. If there is a transformation, it precedes the artist's art that then becomes the tangible form of cathartic release that proves the transformation took place. All art, as all language, is a reaction of how one feels about what one knows. The reader of a poem is also not transformed by the poet's poem but may be influenced by the implicit answers the poem evokes of the above questions. However, any realization a reader comes to can only come when the mind is prepared to accept it. The poem's catalyzing effect is a serendipitous coincidence, not the cause. As Auden says: "Art cannot teach or even portray examples worthy of imitation. It can only hold a mirror in which each person sees his face reflected; it can, that is, make him conscious of what he is like, but what he is to do about it must be left to his choice to decide, since the way for every person is unique" ("The Dyer's Hand," 260).

To be conscious of what one is like leads one to consider if he likes what he is like. This awareness then becomes a matter of choosing to preserve the status quo or alter it. Choice is individual. Not everyone has the self-awareness required. For many, choices are unconscious reactions to the necessity of survival; little, if any, self-conscious examination or awareness goes into most people's choices. Thus, a pertinent question about the two questions is, who asks them? While everyone makes choices, it is the highbrow who wants to know about his mind and its relation to the universe preemptively, in anticipation of some discovery. The lowbrow seeks to know only about his body in relation to its needs reactively in his immediately present environment and no further. Whatever discoveries the lowbrow makes have to do with personal gratification after having satisfied some need. The highbrow's discoveries are in anticipation of needs for himself and for others. This is not to say the highbrow is selfless, only that he wants others to know about his discoveries and give him approval for them. The artist, the scientist and the historian initiate a new reality by asking the two questions in a public arena. If they are selfless, that is a bonus for mankind, not a requirement that mankind can demand.

Selfish or selfless, it is the highbrow who will ask the two questions, and by doing so find answers that contribute to the perpetuation of the continuum. Gerald Heard believed that all man's acts are leading to a psychic evolution whether he knows it or not, so that even the most egotistically selfish highbrow, if he makes a discovery that benefits others, is closer to some kind of mystical advancement than the lowbrow who discovers nothing and gives nothing. Let it be clearly stated that the term "discovery" is not restricted to the tangible, but herein includes the introspectively intangible, upwardly transcendent kind of self-discovery, if such inner revelations can benefit others by reflection or example. The mystic who discovers something within, can, by his self-illumination, share his light with others. Who is to say which person actually gives more to the world, the "tangibilist" or the "intangibilist"? Both are needed; sometimes the rare miracle happens that both are in one person. Meanwhile, after all the vainglorious artistic, scientific, materialistic discoveries are made, why do so many people remain unsatisfied? After the noise of youth settles into a quest for quiet in middle age and after, why are so many of us "sentient beings" still asking ourselves: *Who am I? Whom ought I to become?* Language, particularly literary language, will be the means to the two questions' ends.

The everyday, illusory world of the body and its senses has not answered to the satisfaction of anyone who has let his body hold dominion over the mind. The answers to the two questions, for the people, for the poet, are not of this illusory world of the selfish ego and body. The answers belong to that mystical world that resides in the world mind of the unified consciousness; a world that is evoked by intimations of *awe*-sociations that suggest God-Awe correlatives intuitively felt before there were recorded texts. These spoken "fabula" evolved into rituals that then were systemized as theologies. Each theological discipline had a mystical component that often (if not always) preceded the dogmatic element. The first recorded spiritual texts—the Vedas—are mystical and have continued through every theology as the Perennial Philosophy. The first creative impulse is to make poetic fables for the tribe that explain awesome events.

These stories were told and later written down to account for the feelings of awe and to recall these feelings through awe-sociations. From the very first story, which is the first link in a chain of evolving consciousness, began the initial impetus from which every subsequent story and variations were derived. This poetic wisdom evolved into the "esoteric wisdom" of philosophy, science, literary theory, and so on. These disciplines record the history of humanity. The creative impulse supersedes esoteric wisdom as the results exemplify spiritual history. Forms change; hence, the creative impulse also supersedes form and genre. The first story inhabits every story thereafter. Sometimes the first story (thesis) leads to a later story that confutes the earlier story (antithesis). Nonetheless, even a confutation of the first story in a later story could not exist without having the first story inspire a response. The result over time becomes a synthesis of the first and second story. The first story, even if forgotten, remains the catalyst for the later story. In an ascending, widening spiral (Yeats called these "gyres," Polanyi, a "hierarchy of comprehensive entities"), like the effect of the stone thrown into a pond, the circles (and the universe) continually expand. The construct of artificial time inclines one to see a line of events as past, present, and future, and one loses sight of how events in the past constitute the present and will affect the future. If one, like Wilder, sees instead the "vast landscape," then all of the Ultimate Reality becomes one continuous, contiguous, comprehensive vision; one that is seen like a map of cause and effect with all events interrelated. The Perennial Philosophy is the first story that initially existed wordlessly in the pre-verbal tribe. Literature is the reflective and spiritual outcome of the Perennial Philosophy. The human psyche is "metaphorized" in literature as a synthesis of the psyche's evolution towards evolving consciousness. The Perennial Philosophy accounts for the creative impulse as one that intuitively seeks transcendence from differentiated particles and particularities to tell through parable how one can reclaim an undifferentiated connection to the whole. If the Perennial Philosophy is the first story, it is also the first literary theory.

CHAPTER 3

Mystical Philosophy as Applied to Philosophers and Literary Theorists

To understand just one life you have to swallow the world. — Salman Rushdie, *Midnight's Children*

THIS CHAPTER PROVIDES EXAMPLES of different writers and philosophers who have expressed their ideas over the past 400 years; one can see the essence that preceded their themes as interconnected variations of mystical philosophy. Since the earliest intimations of the Perennial Philosophy in its initial silent beginnings as "mute logic, then "poetic wisdom," then esoteric wisdom as the Vedas, there has been the intuition that there is an *otherness*, an ultimate reality that will reassert itself through different voices in different ways. Its essence was and is constant from *is*ness to *is*ness. The very fact that the Perennial Philosophy has re-emerged from age to age, and place to place, and often with no knowledge of it by theorists about any antecedents prior to their own thoughts and writings, would seem to indicate that certain similar objective ideas originate due to an inevitable "rightness" that cannot be denied. This in no way gives any less credit to the writers/philosophers that have creatively derived theories that are outcomes of the different zeitgeists in which they live. The argument posed thus far is that since life-is-art, art-is-life. The Perennial Philosophy explains both poetic wisdom (art) and esoteric wisdom (philosophy). If the Perennial Philosophy is first and if it is both the impetus for the creative impulse and for the philosophic impulse, then it is the first and the continuing literary theory from which subsequent literary theories have evolved.

Mystical philosophy as a paradigm for literary theory is not new. Starting with the Reconciliation of Opposites; then Heraclites' Fragments that assert that flux is not really flux; Vico's Poetic Wisdom as first cause of all wisdom; Hegel, who initially thought Buddhism preceded Vedanta and took his "Dialectics" unknowingly from the latter; Schopenhauer, a devoted Vedantist who inspired Nietzsche; Nietzsche's "more eyes," and his "stripping away"; Horkheimer and Adorno's "irritation"; Iris Murdoch's *Metaphysics as a Guide to Morals*, with her admiring chapter on the Vedantist Schopenhauer; and Frederic Jameson's "neo-dialectics" and *combinatoire*, all echo the ancient Hindu Vedas.

Vico: The Divine Ground of Poetic Wisdom Is Formed by Mysticism

Giambattista Vico's *New Science* (1744), a great influence on James Joyce among others, explained his theory of how knowledge began among the first primitive tribes. Before all philosophy, all aesthetic theory, all articulated knowledge of any kind, there was what Vico calls "mute logic" as the first principal that preceded articulation:

> "Logic" comes from logos, whose first proper meaning was fabula, fable, carried over into Italian as *favella*, speech. In Greek the fable was called *mythos*, myth, whence comes the Latin *mutus*, mute. For speech was born in mute times as mental [or sign] language, which ... existed before vocal or articulate [language]; whence logos means both word and idea [*nama-rupa*]. It was fitting that the matter should be so ordered by divine providence in religious times, for it is an eternal property of religions that they attach more importance to meditation than to speech. Thus the first language in the first mute times of the nations must have begun with signs, whether gestures or physical objects which had natural relations to the ideas [to be expressed] [157].

The philosophy of mysticism has also attached more importance to meditation than to speech.

"Mute logic" as the first step in a process of "experiencing," meaning the initial emotional reactions to external stimuli, is thus described by Auden (with the direct influence of Gerald Heard):

> If an Australian aborigine sits down on a pin he says, "ow." Dogs with bones at the approach of other dogs, growl. English, Russian, Brazilian, all mothers, "coo" to their babies. Sailors at any port, pulling together on a hawser: watch them and listen — heaving, they grunt together "ea-ah." This is the first language....
> We generally think of language being words used to point to things, to say that something is this or that, but the earliest use of language was not this; it was used to express feelings of the speaker; feelings about something happening to him (the prick of the pin), or attitudes towards other things in the world (the other hungry dog; the darling baby), or, again, as a help to do something with others of his own kind (pulling the boat in).
> Life is one whole thing made up of smaller whole things. The largest thing ... the universe, the smallest ... the negative electrons of the atom that run around its central positive nucleus, already a group. So too for us, nucleus and cell, cell and organ, organ and the human individual, individual and family, nation and world, always

groups.... The whole cannot exist without the part, nor the part without the whole ["Writing," *English Auden*, 303].

Vico also writes of parts/wholes and particulars/universals in relation to primitive language: "Synedoche developed into metaphor as particulars were elevated into universals or parts united with other parts together with which they make up their wholes" (130). Language is a system of analogous terms, or parts, that have much less meaning as parts individually until there is a contextual referencing to the mind's internal system of wholes, and, by extension, to the whole knowledge of civilization, which no single person knows entirely but people in their multiplicity do—part by part, person to person, group to group, civilization to civilization.

An individual's relation to a mystical whole as signified by Auden and Vico can be more succinctly summarized by the Vedic construct, *Tat Twam Asi* ("Thou art that; that art thou."), which signifies one's continuity/contiguity to a mystical unity with all existence. Vico and Auden also signify that this underlying indivisibility within all existence is first experienced intuitively. The Self becomes a vessel for non-identity or *otherness* that allows everything to pass through the mind and occupy a mystical consciousness that the abnegation of the willful ego has left room for. The ego-full self, with a lower-case "s," gives way to the ego-less Self, with a capital "S," which signifies humanity's journey towards a Jungian/Heardian collective unconscious or, as in Vedic scripture, a mystical consciousness of the Ultimate Reality. Vico writes that the first intimations of a mystical consciousness then became "poetic wisdom."

> Jove was born naturally into poetry as a divine character or imaginative universal, to which everything having to do with the auspices was referred by all the ancient gentile nations which must therefore all have been poetic by nature. Their poetic wisdom began the poetic metaphysics, which contemplated God by attribute of his providence; and they were called theological poets, or sages who understood the language of the gods expressed in the auspices of Jove; and were properly called divine in the sense of diviners, from *divinari*, to divine or predict. Their science was called Muse, defined by Homer as the knowledge of good and evil ... [and] the divination, on the prohibition of which God ordained his true religion for Adam. Because they were versed in this mystic theology, the Greek poets, who explained the divine mysteries of the auspices and oracles, were called *mystae*, which Homer learnedly renders "interpreters of the gods" [148].

The interpretation of the gods became the second language. The first language, as Vico and Auden would have it, was reactionary and intuitive rather than articulate. The second language became the language of poetic wisdom as a reaction to awe-inspired divinations, and, in turn, became the language of parables (Auden) or fables (Vico) from which all human wisdom began. First Vico:

> the histories of the gentile nations have had fabulous beginnings ... [that evolved into wisdom] for the following five reasons. The first was reverence for religion, for the

gentile nations were everywhere founded by fables of religion. The second was the grand effect ... namely this civil world, so wisely ordered that it could only be the effect of superhuman wisdom. The third was the occasions which ... these fables, assisted by the veneration of religion and the credit of such great wisdom, gave the philosophers for instituting research and meditating lofty things.... The fourth was the ease with which they were thus enabled ... to explain their sublime philosophical meditations by means of the expressions happily left them by the poets. The fifth ... is the confirmation of their own meditations, which the philosophers derived from the authority of religion and the wisdom of the poets [135].

Thus the mythologies, as their name indicates, must have been the proper languages of the fables; the fables being imaginative class concepts—the mythologies must have been the allegories corresponding to them. Allegory is defined as *diversiloquim* insofar as, by identity not of proportion but (to speak scholastically) of predictability, allegories signify the diverse species or the diverse individuals comprised under these genera. So that they must have a univocal signification connoting a common quality common to all their species and individuals (as Achilles connotes an idea of valor common to all strong men, or Ulysses an idea of prudence common to all wise men) such that these allegories must by etymologies of the poetic languages, which could make their origins univocal, whereas those of the vulgar languages are more often analogical [159].

Achilles and Ulysses (parts/particulars) are exemplified to be understood by readers/audience (whole/universal) so that all particular instances allow a reader's non-identity (otherness) to *become* the "other," and as such, identify with the "other." Consequently, a reader can possibly learn from the "other," that is, Achilles or Ulysses.

The Gita says: "Whatever a great man [or great character] does, ordinary people will imitate; they follow his example" (*BG*, 56). As regards characters in fiction, Auden said previously: "You cannot tell people what to do, you can only tell them parables; and that is what art really is, particular stories of particular people and their experiences, from which each according to his immediate and peculiar needs may draw his own conclusions.... Parable-art, [is] that art which shall teach man to unlearn hatred and learn love" (*English Auden*, 341).

Auden here means, "love" as the *vision of agape* when one's egoless non-identity feels a love for all existence and where one not only achieves a sense of "otherness" but also *loves* otherness. The above quote from Auden was written after Auden had, by his estimation, a mystical experience where he learned viscerally what it means to feel a love for all existence.

Fables and parables are told in accessible language, but in a manner, as Auden would say, via Yeats, that convey the thoughts of the wise man in the speech of the common people, which is the vernacular, or the vulgar, in the original meaning of the word, which now often connotes a negative definition but merely means common everyday language and customs. And as Vico explained, "it will be shown that as much as the poets had first sensed in the way of vulgar wisdom, the philosophers later understood in the way of esoteric

3. Mystical Philosophy as Applied to Philosophers and Literary Theorists 67

wisdom; so that the former may be said to have been the sense and later the intellect of the human race" (138).

Vico's "sense" was derived from a poet's visceral intuition of "vulgar wisdom." In the hands of a poet, vulgar, profane, and lowbrow language can connote the numinous, sacred, and highbrow. "The first men who spoke by signs, naturally believed that lightning ... and thunder ... were signs made by Jove; whence from *nuo*, to make a sign, came *numen*, the divine will by an idea more sublime and worthy to express the divine majesty" (Vico, 147). The artist/poet attempts, by analogous abstraction, to infer the reverential, ritualized awe of the tribe/group that lies in the unified consciousness. This awe existed first as "mute logic" before words were invented to recall the awe.

Before words there was *wonder*; a wonder inspired by Vico's divine awe that was felt with a "mute logic" before it was spoken of. Vico and Huxley provided their views on how mystical awe-sociations are at first intuited rather than articulated in a manner that is not within any boundary of sensory recognized cognition. First Vico:

> Divine providence has been so conducted that human institutions, starting from poetic theology which regulated them by certain sensible signs believed to be divine counsels sent to man by the gods, and by means of the natural theology which demonstrates providence by eternal reasons which do not fall under the senses, the nations were disposed to receive revealed theology in virtue of a supernatural faith, superior not only to the senses but to human reason itself [139–40].

One can relate Vico's theories to a reiteration of tenet 2 of Huxley's Minimum Working Hypothesis of the Perennial Philosophy:

> *human beings are capable not merely of knowing* about *the Divine Ground by inference* [intimating the *awe*-sociations]; *they can also realize its existence by a direct intuition* [i.e., meditation, art] *superior to discursive reasoning. This immediate knowledge unites the knower with that which is known.*

Vico wrote above: "the nations were disposed to receive revealed theology in virtue of a supernatural faith, superior not only to the senses but to human reason itself." There are different means by which one can "receive revealed theology in virtue of a supernatural faith"—art is one. These means recreate awe and lead to a desired end, which is a conscious or unconscious intuition of mystical transcendence. Consciousness is both within and without an individual and is an integral benefit to humanity when it is achieved by the one or the many. Vico writes of the results of Poetic Wisdom: "The highest institutions in this universe are those turned toward and conversant with god; the best are those which look to the good of all mankind" (110).

In 1997 Satya Mohanty wrote: "[Art] ... is valuable because it is one of the several ways that humans gain access to a deep aspect of themselves. Aesthetic experiences point beyond themselves to other, fuller experiences and possibilities—like those available only, to say, a mystic.... On this view, genuine aesthetic experiences are unavoidably linked to ethical and metaphysical values and perspectives, and they can enlarge our existing conceptions of human flourishing" ("Can Our Values Be Objective," 48). Mohanty signifies that a mystic has "fuller experiences" that lead to greater "possibilities" than one who isn't a mystic can achieve. Art, however, is a reasonable alternative.

Joyce Influenced by Vico: Portrait of the Artist as a Young Man *and Vico's View of Human Creative Powers*

If one agrees with Vico—who himself agrees with aesthetic theories postulated much earlier—then one will find in all artistic endeavors the impetus of mythmaking through fables from which poetic wisdom, then all wisdom, is derived. (One may disagree on what constitutes art but even anti-art is a reaction to previous statements of art; hence, even bad art is another incremental pressure expanding on the widening circle begun with a metaphoric initial impetus—or first cause, if one wishes to see it as a mystical origin.)

Still, some examples of art elucidate Vico better than others and Joyce's *Portrait of the Artist as a Young Man* is one, which is apparent in searching among the over 1,100 Vico entries in MLA and seeing the fairly large number of those that include Joyce as having been influenced by Vico. In *Portrait*, the Vico parallels or parables are more manifest because Joyce's subject is art itself and the creative impulse. His autobiographical "character" Stephen, as a young child, like all children in re-creating the world, first learns by imitation, which Joyce's technique of incantatory repetition emphasizes as he repeats Stephen's father, his friends, his teachers, and his priests. He absorbs information and derives his highest forms of imitation from reading. He becomes the Count of Monte Cristo and courts Mercedes in the old, courtly way of *fine amor*, which will contrast with his much less romantic meeting with the prostitute later in the book. *Monte Cristo* is a derivation of the basic revenge parable that began in a chain of evolving parables derived from Vico's account of the earliest fables. Stephen absorbs the message of the novel's parable and much more information from which he selects and modifies as he begins to imitate less and create more—mainly in his imagination. Stephen, after many pages of listening to sermons, lectures, admonitions, and a laudatory offer to join the priesthood, discovers that the form of truth he would rather obey is none of the preceding cants and rants. Stephen instead prefers the primitive and much more viscerally appealing banter of his childhood peers:

> He recognised their speech collectively before he distinguished their faces.... He stood still in deference to their calls and parried their banter with easy words.... What did it mean? Was it a quaint device opening a page of some medieval book of prophecies and symbols ... a prophecy of some end he had been born to serve and had been following through the mists of childhood and boyhood, a symbol of the artist

forging anew in his workshop out of the sluggish matter of the earth a new soaring impalpable imperishable being? His heart trembled; his breath came faster and a wild spirit passed over his limbs.... This was the call of his life to his soul not the dull gross voice of the world of duties and despair, not the inhuman voice that had called him to the pale service of the alter. An instant wild flight had delivered him and the cry of triumph which his lips withheld cleft his brain.—Stephaneforos!" [184].

For Stephen this was his epiphany or mystical moment of allness. There has always been a proclivity by young people with creative imaginations to reject their immediate precursors by rejecting the very language they have absorbed and from it deriving new terms as a self-contained lexicon that gives identity to themselves as individuals and as a group striving to emerge from the "world of duties and despair." The new nomenclature is a claim of independence and from this new nomenclature, which is a form of creativity, begins a new impetus to create, through modifications, the knowledge that has come before as per Vico: mute logic to fables to poetic wisdom to esoteric wisdom to the next generation which recreates in the same pattern — mute logic to fables to poetic wisdom to esoteric wisdom. Joyce's *Portrait* exemplifies this pattern.

Nietzsche: Beyond Good and Evil to Ressentiment *as an Outcome of the Mysticism's Reconciliation of Opposites*

The measure of a philosophy is its applicability to life, and, if it is, indeed, applicable, then it will also apply to literary art, which is the mirror of life, even if that mirror refracts the image to reflect a given moment's unique nuances between an artist and audience. Nonetheless, the art, however refracted, will work best if the image or narrative is continuous and contiguous with the logical reasoning of real life; that is, the art compares to life so that its audience can correlate or juxtapose from one's own sense of perspective based on one's own internal logic derived from one's own experiences. Art comes from life; a writer cannot write without having experiences of living. Huxley considered language an implied philosophy of the society it represents. Language applied to art becomes art as a parable of the implied philosophy that reflects society. This is not to say, nor does Huxley mean, that the implied philosophy is good or correct or true — it just *is*, like the whiteness of Melville's whale, which was evil only so far as Captain Ahab said it was. Within this *is*ness, or present moment of being, the implied philosophy exists, and it is at once both explicit and tacit. The "tacit dimension"— Michael Polanyi's phrase but also a Nietzschean premise — infers meanings connotatively between the words, and these meanings and the messages they entail are much more important than the possibly obsolete literalness that the words may no longer denote. This implied philosophy belongs to the *is*ness as meanings depend on cognition, and cognition is action, and action is a transition from one continuous-contiguous *is*ness, or new present moment of being in the eternal now, to another moment of continuous-contiguous *is*ness—moment to moment to moment.

Perhaps a difference between action and *is*ness can be seen as the difference between observing knowledge and perceiving understanding as posited by Huxley: "Knowledge is acquired when we succeed in fitting a new experience into the system of concepts based upon our old experiences. Understanding comes when we liberate ourselves from the old and so make possible a direct, unmediated contact with the new, the mystery, moment-to-moment of our existence" (Knowledge and Understanding," 33). *Is*ness is the "unmediated contact with the new, the mystery, moment-to-moment." From *is*ness, understanding, and a new moment of being, action derives to become new knowledge that is fit into the already known but then liberated from the old through a perceived Joycean epiphany of emancipating understanding and then transited to a new present moment of being, or *is*ness. Joyce defined "epiphany" in *Stephen Hero*: "By an epiphany he meant a sudden spiritual manifestation, whether in the vulgarity of speech or of gesture or in a memorable phase of the mind itself. He believed that it was for the man of letters to record these epiphanies with extreme care, seeing that they themselves are the most delicate and evanescent of moments" (187–88). From these epiphanies new actions follow and included among these actions are the making of morality (values) and art (reflection of values).

Morality and art, while symbiotic with explicit and tacit philosophy are meanings derived from the explicit and tacit philosophy through actions that are outcomes of thoughts, resulting in effects—which means they co-exist with *is*ness, but are not *is*ness unto themselves independently. (A writer writes as a cause inspired by thought; an ensuing book is the effect.) "Philosophy" herein is not restricted to the relatively recent formations—the last 3000 years more or less—but includes and begins with the crude initial impetus of the Viconian mind/body intuition, then fables of poetic wisdom, then esoteric wisdom and finally evolves, continuously and contiguously, into our present intellectual complexity. Morality and art derive from the fission of opposition created from actions that are reactions to explicit and tacit philosophy. For Nietzsche, in his *Genealogy of Morals*, a key component of his philosophy, his sense of *is*ness, or that, which is always in the present moment of being, is the concept of *ressentiment*. *Ressentiment* is both independent of action as an explicit and tacit philosophical state of being (*is*ness); yet, also the cause of action through opposition. Before turning to *ressentiment* proper, one can continue with the conceptions, misconceptions, and oppositions of language (as an implied philosophy) that exist in a language's tacit dimension.

Huxley read Nietzsche, deriving many of his ideas from Nietzsche. Nietzsche wrote, concerning the formative power of opposition and the role of language coextensive with opposition, that "To demand of strength that it should *not* express itself as strength, that it should *not* be a desire to overcome, a desire to throw down, a desire to become a master, a thirst for enemies and resistances and triumphs is just as absurd as to demand of weakness that it should express itself as strength. A quantum of force is equivalent to a quantum of drive, will, effect — more, it is nothing other than precisely this driving, willing, affecting, and only owing to the seduction of language (and of the fundamental errors of reason that are petrified in it) which conceives and misconceives all effects as conditioned by something that causes effects, by a 'subject,' can it appear otherwise" (*On the Genealogy of Morals*, 25).

This is also a message from Krishna (spirit) to Arjuna (human) in the Bhagavad-Gita, which Nietzsche read through the influence of Max Mueller, a translator of the Vedas. The great warrior, Arjuna, tells Krishna that he no longer wishes to fight. Krishna tells Arjuna that a warrior is a warrior and that this is his role. An individual only imagines that he is the "doer" and thus, that his interpretations of what one does are subjective, and through language this subjectivity is disseminated as being "truth" even if the perception is askew due to the subjectivity that is ego-bound. *Krishna*: "Feelings of heat and cold, pleasure and pain, are caused by the contact of the senses with their objects. They come and go, never lasting long. You must accept them [rather than interpret them]. A serene spirit accepts pleasure and pain with an even mind and is unmoved by either. He alone is worthy of immortality" (40). In effect, he alone who can see objectively without the ego's influence can supersede language and see the Ultimate Reality that transcends the material world.

Both Huxley and Nietzsche understand that the "implied philosophy" within the tacit dimension that a malleable language represents is to some degree constituted of "fundamental errors of reason that are petrified in it." Yet, fossilized or not, language — utilitarian and literary — derives from the past experiences of its creators, even if the *creation*— language — over time, becomes the *creator*, the conceiver and then misconceiver of new experiences by its influence on these new experiences. It is in the tacit dimension, and the "slippage" between conceive and misconceive, that a subsequent influence is most strongly derived. It is in this vast interstice of slippage, which constitutes the historicity of all human activity, that a reconciliation will need to take place. Indeed, misdirection in language causes the users of language to move away tangentially from the immediate past in a not entirely predictable way rather than in a fixed path of mapped certainty. The new tangent will itself not be fixed in its new direction but bend from the force of all the influence it contains to become a curve of circularity that will widen around an initial impetus (first cause or "big bang") but never lose sight of the impetus as a straight line would. The discerning few follow the curve; the straight line represents the mass that are unable to achieve Nietzsche's "forgetfulness" or Huxley's "liberation." The few that are discerningly "forgetful" or "liberated" perceive causes and effects and the steps in between to arrive at a new understanding while the mass observes only the effects or present knowledge at its face value as dogma. One can say that the discerning are highbrows because they choose to enter into, understand, and act upon their physical and metaphysical environment while the mass are passive lowbrows. The distinction of highbrow to lowbrow has little to do with education, material means or rank in and of themselves, but rather how one from any background can apply natural intelligence to become a maker and not just a consumer, a creative actor and not just a follower. Nature can provide an inquiringly perceptive and active intelligence that can overcome an inauspicious nurture (material means); but nurture cannot overcome an inauspicious, less intelligent and passive nature.

Whether life is a history of human experience or a parabolic reflection of human experience as art, one must, if he is perceptively and inquiringly intelligent, exhume the petrified language of the past and through Nietzsche's intensely analytical *remembering* apply the "more eyes" of discrimination, which when followed by Huxley's "liberating" and Nietzsche's "forgetting" reconstitute language to override the "fundamental errors," the slippage, the conceptions and misconceptions. Only then can observed knowledge become perceived understanding transited to a new moment if *is*ness. Nietzsche writes, "There is *only* a perspective seeing, *only* a perspective 'knowing'; and the more affects we allow to speak about one thing, the *more* eyes, different eyes, we can use to observe one thing, the more complete will be our 'concept' of this thing, our 'objectivity,' be" (79). Many of the conceptions and misconceptions of language, and by extension, extrapolation and evolution, and the life experiences that are strongly influenced by language's pervasively collective subjectivity are the result of conflict and opposition between "strong" and "weak." For Nietzsche, these terms of "strong" and "weak," just as with "good" and "evil," are among the "fundamental errors" pervasive within the *is*ness of language and life. (The *is*ness is not in error because it just *is*; only acts of cognition can err or seek to overcome error.) Any value of the words *strong, weak, good, evil* cannot be understood through static definition, which, for these words, is an impossibility. These words can only be understood in terms of causation and opposition. These words cause opposition by the very fact that they are intangibly subjective concepts, and their interpretation depends on which end of the power structure the perspectival eye of the beholder is looking out from.

Cause and effect, action and reaction, strength and weakness are Nietzsche's dialectic (reconciliation of opposites) from which his philosophy of *ressentiment* takes its impetus. Opposition is the central pivot for Nietzsche, as without opposition there is no challenge to the powerful's notion of good; conversely, for Nietzsche, "good" determines that evil (in the eyes of the people in charge) is whatever the subjugated class does and thinks, which is really anything that threatens the power structure that was set up by the "good" people in charge. The strong (really weak) fear the weak (potentially strong), and

3. Mystical Philosophy as Applied to Philosophers and Literary Theorists   73

through the former's oppression of the latter there may derive that which the strong fear most — rebellion — if not by force then by an undercurrent of emerging ideas that can undermine the falsely "moral" imperatives that the power group's notions of "good" (not really good) seek to preserve.

To preserve what is false, the powerful must discount and discredit the notions of others through force if necessary in the typical oppressor-oppressed, colonizer-colonized dichotomy that is opposition waiting to be reconciled. Subjugation makes one angry. Anger that cannot be manifested (impotence) makes one bitter. Bitterness foments into self-hatred. This self-hatred derived from impotence internalizes as guilt. Subjugation, anger, impotence, bitterness, self-hatred, and guilt ferment into *ressentiment*. *Ressentiment* begins with individuals one by one, led by the priests/seers in general or such as the elders in the play *Antigone* as a particular case, and through their influence this becomes group *ressentiment* that at some point will be mirrored through art such as *Antigone*. The internalized energy formed from self-hatred becomes creative hatred one by one against the powerful. Creative hatred becomes organized hatred. Organized hatred starts revolutions.

This process here described is the macrocosmic view of *ressentiment*. Within this macrocosm of society's *is*ness are the microcosms, the *is*ness of individuals — duplication by duplication (but each with nuances) — that are microcosms in a "what-comes-first-the chicken-or-the-egg" circularity of ever bending and circle making tangents, without which there would be no macrocosm. The individuals in society represent the life of society; the subjugated individuals in society resent their subjugation, which results in individual moral indignation in reality and in art by reflection. An artistic example of individual indignation is Antigone's token burial of Polynices against the king's command; and then there is the collective indignation of the elders (priests) that resent Creon's hypocritical duplicity. The collective moral indignation of a subjugated group can be acted upon differently by the individuals (microcosms) within the group (macrocosm). A minority of individuals will lead an actively creative resentment — some as artists — while most will listen and follow; but whether initiating or agreeing with the feelings of resentment, this collective resentment becomes the force of Nietzsche's *ressentiment*.

> The slave revolt in morality begins when *ressentiment* itself becomes creative and gives birth to values: the *ressentiment* of natures that are denied the true reaction, that of deeds, and compensate themselves with an imaginary revenge. While every noble morality develops from triumphant affirmation of itself, slave morality from the outset says No to what is "outside," what is different," what is not "itself": and this *No* is its creative deed. This inversion of the value-positing eye — this *need* to direct one's view outward instead of back on oneself — is of the essence of *ressentiment* [Nietzsche, 19].

Ressentiment is an opposition such that the interpretation of words such as strong, weak, good, evil, bad, depends on who is in charge — and for Nietzsche, it is the looking *out* that counts for the relentless focus fixed on the cause of *ressentiment*—the subjugators; or, as Sicilians say about an absent enemy who, nonetheless, still has a powerful psychological effect, "I can see that (choose your expletive) right at the end of my nose."

Nietzsche's term *ressentiment* is a factor in the macrocosm of the whole of *isness* at any present moment of being. Within the macrocosm are the microcosms of actors and their actions that derive ever-evolving moral imperatives and their mirror of ever evolving art. Nietzsche's *ressentiment*, as an outcome of oppositional conflict, is an applicable philosophy that exists within all the moments of *isness*. This is clearer, particularly if one considers time not as a river carrying moments away from their impetus until the impetus is out sight but as that "vast landscape," in which, if one could only stand back far enough, one could see the *isness* (whole as macrocosm) as well as all of the actions and consequences (parts as microcosms) indivisibly, giving to life and art the truest sense of continuity and contiguity summed up in the axiom: *any given event in any part of the universe has as its determining conditions all previous and contemporary events in all parts of the universe.*

The universe is a continuous and contiguous *isness*; *ressentiment* is *isness*; *ressentiment* becomes opposition derived from events (actions and reactions) that evolve in a never-ending cycle. To perceive an understanding of *ressentiment* as a causative philosophy affecting life's actions and reactions, rather than just observing the knowledge of the actions and reactions, is to see into human nature's enduring—from caveman to modern man—perpetual reconciliation of opposites. To understand *ressentiment* as the cause of events (actions and reactions) is to apply that understanding to actors, actions, and reactions that *are* life; events include art as the mirror of life. If *ressentiment* can be applied as an evaluation of life, then *ressentiment* can be applied to evaluate literary art.

Antigone: *Vico (Poetic Wisdom) and Nietzsche* (Ressentiment) *as Interpreted through Mystical Philosophy*

For Vico and Nietzsche the body is the source of the mind's activity; consequently, the body of Polynices, even more in death than life, becomes for Antigone's body/mind a central symbol from which Vico and Nietzsche could support their philosophical perspectives.

A Viconian View: The body derives sensations that the mind seeks explanations for; the mind "mythifies" these explanations to rationalize fear and awe, and thus give some sense of control to these emotions. Over time, myth detaches from fear and awe and becomes ritual; ritual, nonetheless, holds enormous psychological importance even if long removed from the initial impetus that led to the myths that preceded the ritual. The body is sacred, and the rituals associated with the body — dead or alive — are sacred. The greatest affront to an individual is to demean the psychological importance of rituals, which an individual correlates to the most basic intuitions and rationalizations that give meaning to existence. King Creon must assert his oppositional strength by denying a ritual burial to the rebel Polynices. This hubristic power play strikes at the very essence of Antigone's — and by extension her society's — self-worth. This self-image has been ingrained through generations of the self-explanations that were originally mythified to rationalize fear and awe in order to replace the fear and awe with self-esteem by removing the fear through parables. To deny a sacred ritual to the temple of the body denigrates the memory of the mind that the body created and renders the living mind or minds as impotent. Impotence leads to anger; anger leads to guilt; guilt leads to Nietzsche's *ressentiment*.

A Nietzschean View: If the powerful (Creon) not only defeats an enemy but also chooses to humiliate the enemy by denying the vanquished an elemental ritual that heretofore had been sacred, this act — even if applied to an individual (Polynices) — strikes at the entire society that honors this ritual. The powerless can react in protest and symbolic defiance (Antigone with her token burial of her brother) but for the most part the society will react through moral indignation that is led by the priests or seers who are the bearers and teachers of the sacred knowledge of ritual law. The priests or seers remind the subjugated populace of the affront and foster their indignation into a new ritual — *ressentiment* as a collectively oppositional moral law that sustains the subjugated society so that it can retain its collective identity, which might otherwise be lost. This identity has lasted through storytelling for untold generations. If a subjugated populace has no power to overturn their rulers, its only outlet for preserving some degree of self-esteem is to believe in their moral superiority. This is achieved by creating new myths that are a response to their subjugation with these myths "punishing" the inequities and iniquities of their rulers by punishing them allegorically. (A classic example is the Jewish myth of The Golem, the giant clay man who comes to life as a protector.) In sum: Sophocles makes the evil ruler (Creon) witness the folly of his immorality (according to the subjugated) through the suicides of Antigone, his son, Haemon (Antigone's affianced), and his wife, Eurydice, who grieves for her son.

Antigone's plot (as with all plots) evolved from the original tribe's storyteller. The fact that Sophocles first wrote *Antigone*, then Brecht, Anouilh and Malina wrote versions adapted from Sophocles, is evidence that a story can last 2,000 years, or 400 years as do Shakespeare's plays, which he adapted from earlier sources, or as with *King Kong*, filmed for the third time. This is proof enough that seminal stories and seminal philosophies are perennial.

Huxley, Horkheimer and Adorno and "The Culture Industry"— When Cultural Opposition Seems Scarce and Reconciliation into New Forms Even Scarcer

> Orwell feared that the truth would be concealed from us. Huxley feared the truth would be drowned in a sea of irrelevance. Orwell feared we would become a captive culture. Huxley feared we would become a trivial culture, preoccupied with some equivalent of the feelies, the orgy porgy, and the centrifugal bumble puppy.... In 1984 ... [p]eople are controlled by inflicting pain. In Brave New World, they are controlled by inflicting pleasure. In short, Orwell feared that what we hate will ruin us. Huxley feared that we love will ruin us.—Neil Postman

Horkeimer and Adorno agree with Huxley more than Orwell; in fact, their essays, particularly the well-known "The Culture Industry," were influenced by Huxley's *Brave New World*, and his essays.

In Horkheimer and Adorno's essay, "The Culture Industry," the "industry" is the mass proliferation of pop "art" and pop "culture" as mind candy made ubiquitous by mass production. The pop (pap) is served up by mass media to a mass that has been largely homogenized through an evisceration of personal responsibility and accountability. Individuality is replaced by an amorphous and anonymous "public."

The anonymous public is the stepchild of the Industrial Revolution, universal education, and mass media. The public is appealed to and influenced by news, advertising, and propaganda, but can never be directly blamed for any of its consequent behaviors that might be provoked by these appeals. This is because media can influence the public's constituents in general, but as individuals no one need admit to anything in particular. The Industrial Revolution mechanized society. Mass production required regimented workers made so through the conformity of universal education—just enough of it so they could cope in the city, run the machines, and produce goods to be consumed in a vicious cycle. Workers are educated just enough to be easily moved about or replaced as needed by the corporate structure and to read advertisements that perpetuate the consumerism vital to that structure. The industrial city heightened the public's anxiety while shift work and more efficient mechanization increased the leisure time workers had in which to worry. The answer to how this time would be filled was that to an anonymous mass mostly unknown to each other, a mass that could now almost all read, if not all read well, only the fodder mass media provides would do—but of what?

Primary education for the many permitted them to read, but their comprehension and/or attention span was limited and/or distracted so that what they read needed to be primary as well. This meant simple, slight, fast, and escapist—in other words, junk reading or listening or viewing.

Certainly, a mind candy culture that deadens and diffuses by design prevents people from thinking seriously about their own existences, which is exactly what the mass wants to forget. An anxious, tired, stultified, universally — but minimally — educated work force demands "junk" that can be consumed quickly and replaced rapidly by new fodder that the industrialized mass media is only too happy to provide. This depersonalized and malleable mass is manipulated to believe that they want what they don't have through advertising and propaganda. Auden wrote, "our age is highly educated / There is no lie our children cannot read" (*Letter to Lord B*yron, 83). This mass becomes Soren Kierkegaard's anonymous public, that anonymous pseudo-person hiding its face behind a newspaper while reading the advertisements and gossip columns. Huxley dubbed this public the "new stupid," because they had just enough education to be easily manipulated.

In this study the term "public" is influenced by Kierkegaard, the 19th century existential Christian philosopher and polemicist:

> The Public is a concept which could not have occurred in antiquity because people *en masse, in corpare*, took part in any situation which arose and were responsible for the actions of the individual, and moreover, the individual was personally present and to submit at once to applause or disapproval.... Only when the sense of association in society is no longer strong enough to give life to concrete realities is the press able to create that abstraction "the public," consisting of unreal individuals who can never be united in an actual situation or organization — and yet are held together as a whole.... A public is everything and nothing, the most dangerous of all powers and the most insignificant [Auden, *The Living Thoughts of Kierkegaard*, 41–43].

As Huxley explains, it is to this definition of "public" that advertisers (and propagandists) appeal:

> Advertisers have come to know the potentialities and limitations of what you can do by mere statement and repetition [Horkheimer and Adorno, "The Culture Industry," p. 148: "Anyone who doubts the power of monotony is a fool."]; by appeals to such well-organized sentiments as snobbery and the urge towards social conformity; by playing on the animal instincts, such as greed, lust and especially fear in all its forms, from fear of sickness and death to the fear of being ugly, absurd or physically repugnant to one's fellows. Thus, I need soap; but it makes not the smallest difference to me whether I buy X or Y. I can allow myself to be influenced by such entirely irrelevant considerations as the sex appeal of the girl who smiles so alluringly from X's posters. In these cases commercial propaganda is an invitation to give in to a natural or acquired craving. In no circumstances does it ever call upon a reader to resist a temptation; it always begs him to succumb. It is not very difficult to persuade people to do what they are all longing to do ["Writers and Readers," 4–5].

Horkheimer and Adorno say of the culture industry that, "advertising is its elixir of life." They also say, "The consumer becomes the ideology of the pleasure industry" (s/ge/adorno.htm).

Huxley posited this theme many years earlier:

> Mass production is impossible without mass consumption. Other things being equal, consumption varies inversely with the intensity of mental life. A man who is exclusively interested in the things of the mind will be quite happy (in Pascal's phrase)

sitting quietly in a room. A man who has no interest in the things of the mind will be bored to death if he has to sit quietly in a room. Lacking thoughts with which to distract himself, he must acquire things to take their place; incapable of mental travel, he must move about in the body. In a word, he is the ideal consumer.

Now it is obviously in the interest of the industrial producers to encourage the good consumer and discourage the bad. Long live Stupidity and Ignorance!

The new snobberies of stupidity and ignorance are now strong enough to wage war at least on equal terms with the old culture-snobbery. In the meantime the battle between the rival snobberies comically rages. A sham fight still; there is as yet no actual persecution of highbrows ["Foreheads Villainous Low," 202–203].

Both of Huxley's quotes are from 1931, so the caveat "as yet" was prophetic. Very soon after, the Fascists and Stalinists would persecute "highbrows" because, throughout history, totalitarian regimes have always known that the intellectuals are the only barrier that stands between the liars and the lies that are fed to the rest of the anti-intellectual Public.

"The Culture Industry" does not just account for pop art, which dominates and makes it difficult for new art to emerge, but accounts for how "good" art can still evolve in a modern society as a result of forms in opposition. The old form of an artistic genre that has become diminished by ubiquitous imitation rubs up against a new form. The new form is in conflict with the public's inability to accept any new form that does not conform to their habituated comfort level of what they know compared to what they don't know. A minority in the public that wishes to challenge their environment and not just passively live in it will be more amenable to hearing and seeing a new form. They will recognize the "irritation" of a new form that evolves from rubbing in opposition to the standard form. If the new form is pleasing, the few will spread the word, and that word, and the new form being advocated, will often be initially disparaged by the majority of lowbrows that are by nature in opposition to the highbrows. Since the public is always expecting what it already knows by the repetition of mass-produced formulas that they are comfortably and numbingly used to, true originality in art that too sharply deviates from accepted norms of packaged style may at first be rejected as failure because to the public it is unfamiliar. Unfamiliar is not the same as "good" or "not good." Beckett's *Waiting for Godot* was booed; Stravinsky's *Rites of Spring* was booed. Rock 'n' roll was the devil. The acceptance of these new forms as "art" was only accommodated after imitators began to make inroads into the old "style" and through repetition of these new styles, now adulterated, the public slowly saw their worth. Often, it is not until mainstream imitators adapt the new forms from the original source such as Gershwin's version of Harlem jazz or rock 'n' roll's appropriations of the blues or Eminem's riff on rap that the form becomes accepted by the many. (If one sees a pattern here, it is intended.) Yet, over time, this originality is imitated to such a degree that, while still giving homage to the originals of Beckett, Stravinsky, and Muddy Waters, the imitations became mass-produced into familiar formulas as per Horkheimer and Adorno:

However, only in this confrontation with tradition of which style is the record can art express suffering. That factor in a work of art which enables it to transcend reality certainly cannot be detached from style; but it does not consist of the harmony actually realised, of any doubtful unity of form and content, within and without, of individual and society; it is to be found in those features in which discrepancy appears: in the necessary failure of the passionate striving for identity. Instead of exposing itself to this failure in which the style of the great work of art has always achieved self-negation, the inferior work has always relied on its similarity with others—on a surrogate identity [www.marxists.org/reference/subject/philosophy/works/ge/adorno.htm].

Herein, "self-negation" is not a negative position but an attempt by an artist to negate or remove himself from the accepted forms that the culture industry has conditioned the public to expect. The superior work is an opposition to the "inferior" work and has resulted from the artist's dissatisfaction with the known and accepted forms so that the artist is motivated to oppose the norm so that originality will be the outcome. Here again is the difference between knowledge and understanding, the lowbrow and the highbrow. The passive public knows what already exists and only wants to access the familiar. True artists perceive new understanding of what can be genuinely created. Still, in the culture industry, and its influence on the public, opposition is scarce.

> The reconciliation of the general and particular, of the rule and the specific demands of the subject matter, the achievement of which alone gives essential, meaningful content to style, is futile because there has ceased to be the slightest tension between opposite poles: these concordant extremes are dismally identical; the general can replace the particular, and vice versa [www.marxists.org/reference/subject/philosophy/works/ge/adorno.htm].

When a culture is subsumed by sameness in form, stagnancy in creativity follows. Sameness of style and form obviates opposition, without which a "discrepancy" by an artist who deviates from the norm and seeks originality is less likely to occur. A tangential artistic deviation that emerges from resistance to the norm, whether it is successful or not, is a measure of an attempt *not* to fit in. These artists face much resistance and often feel like outsiders. Goethe recognized this with his terms, *Weltschmerz* (a feeling of being ill-at-ease with the world) and *Ichschmerz* (self-dissatisfaction), that are factors in his autobiographical novella *Werther*. The terms can refer to many artists who, "ill-at-ease," resist the past and use art to create a new future. (The Auden Generation of the 1930s is a paramount example of societal dissatisfaction that became artistic responses.) Without resistance and opposition to conformity, conformity reigns. Massive conformity is safe and simple for mass producers in the culture industry, but without innovation there is no artistic or social or philosophical progress toward an advance in consciousness. Since art reflects its society, new art reflects a society open to change and progress. Art, indeed, is the metaphor of an artist's *Weltanschauung* (his particular vision and attitude) towards his era's zeitgeist. Art's inclusiveness represents the entire society's influences that formed the artist making the art. Even when an artist is reacting to old forms by rejecting these forms, the artist's opposition and the new form that emerges could not happen without something to reject. Rejection of old art forms often corresponds to concurrent rejections of the society itself. There is no separation of art from the rest of the world from which it came. Fredric Jameson holds the same view.

Fredric Jameson's Take on "Ultimate Reality" in "Magical Narratives: On the Dialectical Use of Genre Criticism"

Fredric Jameson is a Marxist literary critic in that he takes dialectical materialism as a basis for literary theory. In his study, *Marxism and Form: Twentieth-Century Dialectical Theories of Literature*,[1] Jameson writes:

> dialectical judgments enable us to realize a momentary synthesis of the inside and the outside, of intrinsic and extrinsic, of existence and history [346].
>
> totality and individuality — are common both to the analysis of concrete social life and to that of the work of art.... It is clearly the most urgent task of a genuinely dialectical criticism to regain, on the occasion of a given work of art, this ultimate reality to which it corresponds [354].

Jameson is interpreting "dialectical criticism" in terms of a wholeness, within which part and whole are particles revolving within and around each other in an undifferentiated unity of electrons and nucleus, microcosms and macrocosm. His "ultimate reality" is the same as mystical philosophy's Ultimate Reality.

In his essay "Magical Narratives: On the Dialectical Use of Genre Criticism," Jameson posits that recent genre criticism is either semantic or syntactic and that these are forms in opposition. The semantic deals with the "spirit" of a genre as per Frye; the syntactic (Propp) concerns parameters defined by "mechanisms and structure" (169).

Jameson says that the semantic is about what something means and the syntactic about how it works. This opposition is one of many "antinomies in the very nature of language (170)." Yeats used the term *antimonies* in the same manner but he derived the word after studying the Vedas — the seminal writings of the mystical philosophy. Jameson's dialectic in his essay is a reconciliation of opposites.

When Jameson writes that "the apparently philosophical alternative between the two 'methods' was in reality the projection of objective antinomies in language" (170), he is describing the ongoing nature of metaphysical opposition that underlies the subjectivity of all human communication, which, however complex it has become, is originally based on Auden's proposition that "I am *I* and *you* are not I." Jameson says, "every universalizing approach ... will from the dialectical point of view be found to conceal its own contradictions and repress its own historicity by strategically framing its perspective so as to omit the negative, absence, contradiction, repression, the *non-dit* [not-spoken]" (170). The "not spoken," as in Vico's mute logic, is much more profound than the spoken. The spoken or written is just the trace of what is not actually said or written. Words are an outcome of the psyche and they contain both presence and absence, with absence dominating. The "not spoken" has two components: (1) Michael Polanyi said that "we know much more than we can tell," meaning that language is inadequate to represent all of a person's memory and intuitions that go into his speech or writing. (2) When the "I" speaks to the "you," egos are involved so that often the words of an *I* are informed — for the most part unconsciously — by how the *you* will react to them. Moreover, the *I* and the *you* are not autonomous actors but creatures of their societies upon whom the influence of collective subjectivity acts to give the words spoken or written by the *I* and heard or read by the *you* all of the incrementally accumulated shadings inherent in language. Collective subjectivity is the notion that Jameson is dealing with when he writes that "Frye's entire discussion on romance turns on a presupposition — the ethical axis of good and evil — which needs to be historically problematized in its turn, and which will prove to be an ideologeme that articulates a social and historical contradiction" (170). For Jameson, "good and evil" are terms exemplified as opposites that very much need to be reconciled, although this doesn't mean they will be reconciled in his or our lifetimes.

Jameson sees Good and Evil as Nietzsche did. Good is determined by who is in charge and good is the idealized perpetuation of the powerful's notions of their own self-image. Jameson asserts via Frye that the romance is the wish-fulfillment fantasy of this self-image. The folks in charge are a collective *I*, which means there must be a collective *you* as the "other" against which an image of good can be compared and justified. The *you* (other), if not like the *I*, is different, and difference amounts to opposition, which the *I* attempts to eviscerate by demonizing the other (*you*), and by contrast elevating its own image and position as not only "*I*," but *I* am right; *you* are wrong.

The Other, Jameson writes, is "evil *because* he is Other, alien, different, strange, unclean, and unfamiliar" (174). For Nietzsche and Jameson Good and Evil are not in opposition due to any philosophically objectivist universal notions, they are in opposition by manufactured notions based on who is in charge and who isn't.

In sum: when the *I* in charge derives a self-image by self-praise that is created largely at the expense of, and comparison to, a subjugated Other (*you*), the *you* (Other) really gets ticked off but cannot rebel overtly; instead, the Other seethes in bitter resentment and from this resentment — Nietzsche's *ressentiment* — comes an internalized creative energy that over time will challenge the powerful on a moral basis by appealing to the powerful's sense of guilt, a guilt derived from the conflict of their romanticized self-image with the contrast of their actual repression of the Other who is causing the guilt.

Jameson now arrives at the Marxist-inspired dialectic that is the point of his essay: The romance genre — in its many derivations such as the American Western — is a subjective creation of self-affirmation that must have heroes and villains who are really the mirror of the collective *I* against the collective *you*. This dialectic of opposition provides the fission needed to fuel evolving consciousness, of which "historical texts are not the last word, but merely prodigious anticipations of the thought mode of a social formation of the future, which has not yet come into being" (176). On the way to the future will be Jameson's "ideologeme," a construct that he writes "remains a conceptual *antimony*, [and] must now be grasped, on the social and historical subtext as a *contradiction*" (176).

Here Jameson returns to Frye and Propp and to Jameson's preference for the spirit (Frye) over the formal (Propp). This is still in line with Nietzsche, who also preferred the spirit to the formal. For both Jameson and Nietzsche, the formal is encrusted with fossilized language from which society is influenced by the collective subjectivity that language entails. Nietzsche asked that one achieve an intellectual state akin to the Zen *no mind* by stripping down (or in the recent mode "deconstructing") formalized notions within language in favor of the spirit — or *Weltanschauung*— to be found within the writer or speaker individually. This spirit is the *Istikgeit* or "*is*ness" of a given moment in time and this spirit evolves from moment to moment or "*is*ness" to "*is*ness," and from zeitgeist to zeitgeist, which *is is*ness.

In contrast to spirit, Propp's formalism suffers from the societal influences of *his* time even though he is looking back on previous times. Jameson makes his point by referring to Levi-Strauss and Greimas, "who insist on a radical distinction between the narrative surface (manifestation) and some underlying deep narrative structure" (180). In effect, the manifestation of an external formal structure is less important than the spirit represented by the "underlying deep narrative structure"

Spirit supersedes structure, just as the artistic impulse that moves the spirit supersedes genre. The message is more important than the process. The structures of a poem, a play, a novel, a song, are all means to the end of an artist's creative impulse to *say* something. (No matter how many different genres are used to tell the story of King Arthur, the symbolism and message of the sword coming out of the stone is going to be there.) Nonetheless, form *can* be important (181) if a shift in spirit, or a new moment of *is*ness, is signified by a change in form (i.e., the advent of cinema or *The Waste Land* or *Waiting for Godot*). Then, as per Horkheimer and Adorno's "The Culture Industry," a new oppositional modification of an art form provides a discrepancy or, for Jameson, a "deviation" (185) from an existing form and irritates this into a pearl of new art over time. The irritation emerges from a reconciliation of opposites (or antimonies or contradictions). The modified art is a reaction to existing art. Action and reaction occur within the perpetual continuum in a circular rather than a linear movement. Jameson's example of such an artistic deviation is Stendhal's *Le Rouge et le Noir* (185–86).

Jameson talks about "the play of structural norm and textual deviation" as two terms in a "three-term process":

> What is dialectical about this more complete structural model is that the third term is always absent, or more properly, that it is nonrepresentable as neither the manifest text, nor the deep structure tangibly mapped out before us in a spatial hieroglyph, the third variable in such analysis is history itself, as an absent cause.
>
> The relationship between the three variables may be formulated as a permutational scheme or *combinatoire* [187].

Jameson here signifies that the external force — historicity — of a society's collective subjectivity acts as a form of "play" between the norm and the deviation. This historical subjectivity, whether conscious, or more likely unconscious, tacitly influences spoken or written outcomes even while being explicitly absent from these outcomes. Thus, what is present as speech or text, and what is absent from the speech or text — the influences that played in the formation of the speech or text — combine as a *combinatoire* that one must analyze before one can fully understand a speech or text. In effect, the outcome of a reconciliation of opposites is the tip of the iceberg of historicity's influence; the *combinatoire* is the transition of a present moment of being or *isness* to a new present moment of being or *isness*. Contained in the *combinatoire* is all of the past that now combines influences in a way chosen and acted upon by the artist, consciously and unconsciously, to make a new outcome. The outcome is *not* the historicity of the *combinatoire*; yet, the outcome could not come into being without the influence of the *combinatoire*. The outcome is the tip of the iceberg; the *combinatoire* is the massive, unseen iceberg itself. The outcome is a moment of *isness* in the *eternal now*; the *combinatoire* is the historicity contained in all of the moments of *isness* that have formed the new outcome, which, simultaneously is integrated in the new *combinatoire* that will lead to more outcomes. One can refer again to Eliot's "Burnt Norton," "And all is always now."

Eliot's conception in words of an eternal now is an outcome of his life lived and experienced intellectually. He has combined diverse influences (one of which was the Vedas) to formulate his outcome as art. "Burnt Norton" reflects the boiling over of thought from a large pot of water (or ocean) where individual drops of history, philosophy, and previous art (Donne and the Metaphysical poets) have merged into the *combinatoire* from which Eliot has produced the outcome called "Burnt Norton." We cannot *see* or *know* the influences from the words of the poem alone; nonetheless, we can *feel* the influences, and this is what we call the spirit of the poem:

For a genuinely dialectical criticism, indeed, there can be no pre-established categories of analysis: to the degree that each work is the end result of a kind of inner logic or development in its own context, it evolves its own categories and dictates the specific terms of its own interpretation [Jameson, *Marxism and Form*, 332].

The reconciliation of opposites of mystical philosophy precedes dialectical criticism.

Jameson owes a great deal to Christopher Caudwell's 1937 Marxist literary study, *Illusion and Reality*. This book would forever affect Auden's view of history. His "Spain" (1937) and the sonnet sequence, "In a Time of War" (1939), are examples of Caudwell's theory influencing art with the art synthesizing the theory's essence. Caudwell was killed in the Spanish Civil War so that Auden's poems were homage and memorial, not just for Caudwell, but also for Julian Bell (Virginia Woolf's nephew), Christopher Cornford, Ralph Fox, and so many more.

Iris Murdoch: Metaphysics as a Guide to Morals

Iris Murdoch was a novelist and philosopher. Or was she a philosopher and novelist?

Did she hold one or the other as her paramount avocation? As either or the other, her philosophy was concerned with morality and goodness. This study has asserted that that viscerally felt awe-sociations became intuitive accounts, through storytelling, of basic, primal emotions. These stories, as per Vico, became the "poetic wisdom" that preceded philosophy. When "poetic wisdom" became ritualized myth in the life of the tribe, and when these rituals or myths became "esoteric wisdom," the priests or seers of the tribe emerged to give analytical, spiritual, philosophic, and classifiable meanings to the feelings that were engendered by these now "mythified" stories. A principal theme of the stories was to describe metaphorically and analogously what was good and what was not good. A principal theme of the emerging esoteric wisdom (philosophy) was to explain *why* what was good was good, and what was not good was not good. From these explications morality was derived.

Over generations, the configurations of morality and philosophy were expanded along with the expansion of humanity, and these analyses were wide and diverse. Each generation's highbrows—those who actively pursue an understanding of their role in a present environment—seek answers to questions. Some measure their environment; others "metaphorize" their environment into artistic parables, which are an intuitive return to that state of awe that began the ongoing dialectic of the evolution of consciousness. Art is a mirror to life, and art is the true synthesis of the spirit or zeitgeist of particular eras and generations. Murdoch does not disagree:

3. Mystical Philosophy as Applied to Philosophers and Literary Theorists

I think that though they are different, philosophy and literature are both truth-seeking and truth revealing activities. They are cognitive activities, explanations.... Of course, good literature does not look like analysis because what the imagination produces is sensuous, fused, mysterious, ambiguous and particular. Art is cognition in another mode [*Metaphysics*, 10–11].

Murdoch explains that characters in fiction are the bearers of evocations in morality:

It is difficult in life to be good, and difficult in art to portray goodness. Inspiration from good characters may be rarer and harder.... [Shakespeare] portrays moral dilemmas.... He doesn't portray religion directly..., but it is certainly there, a sense of the spiritual.... [We] invent characters and convey something dramatic which at the same time has deep spiritual significance. ["Interview," *ParisReview*.com, www.theparisreview.com/tpr115/murdoch.html].

A novel can lead to truth if a reader is so inclined to analogously correlate the parabolic message to one's own life. A novel can intimate for an individual one's own sense of what is good and what is not good. A novel is never "good" (in the moral, not aesthetic sense) unless a reader believes it is good. Truth is not truth unless a reader sees the truth. Art as an imitation of life has no meaning until an audience gives it meaning. The meaning is independent of the art; the novel stimulates *thoughts* about what is good or not good but cannot create the good or not good as that is entirely conditioned by what the reader already knows or doesn't know. Art *can*, however, take a reader's present knowledge and evoke a response so that this present knowledge becomes understanding. This understanding would be evoked by the historicity of Jameson's *combinatoire*, which would take the reader's body of knowledge, and by provoking correlations about that knowledge, combine that previous knowledge to create an outcome of new understanding.

On thoughts, Murdoch writes:

What is observable is that we need and use the idea that thoughts are particular inner experiences. This is an idea which connects up with our notion of the privacy and the unity of our "selves" or "personalities." There is here, if I may borrow a psychological term, an important and necessary "illusion of immanence"; only to call it an 'illusion' risks giving the description an ontological flavour. It is rather a necessary regulative idea, about which it makes no sense to ask, is it true or false that it is so? It is for us as if our thoughts were inner events, and it is as if these events were describable either as verbal units or in metaphorical, analogical terms [*Existentialists*, 38–39].

Metaphorical and analogical terms are supernatural. That is, one thinks about that which is no longer immediate experience or is not yet immediate experience (or may never be) by spontaneously reacting to stimuli that are not yet words but are at first *thoughts-as-inarticulate-understandings* as first felt intuitively without words. Then, as often happens, almost in an immeasurably slight duration following these *thoughts-as-inarticulate understandings* without words, the *thoughts as-articulate-words* come into play to give a category to whatever the feeling was just a millisecond before. For example, a gunshot may evoke the feeling of fear, after which the mind will form words to evaluate both the cause of the gunshot and the fear evoked by the gunshot (What was that?). *Thoughts-as-inarticulate-understandings* precede *thoughts as-articulate-words.* Concurrent with the articulate thoughts, judgments are made about the thoughts. These judgments are based on previous knowledge of what one believes is good or not good, moral or not moral.

> Morality has always been connected with religion and religion with mysticism. The disappearance of the middle term leaves morality in a situation which is certainly more difficult but essentially the same. The background to morals is properly some sort of mysticism, if by this is meant a non-dogmatic essentially unformulated faith in the reality of the Good, occasionally connected with experience [Murdoch, *Sovereignty*, 74].

Thoughts-as-inarticulate-feelings come from intuition, and intuition is mystical and non-dogmatic; *thoughts-as-articulate words* are derived from the known or the dogmatic. If both the thoughts-as-inarticulate (mystical) and the thoughts-as-articulate (dogma) combine to synthesize a new outcome, this is understanding derived from a mystical intuition informing previous knowledge. Words are the outcomes of rituals that preceded the words; rituals were preceded by intuitive awe-sociations from which the rituals were derived.

> A sacrament provides an external visible place for an internal invisible act of the spirit. The apprehension of beauty, in art or in nature, often in fact seems to us like a temporarily located spiritual experience which is a source of good energy [Murdoch, *Sovereignty*, 69].

Here Murdoch defines what is meant by spiritual experience:

> We need a theology which can continue without God. Why not call such a reflection a form of moral philosophy? All right, so long as it treats of those matters of "ultimate concern," our experience of the unconditioned and our continued sense of what is holy. [Paul] Tillich refers to Psalm 139. "Whither shall I go from thy spirit, whither shall I flee from thy presence? If I ascend into heaven thou art there, if I make my bed in hell, behold thou art there. If I take wings of the morning and dwell in the sea, even there shall thy hand lead me, and thy right hand shall hold me" [*Existentialists*, 511–2].

For Tillich and Murdoch, spirit is everywhere. The principle of *tat twam asi*— thou art thou; that thou art — also signifies that the realm of spirit pervades all of existence, and one is never removed from spirit physically if one chooses to retain spirit psychically via intuition. Murdoch's "moral philosophy" is a theology without God — or so it would seem. Yet, one can interpret that "without god" refers to those versions of god that are the various permutations of human-devised god-as-dogma that long followed the awe of poetic wisdom. The mystics East and West in many ways have said that the more one talks of God the more God cannot be found.

> *Kena Upanishad*: If you think you know It well, you indeed know It very little. That whom you see in the beings and gods, you see but very little [portion] of It [hinduwebsite.com.isha.htm].
>
> *Isha Upanishad*: Self is One, unmoving, and faster than the mind. The senses cannot overtake It, since It is already there when we try to reach it" [hinduwebsite.com.isha.htm].

God (or spirit or consciousness) is felt with the intuition of "mute logic." The purpose of meditation is to empty the mind of sense-associated articulated words that flit about in a stream of chatter. And certainly, with or without god, meditation has been amply studied for its health benefits in reducing stress and inducing serenity. Duke University Hospital's Center for Integrative Medicine regularly has workshops for meditation as part of a holistic process of good health. Holism is Murdoch's concern as well; "ultimate concern" sounds like Ultimate Reality, particularly when Murdoch attributes to "ultimate concern" that which is the "experience of the unconditioned." Unconditioned is the perception of understanding untainted by knowledge-as-dogma, just as the Upanishads, the Bhagavad-Gita, Nietzsche, Huxley, Auden, and mystical philosophy have long asserted.

In her essay, "'Seeing' Human Goodness: Iris Murdoch on Moral Virtue," Ana Lita writes:

> One recent advance in contemporary moral philosophy is Iris Murdoch's unique understanding of the concept of the moral self. Murdoch attempts to remedy the account of the moral self she associates with traditional ethics, which mainly focuses on the will. Drawing from the world of art appreciation, Murdoch holds aesthetic perception to be the necessary component of moral regard for others. She claims that a moral person becomes suitably other-directed through the practice of aesthetic perception through ego "unselfing." In contrast to the Aristotelian emphasis upon the rewards of virtue, Murdoch posits the self-interested "ego" as the chief obstacle to correctly seeing others and, following from this, not rightly exercising virtue towards them, for the ego cannot love. Hence, Murdoch's concept of virtue is a rigorous one, since it advocates the perfection of one's moral vision as an end-in-itself, thus presenting a concept of virtue that comes much closer to the holiness of the saint than to the excellence of a hero. However, the critical question remains: Can an aesthetic construct of the goodness in others become a sufficient basis for knowledge claims about virtue? To answer this question, [this] article analyzes Murdoch's process of obtaining aesthetic "seeing" through development of a "virtuous consciousness," a process of empathic experiencing, that provides the only true path of practicing virtue towards others [*Minerva*, www.ul.ie/~philos/vol7/murdoch.html].

The "process of empathic experiencing" is ultimately the same as the construct of thou art that; that art thou. In effect: If I hurt you, I hurt myself. Lita asserts that for Murdoch the "ego" is the obstacle to "virtuous consciousness."

Katha Upanishad: May we light the fire ... that burns out the ego and enables us to pass from fearful fragmentation to fearless fullness in the changeless whole [hinduwebsite.com.katha.htm].

Mundaka Upanishad: Like two golden birds perched on the selfsame tree, intimate friends, the ego and the Self dwell in the same body. The former eats the sweet and sour fruits of the tree of life while the latter looks on in detachment. As long as we think we are the ego, we feel attached and fall into sorrow. But realize that you are the Self, the Lord of life, and you will be freed from sorrow. When you realize that you are the Self, supreme source of light, supreme source of love, you transcend the duality of life and enter into the unitive state [hinduwebsite.com.mundada.htm].

Murdoch, a fan of Schopenhauer-the-devout-Vedantist via the Upanishads, was a closet Vedantist.

Mary Louise Pratt's "The Contact Zone," and Chinua Achebe's "Dead Man's Path"

Mary Louise Pratt's 1991 essay, "Art of the Contact Zone," connotes the "contact zone" as the place where contact, sometimes oppositional, can become a useful synthesis of ideas and views. Art imitates life; sometimes life imitates art. One is not separate from the other; neither can exist without the other. If art is the mirror of life then Chinua Achebe's short story, "Dead Man's Path," is something of an inverse parable version of similar issues raised in Mary Louise Pratt's essay. Pratt's "Contact Zone" represents the potential for a meeting of minds and, by extension, cultures, that is missing in the failure to communicate that ends disastrously in "Dead Man's Path." Indeed, Pratt offers a means to the end of individuals and communities learning how to coexist with her example of Guaman Poma's letter to the King of Spain, which suggests how any individual, including, and perhaps especially intellectuals, can contribute to their communities. People are similar; no two people are alike. Human nature is consistent; individual humans are not necessarily consistent. One can have expectations of how people will behave based on patterns that have asserted themselves throughout history; conversely, one can never be sure of how any single person will react to both present and past history. Pratt and Achebe write of individual cases that refer to universal situations.

Mimicry is the normal process for human learning between the two (parent-child, teacher-student, master-servant, colonizer-colonized) that is replicated by the vast multiplicities of two times two into the tribe, group, community, culture, and nation. The microcosm of the "two" is replicated into the macrocosm of the many. Yet, the psychology of the two, while having its own particular nuances (such as those that we examine as colonizer/colonized,) is fundamentally the same as the psychology of the many. Collective subjectivity influences the psychology of the two so that this becomes the psychology of the many through mass mimicry. The majority of the mass conforms in the public forum. The private dynamic between any particular two may or may not match the deportment in the public forum but this dynamic is always responsive to "public" performance (mimicry/conformity) if it is inverted. For example, the worker who is browbeaten by his boss into repressed frustration and fear may then express this resentment by aggressive behavior in private towards others.

In effect, Pratt's essay and Achebe's story are two discussions of how the psychology of the two is replicated by the many. *Otherness* is the first and dominant relation that dictates human nature. "I am I; you are not I" is extended to "We are us; you are not us." Pratt and Achebe's descriptions are local (colonizer-colonized) but the depictions of "mimicry" are global in analyzing Achebe's story and Pratt's essay, which point out that fiction and essay are not necessarily different in message, just in their presentation.

The dichotomy of master/servant and colonizer/colonized — an opposition that needs to be reconciled — is not exclusive to colonization. In England, particularly before World War I, the upper class "colonized" the working class and treated them as inferiors in a manner only slightly better than they treated the indigenous inhabitants of their colonies. (See Orwell's "Shooting an Elephant" and "A Hanging.") When Pratt and Achebe infer the notions of slippage, difference, and hybridity (different nomenclature but equal to Jameson's *combinatoire*), they are dealing with *Otherness* no differently than the Vedic Reconciliation of Opposites (or Hegel's dialectic or Jameson's neo-dialectic). The synthesis of colonizer-colonized for Pratt and Achebe derives from a psychology that is not unique to colonization but is deeply, and irrevocably, continuously representative of human nature from caveman to modern "mimic" man. Past and present, global and local, are one and the same. Nuances change in the details but human psychology, in total, has an evolving, yet fundamentally comprehensible, process that has a consistent essence from primal tribe to modern nations that is only different in scale.

For Pratt the contact zone may initially be a place of conflict, but she also asserts that the contact zone can overcome conflict and become an intellectual demilitarized zone where individuals and cultures can make a mutual effort to promote mutual understanding and a correlative acceptance of their similarities rather than their differences in a manner that is beneficial to both sides of the zone. Conversely, in Achebe's story, "Dead Man's Path," difference is not overcome and tragedy follows. The protagonist is a native schoolmaster, Michael Obi (a native with a colonizer first name, native last name, itself a conflict). He had been trained in the colonizer's schools, and he has been afforded this opportunity to be headmaster of a native school by abdicating both his heritage and independence. He will run the school in the manner he believes the colonizers expect of him, and this includes the colonizers' insensitivity to native customs and traditions. Obi is going to close "the dead man's path" that runs through the school grounds. The tribal elder asks him not to close the path as the natives consider it the spiritual corridor to their concept of transcendence. The native schoolmaster refuses to acknowledge what he now believes is a silly superstition and closes the path. There is no further effort to continue the dialogue. The natives respond to the closing of the path by destroying the school. The Elder and Obi might have learned a better way to deal with their disagreement if they had read Pratt's essay.

Pratt offers the historical example of Guaman Poma, an Andean under the rule of imperialist Spain. Poma chooses to write to King Philip III of Spain, and he not only learns Spanish in order to do so, he also creates an Andean "written" language that did not actually exist in the Andean culture. Pratt writes, "Guaman Poma's *New Chronicle* is an instance of what I have proposed as an ethnographic text, by which I mean a text in which people describe themselves in ways that engage with representations others have made of them" (this and all Pratt quotes from web.nwe.ufl.edu/~stripp/2504/pratt.html).

Pratt's point is that Poma must engage Philip (Spain) in terms that can be understood by his Spanish conquerors. Only then (and if he is successful in his explications) can the intellectual Poma's Spanish version offer an Andean perspective that might be listened to so that his Andean "text" (mainly drawings) could enter into a contact zone of mutual understanding.

When, as Pratt writes, "Poma's *New Chronicle* ends with a revisionist account of the Spanish conquest, which he argues should have been peaceful encounters of equals with the potential for benefiting both but for the mindless greed of the Spanish," Pratt is explaining how Poma meant to enter the contact zone so that Andeans and their ignorant conquerors might have reached a mutually beneficial merging of cultures.

"Mindless" is also the mind-set of schoolmaster Obi, who has intelligence — knowledge — but an intelligence that is too inflexible to understand that there might be room for a contact zone with the natives and a reconciling of their opposition. Conversely, Poma is flexible and proves it by learning Spanish in order to teach Andean culture to the Spaniards. History knows that Poma's efforts never reached Spain, but in the much later discovery of his writings, Poma still can teach along the path of the perpetual continuum of evolving consciousness. His message is still valid hundreds of years later.

W.H. Auden said that a highbrow (intellectual) is someone who takes the initiative to measure his or her environment and seeks to challenge that environment by learning from it rather than being passive to it. Consequently, both the desire to learn and the wish to use that learning for some constructive activity in a contact zone where others can benefit are traits of an intellectual. Obi did not wish to learn or to enter the contact zone in order to find a constructive reconciliation. Poma learned Spanish and created a written Andean language so that he could try to get better treatment for his people. In the vast landscape *time must have a stop*, and in the bigger picture Poma, through Pratt, has achieved some of the purpose that he originally intended by his example as a reconciler.

Satya P. Mohanty: "Can Our Values Be Objective?"

Mohanty's essay of the above title was published in 2002 and was quoted previously in the section on Vico. It is most interesting, and in fact gratifying, that Mohanty is Indian, and that his idea of objectivity is one he ultimately relates to his readings of a 10th century Indian philosopher.

> Thus, while many traditional societies may have a view that the response to beauty is a deep and universally valid one, in principle available to all humans, they often also argue that to isolate such a response would be to grossly misperceive the nature of which it is a (limited) part. To take merely one instance, Abhinavagupta, commenting on Bharata's Natyashastra[1] and contemporary Indian aesthetics and metaphysics in his tenth-to-eleventh century treatises, can be read as suggesting that even our full response to beauty ("aesthetic relish") is only a small part of a more complex and meaningful meditational-contemplative response to this world. The latter response, it can be argued, should inform all aesthetic inquiry as well, since to see the aesthetic response as autonomous would be (according to this tradition) to make a serious error about the nature of human beings and their welfare [55].

Mohanty is saying that art and life are integrated and the former cannot be considered as independent of the latter. In effect, this is the nature of the Ultimate Reality of undifferentiated unity.

One is grateful that Mohanty alludes to the East, however indirectly, albeit without the substance that it would seem he is well aware of with his reference to Abhinavagupta's commentary on Bharata's Natyashastra. Mohanty's sense of "objectivity" relates to, and is inseparable from, the question of "non-identity" as it is understood in mystical philosophy. Mohanty's view of aesthetics is that there is an underlying desire for human beings, whatever their origins in a multicultural world, to seek some form of transcendence that takes each individual out of his singular identity and into a realm of non-identity. (And non-identity herein is equated to the mystic's interpretation as that of a dying to the self, where one abnegates the willful ego and becomes a vessel that allows *Otherness* to mediate his connection to mystical unity.)

CHAPTER 4

Mystical Theory Applied to 20th Century British Literature

ALL LITERARY ARTISTS ARE REFLECTING the Perennial Philosophy when they put pen to paper or fingers to keyboard. Most do so unconsciously; some do so consciously. In sections to follow there will be examples from modern literature of authors who express the Perennial Philosophy (or derivation) in their art.

Yeats: *The World* Seems *to Fall Apart, But the Center* Does *Hold*

> Turning and turning in the widening gyre
> The falcon cannot hear the falconer;
> Things fall apart; the centre cannot hold;
> Mere anarchy is loosed upon the world,
> The blood-dimmed tide is loosed, and everywhere
> The ceremony of innocence is drowned;
> The best lack all conviction, while the worst
> Are full of passionate intensity [Yeats, "The Second Coming," 1919].

Yeats was deeply influenced by Vedanta. Yeats, however, took the Irish Renaissance very seriously and chose to see everything through a Celtic prism. Fellow Irish poet Louis MacNeice wrote in his 1941 study of Yeats: "it is difficult to be Irish because the traditional Irish aim is to be spiritually self-supporting. And in the modern world this is as impracticable — for an individual or small country — as to be materially self-supporting. Yeats nominally accepted this aim but in following it practiced a good deal of sleight-of-hand. When he borrowed something (say) from India, he would excuse himself by the supposition that India is essentially Irish" (47). MacNeice, however, abetted Yeats in his ambition by offering no further mention of how Yeats's borrowings from India influenced Yeats's verse and, even more so, his prose work of neo–Celtic philosophy, *A Vision*, written in 1925 and revised in 1937.

Yeats's journey to *A Vision* followed a typical path for his time. In 1887 Yeats met with Madame Blavatsky; in 1888 Yeats joined the Esoteric Section of the Theosophical Society. He was already a good friend of Æ (George Russell), a theosophist turned Vedantist who put his beliefs into his verse and paintings. Æ believed he had visions and his art described them (see discussion on Æ to follow). The influence of Vedanta followed Yeats throughout his career; yet, as per MacNeice, he scarcely credited Vedanta in his work, per se, although in 1913 he would write an introduction to Rabindranath Tagore's translation of Gitanjali's aphorisms. In 1938 Yeats collaborated on a translation of the Upanishads. What is lesser known, and precedes all of the above, is that in 1886 Yeats met Mohini Chatterjee, who was visiting Dublin. Chatterjee would make such a lasting impression that in 1933, a poem named after him would be part of *The Winding Stair*.

Vedanta informs *A Vision*, particularly the 1937 version. There are two versions of *A Vision*, designated *A Vision A* (1925) and *A Vision B* (1937). Both incorporate Vedanta but the second version does so more comprehensively, which is not to say Yeats was giving too much direct credit.

The Upanishads' states of consciousness are reiterated in *A Vision A* and more so in *A Vision B*: "Then when I had ceased all active search, yet had not ceased from desire, the documents upon which [*A Vision*] is founded were put into my hands, and I had what I needed" (*A Vision A*, xi). The documents were Vedanta scripture. Later he would add to *A Vision B* how his system of metaphysics had also informed his art: "I put *The Tower* and *The Winding Stair* into evidence to show that my poetry has gained in self-possession and power' (*A Vision B*, 8). Yeats acknowledged that his system in large part is metaphorical, that it should point toward intuition in order to intimate ideas that are not physical but require symbols to be explained:

> Some will ask if I believe in the actual existence of my circuits of sun and moon. Those that include, now all recorded time in one circuit, what Blake called "the pulsation of an artery," are plainly symbolical, but what of those that fixed, like a butterfly upon a pin, to our central date, the first day of our Era, divide actual history into periods of equal length? To such a question I can but answer that if sometimes, overwhelmed by miracle as all men must be when in the midst of it, I have taken such periods literally, my reason has soon recovered; and now that the system stands out clearly in my imagination. I regard them as stylistic arrangements of experience comparable to the cubes in the drawing of Wyndham Lewis and to the voids in the sculpture of Brancusi. They have helped me to hold in a single thought reality and justice [*A Vision B*, 24–25].

The idea of holding "in a single thought reality and justice" is the same as the mystic's vision of all existence being held in a single thought or seen from the perspective of Wilder's "vast landscape." The Vedas describe meditation as a conduit for feeling the Ultimate Reality. The Vedas are Yeats's strongest influence on *A Vision*.

Yeats's first exposure to Vedanta, which then sent him to Theosophy, was through Mohini Chatterjee. Chatterjee was a spokesman for Theosophy to the degree that this allowed him to be a spokesman for Vedanta. He used the former to write about the latter in *Man: Fragments of Forgotten History* (1884 with Laura Holloway), which promoted Eastern philosophy. He would translate and comment on Indian philosophy for a Western audience. Chatterjees's initial influence on Yeats was retained and expanded upon by Yeats. In 1915 Yeats wrote of Chatterjees's influence in *Reveries over Childhood and Youth*: "It was my first meeting with a philosophy that confirmed my vague speculations and seemed at once logical and boundless. Consciousness, he [Chatterjee] taught, does not merely spread out its surface but has, in vision and in contemplation, another motion and can change in height and depth" (91–92). Chatterjee wrote of the Upanishads' levels of Consciousness in *Man: Fragments of Forgotten History*:

> Following the mystic idealists, we may divide the whole range of existence into different states of consciousness, with their appropriate objects or functions.... the consciousness of a man awake, the consciousness of a man dreaming, and the consciousness of one in a state of dreamless slumber.... Besides these three states ... there is a fourth state of consciousness, which may be called transcendental consciousness [5].

Chatterjee defined the mystic's Ultimate Reality of absolute consciousness as comprised of a mystic union of Prakriti (Matter) and Purusha (Spirit; *Man: Fragments of Forgotten History*, 8). This definition of consciousness can be found in *A Vision*.

Indian influence remained with Yeats but took a firm hold again in Yeats's last ten years with his friendship and work with Shree Purohit Swami. Yeats took on "consciousness" again in the 1930s in his introductions to *The Holy Mountain* and the Upanishads. Generally, Yeats's understanding of Vedanta was enriched by the Swami, and they collaborated on a translation of the Upanishads in 1938. Yeats also wrote introductions to Purohit's other works, including Gitañjali's *Aphorisms of Yoga*. Yeats's efforts would help him form the *Principles* in *A Vision B* (*AV B*).

The Upanishads were a major source with their explications of the different states of consciousness. Yeats draws from the *Brihadâranyaka Upanishad*, where the teacher explains that the Self or soul (*âtman*) is both inner and outer consciousness whether one is awake or asleep. For Yeats dreaming is a creative state. The stage beyond this is a dreamless sleep, where the sleeper "desires no desires and sees no dream." During dreamless sleep the spirit loses contact with desire, in Yeats's term the *Passionate Body*, to come closer to the archetype of itself in an indifferent "state of pure light or of utter darkness, according to our liking" (*AV B*, 220).

The *Mandukya Upanishad* also explains three states as the elements of the sound A-U-M (*OM*), but dreamless sleep becomes Sushupti, or dark Samadhi, and is extended to a fourth state, Turiya, which correlates to the whole Aum, which is achieved through meditation or, as Yeats writes, "in contemplation and in wakefulness"(*AV B*, 222).

Yeats, while deriving his own idiosyncratic perspective in *A Vision B*, forms his system largely from Vedanta. His process is Viconian. The mind learns by looking out and creates the world, as per Vico, to accommodate its own perceptions. This interpretation cannot exist without the Ultimate Reality from which the mind makes its correlations. The mind learns, initiated from its spark of transcendental consciousness, what it already knows intuitively; the mind and the Ultimate Reality could be said to interrelate but this is not quite what would be the actual case from the Vedantic (mystical) perspective, in which mind and Ultimate Reality are undifferentiated and only the appearance of separation keeps the mind from perceiving this undifferentiated union. The "interrelating" is metaphorical, a process of tearing down the barrier of sense perceptions that the mind creates because the senses work from the outside-in by seeing, hearing, touching, tasting, feeling the physical world. The Vedantic concept of *neti, neti* (not this, not that) is the inverse of *tat twam asi* (thou art that; that art thou): For example: A child asks the seer, "Is God in this rock I sit on?" The seer answers, "*Neti*—not this." The child points to a tree. "Is God in that tree?" The seer answers, "*Neti*—not that." When the seer says *neti* to every external object the child points to or names, the child learns that God is not *in* any one thing, but exists in everything without exception or distinction.

Differences seem to exist to dramatize the oppositions that need to be reconciled. Tearing down differences, or emptying out the false idea of duality that the senses create, must precede the building up through intuitive contemplation the unity of the Ultimate Reality. Yeats, as a poet, understands the differences that utilitarian language denotes about the material world; Yeats's vision sees past differences and sees into the power of words as art that symbolizes the de-individuation of the undifferentiated unity of the Ultimate Reality.

Yeats writes of the duality of Purusha and Prakriti in terms derived from Gitañjali's aphorisms in his introduction to *The Holy Mountain* (1934), translated by Purohit: the "Spirit, the Self that is in all selves, the pure mirror, is the source of intelligence, but Matter is the source of all energy, all creative power, all that separates one thing from another ... almost what Schopenhauer understood by Will" (*Essays and Introductions*, 461). From this idea Yeats derives his Principles and Faculties, primary and antithetical, Solar and Lunar, Daimon and human.

Yeats knew he had not solved, nor had anyone else solved, all of the mysteries of consciousness. He did believe that it was "only in India'" that he could "find anybody who can throw light upon certain of its problems" (letter to the Swami, on microfilm, University of Delaware Library; see Saddlemyer, 527–535).

Yeats and the mystics understand that the best an artist/philosopher can do in attempting to explain the ineffable is to point towards a sense of what cannot be known empirically but only intuitively. This "pointing "of writers through the ages is an inspiration at best but can never be a methodology to a transcendent consciousness. The mystical sages have all agreed that the Ultimate Reality is beyond words. In Yeats's papers there is a draft of a translation of a Hymn of Creation from the *Rig Veda* (Tenth Cycle, Hymn 129). The *Rig Veda* is among the oldest literature in the world. The translation almost certainly dates from his last decade in the 1930s during his work with Sanskrit writings and it shows many traits in common with his work on the Upanishads with Purohit Swami,[1] where Yeats was using literal translations and attempting to find natural and direct forms of expression, and the translation, though still very much a draft, has a poetic immediacy and effectiveness (State University of New York at Stony Brook University Libraries, West Campus, William Butler Yeats Microfilmed Manuscripts and Correspondence Collection).

The totality of Nature and Being existed before the primitive tribe's naming by words began to differentiate this undifferentiated unity. Does the mind react, when fingers touch a hot stove, with an articulation? "A part of me has burned; the part I call fingers." Rather, there is first a non-descriptive reaction that will one millisecond second after the immediate experience be called "pain." As Auden said, however, via Heard, an intuitive reaction will first be the recoil of the fingers perhaps accompanied by a sound formed in the throat: "Ow!" From this reaction words evolved. Within that millisecond between reaction and description is the wordless intuition that is the same as the intuition needed to find the Ultimate Reality. The mystics seek to reclaim the wordless state and try to retain it for more than just a millisecond. Easy to say, hard to do, but the effort in trying has intrigued highbrow human beings since before words replaced awe. Yeats was one of these human beings, and his stature, then and now, has influenced others to try as well.

Yeats's system in *A Vision B* is intricate and complex with many terms and definitions of these terms. Just a few are described below. Ultimately, the system is creatively derivative of the Vedas in the Upanishads and Bhagavad-Gita. There is a good deal of Yeats's creative influence over and beyond the Vedas, but one who knows both can see the similarities.

Antithetical: The impulse to individuation and subjectivity, which is in opposition to the undifferentiated unity of the Ultimate Reality.

Creative Mind: One of the Four *Faculties* (similar to Jung's four faculties), originally termed "Creative Genius." It represents the mind in its consciously constructive aspect (*AV B*, 142).

Daimon: A complex concept echoing the antecedent of Kierkegaard's "demonic defiance," and "demonic despair," which theologian Paul Tillich would also adapt; both influenced Auden's art of the 1940s. For Yeats the *Daimon* is the supernatural opposite of the human being, but part of a single continuous consciousness with the human, and can even be viewed as the same elements in a different dimension. To a certain extent it controls human destiny, but needs its human counterpart to complete its knowledge of the whole. Demonic defiance is more or less the creative aspect of this correlative of continuous consciousness. It powers the imagination to strive. This is not to say that the striving is always constructive. It can also be destructive, as in war. Demonic despair is inertia and depression.

Discord: See *AV B*, 93–94. Oppositions are Discords to each other: Will and Mask, the two fundamentally antithetical Faculties, are the Discords to Creative Mind and Body of Fate, the two fundamentally primary Faculties. This is Yeats's version of the Reconciliation of Opposites.

Gyre: The essential element of growth and life, representing the cyclical nature of the Ultimate Reality with the recurrent pattern of growth and decay, ebb and flow, just like in the Upanishads.

Opposition: A relationship between the two primary Faculties. In each pair one is active, Faculty (Creative Mind and Will), and the other is the goal of its action, the Target-Faculty (Body of Fate and Mask). Within the fundamental gyre, the active Faculty is the zenith of the gyre, while the target-Faculty is the base or widest expansion of the gyre; Oppositions are diametrically opposed to each other. The two Oppositions form Discords to each other from which the evolution of consciousness derives.

Sphere: The absolute and unitary form of being, beyond the gyres. The human mind, fixed in the antinomies (Yeats's terms for opposites), cannot sensually perceive the whole of the Ultimate Reality, but can sense the historical events along the ascending spiral of the gyre. Intuition can "feel" the sphere, of the Ultimate Reality.

Wheel: Yeats perceives time as cyclical rather than linear and, as in the Hindu symbol, the Wheel also represents the cycle of the soul's rebirth. Yeats learned this when Chatterjee visited Dublin in 1886 (see Foster, *W. B. Yeats: A Life*, vol. 1, 47–48; Mann, 164).

Yeats's influence on modern poetry is great; his interpretation of Vedanta through his verse and prose is not a small part of this influence.

Æ (George Russell): Perennial Philosopher

> Goethe, Wordsworth, Emerson, and Thoreau among moderns have something of this vitality and wisdom but we can find all they have said and much more in the grand sacred books of India.
>   The Bhagavad Gita and the Upanishads contain such godlike fullness of wisdom on all things that I feel the authors must have looked with calm remembrance back through a thousand passionate lives, full of feverish strife for and with shadows, ere they could have written with such certainty of things which the soul feels to be sure.—Æ [George Russell]

Æ's vast energy was nourished and nurtured by his mystical consciousness, a source that he deliberately cultivated. This consciousness provided energy along with an endearing personality. James Stephens loved Æ, to whom he owed his career as a fellow poet and writer. Yeats, as far as he could show affection, showed it to Æ. George Moore, normally caustic and verbally pugnacious, gushes over Æ in his three-book saga of the Irish revival, *Hail and Farewell*. In the third volume, *Vale*, Moore, finding himself in an irascible mood (which was the case quite often apparently), thinks of Æ to cheer himself. "A smile began to trickle round my lips as a picture of the dusty room at the end of many dusty corridors rose up before me, with Æ sitting at a small table teaching that there is an essential oneness in all the different revelations that Eternity has vouchsafed to mankind" (232). Later, with mutual friend John Eglinton, Moore, who attacks everyone else, considers if Æ has any faults. He concludes, after four pages listing Æ's many virtues of character, kindness, and generosity, that Æ is, indeed, faultless.

One of Æ's friends was fellow Irishman Gerald Heard. Æ's interest in mysticism, the underlying principle of the Perennial Philosophy, influenced Heard, who went on to be an even greater influence on Aldous Huxley, W. H. Auden, and Christopher Isherwood. Heard and his friends helped spread the gospel of the Perennial Philosophy throughout the world. Consequently, Æ's impact has far extended past the day he left his body in 1935.

Æ was a poet, essayist, editor, dramatist, painter, agricultural economist, legendary raconteur, cheerleader, benefactor, teacher, loyal friend, and mystic. The last encompasses all the rest, and this is how Æ would want to be remembered, as a mystic. And if he was a mystic, then he was a Perennial Philosopher.

George Russell was also a poet of visionary metaphor, and a painter of visionary visions. For Russell, both mediums were a means to a single end, which was to raise his own consciousness and that of his audience, and to praise the divine consciousness for his ability to do so. He felt filled with God and was happy to share the overflow. Those who knew him benefited from the sheer energy of his mystically inspired presence.

Æ's friend Eglinton recalls how Æ explained to him that as a young man he began to realize why one is faced with temptation and desire. It is so one can learn the difference between his ego-bound mortal self and his transcendent heavenly Self, which is the spirit integrated with, rather than separated from, the Divine Ground of all existence.

> This was the beginning of his doctrine of the Ancestral Self or Heavenly Man.... He began to paint his visions, and had been attempting an ambitious series of pictures on the history of man, in one of which he [and Eglinton quotes Æ] "tried to imagine the apparition in the Divine Mind of the idea of the Heavenly Man," when, as he lay awake considering what legend he should write under the picture, something whispered to him, "call it the birth of Aeon [from which Russell took the pen name

Æ]." Next day the entire myth "incarnated in me.... I trembled because I was certain I had never heard the word before, and there rushed into my mind the thought of pre-existence, and that this was memory of the past" [8–9].

Æ loved God first and wrote about that love second. Æ felt the feeling of "being-thereness" and then attempted to evoke it in words and pictures. Æ was not interested in technique but in transferring passion to paper as it passed from a divine consciousness into his pen. If one does not have the same interests as Æ, then his poems have less appeal. This is no different than a person getting nothing out of reading the Bhagavad-Gita if it is not his cup of tea. Conversely, if one has the same interests as Æ, such as the mystical philosophy, then one can enjoy his poems as devotionals and even as ambient preludes to meditation. For example, to mystics and meditators, dawn and dusk are auspicious times for devotion and concentration on the Absolute. A mystic or meditator can read Æ's "The Hour of Twilight" (1913) and identify with the poet's emotions.

> When the unquiet hours depart
> And far away their tumults cease,
> Within the twilight of the heart
> We bathe in peace, are stilled with peace.
> The fire that slew us through the day
> For angry deed or sin of sense
> Now is the star and homeward ray
> To us who bow in penitence [*Selected Poems*, 51].

Æ believed that spirit creates art and that art should serve the spirit. "I have no interest in people who find in literature anything but an avenue to life. Every thought or mood is the opening or closing of a door to the divine world and who is there we would not laugh at who went to a door and only admired or looked at it forgetting its uses. Art for art's sake is considering the door as a decoration and not for its uses in the house of life" (Foreword, *Letters*, xii). Monk Gibbon, who knew Æ, believed that "the key to Æ's life is the fact that he elected to be a student of esoteric wisdom, and that his interest in literature, in poetry, in painting and in practical affairs were all to a large extent rooted in this original impulse. At the age of twenty-seven he [Æ] writes to Professor [Edward] Dowden, 'I am glad you have regarded me rather as a mystical poet than as a poetical mystic....' Æ's most characteristic utterances invariably reveal him as the natural mystic that he was. He looks always beneath surfaces and towards a Primary Cause, and at the same time he relates his intuitions to the immediate event" (Foreword, *Letters*, xv).

Æ would be consistent in his beliefs as shown in this letter to Dowden:

13th August 1894

To get free; to be able to rise from the region of dependent things into the self-existent spiritual life is the first need of the mystic. He is most able to do this by pondering over statements which for the time draw the mind away from nature and need a self-illumination for their proper significance to be grasped. Such are:

> The Knowledge of It is a divine silence and the rest of all the senses. *Hermes*

And

> The soul is its own witness and its own refuge. *Upanishads*

And

> Iswara is a spirit untouched by troubles, works, fruits of work or desires. *Yoga Aphorisms*

Or

> Night and day are undistinguished on the Path. Whether one would set out to the bloom of the East or come to the chambers of the West without moving is the travelling on this road. In this path to whatever place one would go that place one's own self becomes. *Dynaneshvair.*

All these statements are a chaos to the reason; only the imagination kindled at the inner shrine can realize their truth.

In this letter Æ continues his elucidation of these quotations and touches on karma, reincarnation, and avatars from East and West. Finally, he ends with: "If it is any compensation for a long lecture on mysticism I append verses in which I feel more at home and which you may like better."

IN THE WOMB

Still rests the heavy share on the dark soil;
Upon the black mould thick the dew-camp lies;
The horse waits patient; from his lowly toil
The ploughboy from the morning lifts his eyes.
The unbudding hedgerows dark against day's fires
Glitter with gold-lit crystals; on the rim
Over the unregarding city's spires
The lonely Beauty shines alone for him.
And day by day the dawn or dark enfolds
With dreams of beauty eyes cannot see
How in her womb the Mighty Mother moulds
The infant spirit for eternity [*Letters*, 12–14].

Æ believed his verses and his paintings came from his spirit-inspired imagination and that these said much more than his prose discourses ever could. Mystics believe that if one tries to explain God, then one does not know God, for God cannot be explained, only felt. The western mystic, Meister Eckhart, writes, "The knower and the known are one. The simple imagine that they should see God, as if He stood there and they here. This is not so, God and I, we are one in knowledge" (quoted in Huxley, *The Perennial Philosophy*, 12). The eastern mystic Kabir agrees, "Behold the one in all things; it is the second that leads you astray" (quoted in Huxley, *The Perennial Philosophy*, 10). Hence, Æ, while attempting to explain the knowledge of mysticism to Dowden, knows that he cannot convey the *understanding* of mysticism, which is ineffable and must be understood intuitively or not at all. Or, as Huxley would say, "Even the best cookery book is no substitute for the worst dinner" (Introduction to Krishnamurti, *The First and Last Freedom*, 10).) The poet attempts to be a transducer and purifier of *feeling*. Æ wanted to be a transducer and purifier of spirit-inspired feeling. One can theorize that all art, whatever its content and medium, is inspired from the same spark of divinity within the mind that is both the part and the whole of the Divine Ground of all existence. Æ believed art is the divinely inspired gift of God to man in order for man to best transmute his feelings, particularly feelings about an intuited God.

DUSK (1913)

Dusk wraps the village in its dim caress;
Each chimney's vapour, like a thin grey rod
Mounting aloft through miles of quietness,
Pillars the skies of God.

Far up they break or seem to break their line,
Mingling their nebulous crests that bow and nod
Under the light of those fierce stars that shine
Out of the calm of God.

Only in clouds and dreams I felt those souls
In the abyss, each fire hid in its cloud;
From which in clouds and dreams the spirit rolls
Into the vast of God [*Selected Poems*, 9].

Published in 1932, three years before he left his body, Æ's book, *A Song and Its Fountains*, correlates the impetus for inspiration with the poems that result. His preface states: "In what follows I have tried to track song back to its [the psyche's] secret fountains. As I have thought it unnatural to see together in gallerie pictures unrelated to each other, or taken from the altars for which they were painted, so I have thought it unnatural for lyric to follow without hint of bodily or spiritual circumstance out of which they were born. I have here placed some songs in their natural psychic atmosphere" (v). On the dust jacket copy (which sounds like Æ wrote it as well) it says that the writer "thinks there should be as much interest in the truth about the making of a thing as about the thing being made."

There has been in recent years a much greater interest in how things get made or discovered, particularly in how the person *inside* is made and how he discovers what has brought him to the present. Prior to World War II psychology was still new and reserved for the few. After the war, Auden's *Age of Anxiety* began an era of psychotherapy for Everyman. (For the very young Auden Æ was a favorite.) Presently, it is ubiquitous. Also more common are the self-help books and formulas that ask one to find an inner self, even an inner child, as a guide through outer tumult. Æ has this covered in a *Song and Its Fountains*. His text sounds much like the pop-mystical "find yourself" books that have their own—and not too small—section in bookstores. (*His* text, however, is better.)

Æ opens with an explanation of a "meditation the ancient sages spoke. In this meditation we start from where we are and go backwards through the day; and later, as we become quicker in the retracing of our way, through weeks, through years, what now are passing into what we did or thought the moment before, and that into its antecedent; and so we recall a linked medley of action, passion, imagination or thought.... The sages enjoined this meditation with the intent that we might, where we had been weak, conquer in imagination, kill the dragons which overcame us before and undo what evil we might have done.... It became of myself as if one of those moving pictures we see ... where in a few moments a plant bursts into bud, leaf and blossom, [then] reversed and I had seen the blossom dwindling into the bud.... To see our lives again is to have memories of two lives and intuitions of many others, to discover powers we had not imagined in ourselves who were the real doers of the deeds, to have a sense that a being, the psyche, was seeking incarnation in the body" (*Song*, 3).

The idea of a time as a perpetual continuum that one can embrace as a single totality is a key component of mystical philosophy. Artists in words have also addressed time in this manner. Æ's mind does the same during his meditations. He writes of going back to his childhood and recalling the revelation of the diverse colors one finds in nature. He says that this was the birth of his "aesthetic sense" (*Song*, 4). Æ recalls his inner child and brings this child into present consciousness to renew and revivify a purer self that is the true Self, unencumbered by the exigencies of adult angst. From these meditative excursions guided by his inner child, Æ would emerge with a need to write or paint. The passion derived from his inner journey would suffuse his outer art. "This meditation, he writes, "which discovers another being within us, unites us to it in some fashion; and in retrospect we seem to have lived two lives, a life of the outer and a life of the inner being" (*Song*, 8–9).

As an example of art reflecting a meditation on the inner being, Æ recalls one of his early paintings of a man casting a giant shadow far larger in proportion to the body casting the shadow. This indicated to him that his intuition about the great psyche of memory did, in fact, loom much larger than the mere physical man whose imposing shadow is the aggregate accumulation of multiple pasts—child, adolescent, young man—until old age's shadow seems to stretch infinitely. From this past the understanding of the present follows, but only if one chooses to find it.

Æ said, borrowing from the ancient sages of Vedanta's undifferentiated unity that "wisdom lies in the transmutation or reconcilement of opposites, and, if we were gentle enough, the God would give us a star to lead.... it was from that original fountain of dream that many poems came" (*Song*, 6). He also writes, "One part of us is seer and another is creator" (*Song*, 19). Art comes when the seer part inspires the creator part.

T.S. Eliot Didn't Study All of That Sanskrit for Nothing

> There are some readers who ... regard Asiatic literature as the sole repository of religious understanding; there are others who ... refuse to venture further than a narrow Christian tradition. For both kinds of reader, it is salutary to learn that the Truth ... is not wholly confined to their own religious tradition, or on the other hand to an alien culture and religion.... I am aware also that there are readers who persuade themselves that there is an 'essence' in all religions which is the same. — Eliot, "Preface," *Thoughts on Meditation*, 11

T. S. Eliot read the Bhagavad-Gita and the Upanishads and both influenced his verse. Buddhism was also factored in.

According to Eliot biographies and criticism, around 1912 he read Hegel's *Philosophy of History*, Charles Lanman gave him a copy of the Upanishads, translated by Vasudev Laxman Shastri Phansikar (Bombay, 1906), and he attended a lecture on Heraclites (the Greek reconciler of opposites; see the following discussion, "Heraclites and Guy Davenport"). In 1913 he read F.H. Bradley's *Appearance and Reality* (which in 1937 was responded to by Marxist literary critic Christopher Caudwell's *Illusion and Reality*); he writes a paper, "The Interpretation of Primitive Ritual," and begins writing his doctoral thesis on Bradley; in August he reads Paul Deussen's *Upanishads des Veda*.

At Harvard, Eliot studied Sanskrit and Pali for two years (1910–11), in order to acquaint himself with Indian philosophical texts in the original. As early as 1918, Eliot reviewed for *The Egoist* an obscure treatise on Indian philosophy called *Brahmadarsanam or Intuition of the Absolute* by Sri Ananda Acharya.

T.S. Eliot wrote in 1933 that the great philosophers of India "make most of the great European philosophers look like schoolboys" (*After Strange Gods*, 40).

Krishna of the Bhagavad-Gita appears in Eliot's poem "The Dry Salvages," telling Arjuna to practice selflessness and not to be attached to materiality even while living in materiality. Noted earlier was Eliot's vision of the *eternal now* in "Burnt Norton."

The Waste Land is about the tearing down of civilization until all that is left is the nihilistic emptiness of the void. Yet, the poem ends with "Shanti, Shanti, Shanti," which is all the proof a Vedantist needs to understand that the void will now be filled with a regenerative cycle of building up just as told in Vedantic cosmology.

> From the unreal lead me to the real
> From the darkness lead me to light
> From death lead me to immortality
> Brihadaranyaka Upanishad

While "Shanti" more or less means "Peace," in Eliot's notes he defines it as "The Peace that passeth understanding," or the intuitive peace of the mystic. To the degree that he knew his English translation was spiritually inadequate, in the

1922 edition he added, "our feeble equivalent to this word." In the section of *The Waste Land* titled "What the Thunder Said" Eliot also points to the theme of cyclic regeneration when he describes the Vedic myth of Indra slaying Vritra who had held up the waters in the heavens.

When *The Waste Land* is interpreted through Vedanta there is a mystical amplification that Eliot intended. The poem has been described as difficult and incoherent, but it is not nearly so of one stands back and looks at its "vast landscape." Stephen Spender, in his 1937 critical study, *The Destructive Element*, took the term "destructive element" from Conrad's *Lord Jim* as well as I.A. Richards's essay about *The Waste Land*, in which Richards said that *The Waste Land*, by destroying all belief, urges the reader to antithetically fill the void with new belief. Eliot tacitly expresses beliefs in absentia through stating unbelief, or that by having rejected certain ideas, readers infer new ideas to arrive at a new synthesis from this reconciliation of opposites. Nietzsche said there must be a "stripping away" of dogma before one can see with "new eyes."

Lines 395–422 of "Thunder" refer to the *Brihadaranyaka Upanishad*, in which Prajapati (God) responds to his symbolic constituents who ask Prajapati what "truth" is. The response comes from thunder above, with the sound Da, Da, Da, which the creatures hear as *datta, dayadhvam, damyata* (give, sympathize, control).

Damyata concerns self-control and universal control. This is a counterpoint to the poem's search for coherence and control. Eliot inserts Vedanta deliberately to assert that within the surface chaos there is an alternative reality that is suffused with an inner meaning if only the poem's protagonist — who represents both Eliot and readers of the poem — could fill in this void of nonbelief with an intuitive sense of the Ultimate Reality that is the true existence.

Datta suggests that through an abnegation of the willful ego, consciously or unconsciously, or how one gives to the world instead of just taking from it, a path to the Ultimate Reality can be achieved. The poem can then be taken as a meditation that will help a reader intuit the counterpoint message to the seeming external nihilism that the poem's wisdom is within not without. This reaction by the reader must be felt intuitively before one can apply it cognitively. Intuition will then supersede societally learned dogmatic responses.

Dayadhvam is a reminder that one should not lose the high of an epiphany derived from intuition by then subsequently succumbing to a paralysis by overanalysis, which is a return to self-absorbed egotism. One should carry over the epiphany of intuition as a feeling of sympathy for the world rather than for one's self.

Here is Eliot's note for these three Sanskrit words:

> In the Hindu fable of "The Three Great Disciplines," the Creator God instructs the lesser gods to "control "their unruly natures, men to 'give' alms despite their natural miserliness, and the cruel demons to "sympathize"; that every thing is repeated even today by the heavenly voice, in the form of thunder as "Da," "Da," "Da."

...Therefore one should practice these three things: self-control, giving, and mercy" [in *Norton Anthology of Modern Poetry*, 503].

While Eliot's note gives one of the themes in *The Waste Land* as being an interpretation of Vedanta as applying to the poem as a whole, there has been little or no interpretation by critics of Vedanta's specific impact. Stephen Spender's study, *T.S. Eliot* (1976), was praised for Spender's analysis of Eliot's politics and religion; yet, the religion covered is bereft of any mention of Vedanta, or is spirituality given its due by whatever denomination. (In Eliot criticism there are exceptions, notably McNelly Kearns; yet, the proportion is still small.)

"*Shanti, shanty, shanty*" closes the poem just as the words close the many Upanishads, where they are meant to tell the reader that it is time to meditate on what he has just read and hopefully learned from the content. The three shanties are also a mantra for meditation, often sounded along with *Om*, which represents the sound behind the sound of all existence. That this is his intention is as apparent as it would be for a professor of quantum physics to understand algebra.

The protagonist's quest in the poem, despite the nihilistic meanderings, is not ultimately as futile as the poem might suggest. There are wanderings in the Vedas, Buddha, and the New Testament. From Buddha comes Eliot's impetus for Section III in *The Waste Land (WL)* "The Fire Sermon."[2] Art not only reflects life, but it reflects spiritual life even when that art most seems to be denying life.

Death and rebirth also concern Eliot, which are a burning wheel of suffering if there is no spiritual awareness.

Eliot's Fisher King is often thought to be Christ, the fisher of men; however, in Vedanta and Indic Buddhism, a priest or seer can be a fisherman who draws fish from the ocean of spiritual existence that help lead to spiritual salvation. Salvation gets one off "the Wheel" of temptation.[3] (*WL* 1.51) and into "the heart of light (*WL* l. 41).

The Waste Land metaphorically resembles the steps of meditation. Meditation begins with the mind meandering in its normal stream-of-consciousness distractions. An effort is made to first limit the randomness by inserting symbols of stillness, a mantra or visual image or music. Through concentration and practice, the symbols begin to move out more and more of the distractions and these symbols take over more of the mind's space. Over time, this effort will produce moments— even if in seconds— of the state of *no-mind*, or in 1960s parlance, "Don't Think," which refuted the signs saying "Think!" Eliot refers to the "water-dripping song" (*WL* beginning at 1.331), which emulates the process of meditation as one which goes from concentration upon symbolic external sensations to more internal, less defined sensations, leading to calm. This, as an opposition to nihilism, is the final message of *The Waste Land*, as exemplified and emphasized by *Shanti, Shanti, Shanti*.

Here is a final word on *The Waste Land* and the ascending spiral of consciousness: A key component of this study concerns the nature of influence from moment-to-moment, *is*ness to *is*ness in the path of evolving consciousness. In "The Fire Sermon" (L258), the first line of the Stanza is "This music crept by me upon the waters," which is from Shakespeare's *The Tempest*. In the play, the "music" is a song by the sprit Ariel who offers Ferdinand "a sea-change, / into something rich and strange." Eliot could be thought of as also wishing for "a sea-change into something rich and strange." In 1953, Archibald MacLeish took Shakespeare's "music" line as the title of a verse play (details to follow).

In sum: from Shakespeare to Eliot to MacLeish, there is a continuity that may seem mere chance, but to paraphrase Branch Rickey, chance is the residue of design.

A Short Note on Joyce: A Celtic Buddha via Vico

In her book, *The Sensual Philosophy and the Aesthetics of Mysticism*, Colleen Jaurretche considers James Joyce as part of the medieval mystical tradition. She considers that Joyce was continuing a "negative" mystical tradition that is an effort to transcend physical sensations and attain an altered state of consciousness that could touch the Ultimate Reality. Jaurretche's correlations to Joyce start with the medieval mysticism of Dionysius the Areopagite and the sixteenth-century writings of St. John of the Cross, and that Joyce interprets these Christian mystics through the attitudes of late Victorian and early modern writers, such as William Blake, Walter Pater, Francis Thompson, Gerard Manley Hopkins, Oscar Wilde, and Yeats.

Jaurretche posits a strong case that Christian Mysticism informs Joyce's art. Christian Mysticism, as Huxley aptly demonstrates in *The Perennial Philosophy*, is the same mysticism that goes back to the Vedas. Moreover, Joyce's influences are not limited to Christian Mystics or only to the above artists named; the East and Vico have important roles in Joyce as well.

James Joyce took Vico's *New Science* as a framework for much of his fiction, in which Joyce incorporated the inclusive influence of accumulated knowledge as being the comprehensive "stuff" of each present moment of *is*ness. In *Portrait of the Artist as a Young Man*, Joyce traces Stephen's personal evolution from a youth who learns from others dogmatically to a young man who begins to see holes in the dogmatism to an aspiring artist who has learned to tear down societal influences in order to make room for the intuitive epiphanies of perceived understanding. His beach epiphany, when he hears the cry "Stefaneforos," is his watershed breakthrough that tears down the barriers that stand in the way of mystical understanding.

Vico is strong in Joyce; yet, Vico is not the only source for Joyce's vision. As early as 1901 and through the influences of Æ and Theosophy, Joyce engaged mystical philosophy, particularly in its manifestation as Indian Buddhism, and this can be seen in *Stephen Hero, Ulysses,* and *Finnegans Wake.* One midnight early in August 1902, as L. A. G. Strong writes in "'Æ'—a Practical Mystic," Æ and Joyce "discussed Theosophy, which Joyce considered a refuge for renegade Protestants but found intellectually interesting" (427–28). Joyce at this time was looking for anything that could also be a refuge for renegade Catholics.

Joyce read Henry Steel Olcott's *Buddhist Catechism* (1881), and his copy of the book was dated May 7, 1901. On February 6, 1903, Joyce reviewed H. Fielding-Hall's *The Soul of a People* in the Dublin *Daily Express,* which includes Hall's discussion of Buddhism. Joyce quotes Hall on Buddha: "He was the preacher of the Great Peace, of love, of charity, of compassion" (85). These qualities are retained in Joyce's fiction.

Stephen Hero talks about Buddha; *Ulysses* refers often to Reincarnation and Karma; *Finnegans Wake* incorporates Buddha's biography.

Joyce's knowledge of Buddha informs a Stephen Hero "stream of consciousness":

> The woman in the black straw hat has never heard of the name of Buddha but Buddha's character seems to have been superior to that of Jesus with respect to unaffected sanctity. I wonder how she would like that story of Yaso Dhara's kissing Buddha after his illumination and penance. Renan's Jesus is a trifle Buddhistic but the fierce eaters and drinkers of the western world would never worship such a figure. Blood will have blood [*SH* 190].

In *Ulysses,* Buddha, Theosophy, and mystical philosophy are featured within the theme of the all-inconclusiveness of mystically "seeing" the vast landscape of the *eternal now.* Stephen: "We walk through ourselves, meeting robbers, ghosts, giants, old men, young men, wives, widows, brothers-in-love, but always meeting ourselves" (*Ulysses,* 9.1044–46). This idea of one individual "seeing" oneself as integral to all other individuals is a staple of Joyce and of mysticism. One can refer back to Æ's painting of the man casting a giant shadow that included all of his various lives and the lives of others.

Reincarnation and Karma are found in the 4th episode, "Calypso." Bloom tells Molly: "Some people believe ... that we go on living in another body after death, that we lived before. They call it reincarnation. That we all lived before on the earth thousands of years ago or some other planet. They say we have forgotten It. Some say they remember their past lives" (*Ulysses,* 4.362–65).

Finnegans Wake concerns Maya. (59.14, 80.24, etc.). In Vedanta Maya is the mistaken assumption that the sense-derived evidence of materiality is the *only* reality and this false impression prevents the undiscerning from seeking the Ultimate Reality. Maya is often called the illusion of the material world and this idea of illusion has been misinterpreted as meaning that trees, rocks, chairs, tables, and so on don't actually exist. They do—very emphatically. The illusion does not refer to what's actually there physically but to the ignorance that imagines there is no other form of consciousness or alternative reality. To refer to an analogy used earlier, anyone can see and sit on a chair without knowing or believing that the chair contains atoms that are moving.

Joyce also admired Buddhism's pacifistic principles. Stephen Daedalus does not fight; he chooses self-enlightenment as his rebuttal to dogma.

Interconnections Along the Ascending Spiral

Myth-explainer Joseph Campbell, with Henry Morton Robinson, published *A Skeleton Key to Finnegans Wake* in 1944. In 1942, Campbell edited Swami Nikhilananda's translation of *The Gospel of Ramakrishna* and would later do the same for Swami's four-volume translation of the Upanishads. Campbell and Robinson said that Thornton Wilder's play *The Skin of Our Teeth* is based on *Finnegans Wake*. Wilder studied *Finnegans* Wake for thirty years. Wilder read critic William Empson's work in the 1960s. Empson praised the Perennial Philosophy as outlined by Huxley. Wilder's 1967 novel, *The Eighth Day*, revered in Russia and Germany, and from which the "vast landscape" view of time is defined, is written as an *eternal now*. The book's last paragraph is a paraphrase from the Isherwood-Prabhavananda translation of the Bhagavad-Gita, which has an introduction by Huxley, in which he first states his Minimum Working Hypotheses. This author is a friend of gay spiritual writer Toby Johnson.[4] Johnson befriended and was mentored by Campbell. Johnson wrote a book, *The Myth of the Great Secret* (1987), that includes his memories of Campbell. This author shares the same birthday with Campbell, March 26.

Johnson's central idea is that as outsiders with a non-gender-polarized perspective, homosexuals play an integral role in the evolution of consciousness—especially regarding the understanding of religion as myth and metaphor—and that for many homosexuals gay identity is a transformative ecological, spiritual, and even mystical vocation.

Virginia Woolf: To the Lighthouse

> It is hard for a writer to be objective about another [Woolf] who has had such an influence on me, on other women writers. Not her styles, her experiments, her sometimes intemperate pronouncements, but simply, her existence, her bravery, her wit, her ability to look at the situation of women without bitterness. And yet she could hit back. There were not so many female writers then, when she began to write, or even when I did.
>
> None of that lot, the Bloomsbury artists, can be understood without remembering that they were the very heart and essence of Bohemia, whose attitudes have been so generally absorbed it is hard to see how sharply Bohemia stood out against its time. They are sensitive and art-loving, unlike their enemies and opposites, the crude business class. E. M. Forster, Woolf's good friend, wrote Howard's End, where the battle between Art and the Wilcoxes is set out. On the one hand the upholders of civilisation, on the other, philistines, the "Wilcoxes." To be sensitive

and fine was to fight for the survival of real and good values, against mockery, misunderstanding and, often, real persecution. Many a genuine or aspiring Bohemian was cut off by outraged parents. — Doris Lessing, ["Sketches from Bohemia"]

What else is there to say about her? Critics will place her among the four greatest English women writers. Friends will remember her beauty, her uniqueness, her charm. I am very proud to have known her. Was she a bewitched princess, or the wicked little girl at the tea party — or both, or neither? I can't tell. In any case she was, as the Spaniards say, "very rare," and this world was no place for her. I am happy to think she is free of it, before everything she loved has been quite smashed.. If I wanted an epitaph for her, taken from her own writings, I should use this [from To the Lighthouse*]:*
  "It was done; it was finished. 'Yes,' she thought, laying down her brush in extreme fatigue, 'I have had my vision.'" — Christopher Isherwood, ["Virginia Woolf," 132]

In *Virginia Woolf: Moments of Being-Unpublished Autobiographical Writings* (ed. Jeanne. Schulkind), Woolf recounts two mystical experiences, both as a child with her mother:

If life has a base that it stands upon, if it is a bowl that one fills and fills and fills — then my bowl without a doubt stands upon this memory. It is of hearing the waves breaking, one, two, one, two, and sending a splash of water over the beach; and then breaking, one, two, one, two, behind a yellow blind. It is of hearing the blind draw its little acorn across the floor as the wind blew the blind out. It is of lying and hearing this splash and seeing this light, and feeling, it is almost impossible that I should be here; of feeling the purest ecstasy I can conceive.

The next memory ... still makes me feel warm; as if everything were ripe; humming; sunny; smelling so many smells at once; and all making a whole that even now makes me stop — But again I cannot describe that rapture. It was rapture rather than ecstasy.

But the peculiarity of these two strong memories is that each was very simple. I am hardly aware of myself, but only the sensation. I am only the container of the feeling of ecstasy, of the feeling of rapture [*Moments*, 64–67].

For mystics there is a metaphor of the corporeal body being just a temporary suitcase — "only a container" — that carries the spirit around. One may refer back to Auden's mystical experience and compare it to these — there is a sense of an "all-rightness of being," an "at-homeness in existence," and most certainly the aura of a wholeness in which one is continuously and contiguously integrated. Art reflects this perception of wholeness for art is an outcome of one's wholeness of being, a synthesis of an individual's previous knowledge that is itself a synthesis of a zeitgeist, an *isness*, formed from the multiplicity of human knowledge. Woolf's innovations in narrative technique are her efforts to describe — not history — but consciousness.

Julie Kane, in her "Varieties of Mystical Experience in the Writings of Virginia Woolf," suggests a transition from Woolf as a feminist to Woolf as a mystic. In her analysis, "prior to writing *The Waves*, Woolf maintained a posture of utter contempt toward her fellow 'mystics'" (328). Her thesis is that Woolf developed her own brand of 'natural mysticism' that closely paralleled the beliefs of the Theosophists. Kane analyses Woolf's encounters with mysticism and her psychological relationship to the notion of mysticism.

Like Kane, Madeleine Moore examines Woolf's relationship to mysticism in a biographical framework. In *The Short Season between Two Silences: The Mystical and the Political in the Novels of Virginia Woolf*, Moore examines several of Woolf's novels in the context of Woolf both as a mystic and as a feminist. Each novel concerns implications of mysticism and the role of women in society:

One can look at *To the Lighthouse* as a narrative of a mystical consciousness:

> And what then? For she felt that he was still looking at her, but that his look had changed. He wanted something — wanted the thing she always found it so difficult to give him; he wanted her to tell him that she loved him. And that, no, she could not do. He found talking so much easier than she did. He could say things — she never could. So naturally it was always he that said things, and then for some reason he would mind this suddenly, and reproach her. A heartless woman he called her; she never told him that she loved him. But it was not so — it was not so. It was only that she never could say what she felt. Was there no crumb on his coat? Nothing she could do for him? Getting up she stood at the window with the reddish-brown stocking in her hands, partly to turn away from him, partly because she did not mind looking now, with him watching, at the Lighthouse. For she knew that he had turned his head as she turned; he was watching her. She knew that he was thinking. You are more beautiful than ever. Will you not tell me just for once that you love me? ... But she could not do it; she could not say it. Then, knowing he was watching her instead of saying anything she turned ... and looked at him. And as she looked at him, she began to smile, for though she had not said a word, he knew, of course he knew, that she loved him. He could not deny it. And smiling she looked out of the window and said (thinking to herself) Nothing can equal this happiness—[16].

The tone of this passage is not too unlike that of Woolf's visions described above, particularly the "Nothing can equal this happiness." The capital "N" signifies in a similar way as, *Neti, neti*—"Not this, not that." *Nothing* really means that every material thing cannot add up to a single moment of being in which one feels the *isness* of consciousness.

To the Lighthouse reflects the new age of psychoanalysis and the new woman as represented by the author herself and her surrogate in the novel, Lily-the-artist. Woolf, however, is also a bit of the old woman, Mrs. Ramsay, having married into a "modified normalcy" with Leonard Woolf, while also being an artist. The above passage, in addition to describing the incommensurate ineffability of any two people truly knowing each other, is written with the innovative stream of consciousness that shows just how at odds the perceptions of the man and woman are about each other, and that these perceptions are unable to cross any bridge between them without an awareness of a mystical consciousness.

In describing, *To the Lighthouse*, Woolf considered it as a process of self-psychoanalysis and an expiation of emotions. The novel ultimately finds a completeness that Woolf could not achieve in her life, which ended in suicide. At the novel's end Mrs. Ramsay's son James has made it to the lighthouse, a desire that was denied in the novel's opening, and Lily has completed her painting of Mrs. Ramsey, also begun at the beginning of the novel. British society itself felt incomplete in the 1920s and yearned for solace.

One must consider that in the 1920s Britain was reacting to the horrors of World War I and what this meant to collective and individual psyches. Woolf was the daughter of an esteemed intellectual, Leslie Stephen; Woolf's mother was famous for being a hostess to the literary figures who gathered at the Stephen home. Thus, Woolf had to deal with expectations created by her father's learning and her mother's social graces. Woolf was acutely sensitive, leading to several nervous breakdowns, the first at twelve after her mother's death. This sensitivity, as for many artists, is the double-edged sword that can inspire creativity but also foment psychological difficulty. Woolf's understanding of both of these sharp edges became her art.

Woolf and her siblings were at the center of the artists, writers, and intellectuals known as the Bloomsbury group. They included Lytton Strachey, Dora Carrington (both depicted in the film, *Carrington*, which is an excellent portrait of the Bloomsbury era), J. M. Keynes, and E. M. Forster, another innovative novelist of the period. An enormously important intellectual stimulus for Woolf was that in 1917, Leonard and Virginia bought a hand press and founded Hogarth Press in their home. It published not only some of Woolf's novels, but also T. S. Eliot's poems and other important works. Literally, Woolf saw much of the cutting edge of British literature before the public did and this certainly must have influenced her innovativeness. Hogarth Press also published the first translations of Freud in English — another compelling exposure to consciousness and the life of the mind. Woolf was a tragic figure. Christopher Isherwood, who was published by Hogarth Press, said to the day he died in 1986 that he always believed that she was the most beautiful human being — male or female — he had ever seen. She was, like her precursors Austen and George Eliot, a woman in a man's world, one that was changing, but one that had not yet changed enough. Hence, she endured the same issues stemming from the woman's role as an artist challenging men.

To the Lighthouse is set on an island in the Hebrides off the West Coast of Scotland at the Ramsays' vacation house. The novel is set in a ten-year period, with the first and largest section taking place in one day before the war, a middle period in which all action takes place "off stage" during the war, and a last section taking place in one day after the war; this structure is itself innovative. The island is a physical metaphor for the psychological distance that makes each individual an island in a sea of islands where they can see lights in the distance signifying other life but cannot always get across to truly interact with these lives.

A main theme of this novel is the effect of a male-dominated world on the creative lives of women. Woolf is not histrionic. Much like Forster, she understates the peaks and valleys and instead focuses more on the subtle distortions that a male-dominated society imposes on men, women, and families. Another theme is the male domination of art and the effect this has on women who wish to be artists, like Lily and Woolf. Woolf will inquire as to the nature of art and art's role as both a reflection of society and a recorder of moments in time. Time itself is a theme with the novel's structure revoking the 19th century linear plot in favor of a stream of consciousness narrative that depicts memory as that which can evoke time in a person's mind in the random selection that is the mind's method more often than not. The mind's memory function has an internal hierarchy that prioritizes certain memories over others. To interpret the evocations of these memories and record them is the artist's goal.

World War I was the watershed moment in the lives of Woolf and her contemporaries that, for them, always measured their lives in terms of "before" and "after." And, as above, Woolf also delineated the effect of Halley's Comet as a world-changing moment of being. There is much nostalgia in *To the Lighthouse*, as in much of the British literary art of the 1920s. Very often the nostalgia was countered by its depiction as a burden, a danger, a dilemma that impeded progress, as per T.S. Eliot, Huxley, Forster, Isherwood, Robert Graves, Robert Nichols, Siegfried Sassoon, and many others. Nostalgia is a function of the memory that symbolizes the "before" as better — even if it is not true. DeLillo's *Underworld* and García Márquez's *One Hundred Years of Solitude* are two other novels that feature the symbols of nostalgia as symbols that can impede progress in the present.

Woolf understands the symbolism of nostalgia. Moreover, she derives a new method of narrative technique in her form and structure to deal with nostalgia as real people do, as memories that arise in the mind at random as free association, with each association triggering another association that may seem superficially unrelated but that is, at a deeper level, psychologically related. Woolf's reality is reality as it might emerge in psychotherapy — or in visionary experiences. Woolf's craft is that she puts this method into practice, and this is a deliberate choice to break from the tradition of the novel that peaked in the Victorian era; novels that narrated in the linear mode and mainly from the outside-in instead of the inside-out. As a woman in a patriarchal world, Woolf challenged her readers by going against their expectations. Woolf's challenge was through innovation, which, in large part, was motivated by her feeling that a woman had to be more daring than men in order to get noticed. In this, she succeeded. Indeed, as mentioned above, *To the Lighthouse* is a tacit (sometimes explicit) contest or debate between the traditional Mrs. Ramsay and the new artist, Lily — with Ramsay as the before (pre-war) figure and Lily as the after-the-war persona.

Woolf's essay "A Room of One's Own" argues that in order to write and write well, women needed a room of their own and five hundred pounds a year so that they did not have to earn a living outside of writing or to get married for the money. This can also apply to men as well, who must expend their energy in making a living conventionally instead of artistically. Men, however, still had more options than women. Lily Briscoe knows the pressure of trying to paint when she is expected to be a wife and a mother while her art is demeaned as unimportant and that it can never equal a man's art.

The perception of the woman's role began to change after World War I and Woolf is fully aware of the war's world-changing impact. She conveys this impact indirectly and with great understatement in the middle section, "Time Passes," where the main characters do not actually appear. Yet we learn about them indirectly while the empty vacation house seems an entity in and of itself. World War I is a rupture that changes everything in the flow of the world. Off stage, Prue Ramsey marries and then dies from a sickness in childbirth. Her brother Andrew Ramsey dies from a shell in the war. Mr. Carmichael comes out with a very popular book of poems, and so on. Despite efforts to retain the past, nothing will ever be the same. The horror of the war and its impact cannot be ignored.

Mrs. Ramsay is the actor who holds the family together, giving solace and protection to a degree that Woolf considers a skill or even an art. Mrs. Ramsay may be Woolf's mother. Consequently, Woolf may depict the "old woman" against the new woman, but she does not necessarily say that one is better than the other — each has a role and each should be allowed to thrive as she chooses. (This is a precept of the Bhagavad-Gita.)

The lighthouse is the most important symbol, and it seems to have a two-way effect like Emerson's "transparent eyeball," in which a person can both look out at the world and look back on him or herself in the world. One looks upon the lighthouse and the lighthouse looks back. The lighthouse is longing, hope, desire, difference, and a bridge away from the many isolated islands that are the characters' inner lives. The lighthouse is consciousness. To James as a boy in the novel's opening chapter the lighthouse signified a hidden wish:

> The wonder to which he had looked forward, for years and years it seemed, was, after a night's darkness and a day's sail, within touch. Since he belonged, even at age six, to that great clan which cannot keep this feeling separate from that, but must let future prospects, with their joys and sorrows, cloud what is actually at hand, since to people even in earliest childhood any turn in the wheel of sensation has the power to crystalize and transfix the moment upon which its gloom or radiance rests, James Ramsay, sitting on the floor cutting out pictures from the illustrated catalogue of the Army and Navy Stores, endowed the picture of the refrigerator as his mother spoke with a heavenly bliss. It was fringed with joy [9].

This remarkable passage indicates the book's purpose and method. The lighthouse is a desired object; it is a peace that may only come with death; a mystery that enters the human mind and shapes how the human mind will catalogue memories, thoughts (and thoughts include fantasies) that are both backwards and forwards in time, and the allusion to "Army and Navy" signifies the great rupture of the war to come. The lighthouse, like the vacation house in the middle section, becomes an entity in itself, and it changes as the book develops. The lighthouse is the unifier in a novel that is otherwise not structured with traditional unity. A second symbol and metaphor of importance is the sea, water, and the flow of water that represents the undifferentiated unity of consciousness. The lighthouse, as individual consciousness, shines on the ocean of collective consciousness and its reflection as it moves along the top of the water is evolving consciousness. The visual image is much like the Vedantic spiral or Yeats's gyre.

Woolf, as did many artists and intellectuals in all disciplines, reacted to the rupture of World War I by wanting to re-create the world and move away from the societal influences that had produced the war. The world was abuzz with Freud and psychoanalysis, and also mysticism through the popularity of Theosophy. Perhaps then the world could be changed one mind at a time, one book at a time. Woolf's way was to depict the mind as it really worked so that others might wish to learn how their minds really work. And for Woolf, mysticism *is* consciousness.

The Lasting Influence of Gerald Heard on W.H. Auden (and Huxley, and Isherwood, and Henry Miller, et al.)

If W.H. Auden is either the first or second most important English language poet of the 20th century along with T.S. Eliot, then the importance of Gerald Heard's influence on Auden's mysticism and literature was early, profound, and enduring. Prior to meeting Auden, Heard knew the Irish mystic, poet, painter, and social activist, Æ (George William Russell), who was a Vedantist. Æ was a factor into Heard's earliest theories.

Auden met Gerald Heard through Naomi Mitchison in 1929. Auden's respect for Heard appears in a poetic fragment (first published by Lucy McDiarmid in 1978) entitled "In The Year of My Youth," which can be dated by its mention in Harold Nicolson's diary entry of 4 August 1933; "The idea," Nicolson writes, "is Heard as Virgil guiding him [Auden] through modern life" (*Diaries*, 153). Heard constructed what he called an "outline of the evolution of consciousness" in his 1929 book *The Ascent of Humanity*, in which Heard asserted that our primitive ancestors were not egoistically motivated but rather acted in a unity that precluded "any consciousness of individual separateness" from the group. As Heard writes, the "first human unit is the group, not the individual" (*Ascent*, 23).

Heard called this intuitive group unity "co-consciousness," in which each individual constituent acted as part of a whole. However, at some point in history, this "co-consciousness" was lost. In his 1932 essay "The History of Ideas, or How We Got Separate" (published alongside Auden's "Writing" essay in Naomi Mitchison's *Outline for Boys and Girls and Their Parents*), Heard writes that primitive humans, who "did not think of themselves as self-conscious, separate individuals," felt an undifferentiated unity with all existence.

Human learning, however, while advancing the evolution of consciousness was only possible through what Heard called a "power of separating" ("History," 433), that began to regard the world objectively. The material benefits of this also caused egoistic separation and ended the original sense of unity.

Heard would write that, psychically, "we are divided against ourselves" (*Substance*, 42), by a "threshold," or a "'limen' ... that now divides the subconscious and conscious mind so completely that the conscious mind can generally have no direct knowledge of the subconscious" ("Religion," 145).[5]

Heard believed that humanity had to tear down the wall separating the subconscious and conscious mind to regain the sense of unity with others. Despite being isolated by the conscious mind, the subconscious mind is "still the source of all human energy" (*Substance*, 27). This innate sense of unity is retained dormantly in consciousness, and humans intuitively seek means to re-unify with others.

In 1932, Heard wrote how religious experience was one means to re-unify. "Religious communion" helped individuals seek a "direct sense of the union with their community and through it with eternal life." Re-unified "in a like minded group," Heard believed that the limen in our consciousness could be dissolved, allowing "the individual ... to recover his symbiotic relationship with his fellows." This is the *vision of agape*, which is "supra-personal and unlimited," reaching "at-one-ment" with his or her community.

However, once religion became "infected with the very thing it exists to cure — Individualism" ("Religion," 145) — this just added to the alienation, as personal salvation superseded group salvation.

To overcome separation, Heard described a "deliberate technique" to reach into the subconscious "social and greater self" (*Source*, 17), or a "psychic hygiene" ("Religion," 115), that would "re-mend the fissure in his own psyche and so see himself and his community, it and Life, and Life and the universe as one" (*Source*, 20).

Heard called this a "superconsciousness" (*Ascent*, 6) that could be reached through psychoanalysis and meditative mystical experience. Unity could be obtained by a group of like-minded people. Group meditation would reassert supra-personal unity so that the group could return to its community, feeling part of a larger whole

Auden's early verse contains separating boundaries between sub-conscious unity and conscious alienation. "The Secret Agent" (1928), concerns crossing this border into a hostile frontier in a quest for unity. Auden's "frontier," Mendelson explains, symbolizes "a watershed or divide isolating the mind from the cycles of unconscious nature" (*Early Auden*, 31). The border in "The Secret Agent" describes, "using a barrier to produce energy rather than restrict it" (*Early Auden*, 35). The secret agent furtively seeks the relationship between the conscious and subconscious. For the poem, "In the Year of My Youth..." (uncollected, but see Mendelson, *Early Auden*), Auden co-opts Heard's *Social Substance of Religion* in order to discuss the social implications of this psychic rift. The poem's protagonist tours modern London led by his friend "Sampson" (Heard), observing people that live numbly as robots. This is due to a boundary between motivation and "executive" power.

This term concerns the rational, strictly utilitarian conscious mind. Outer nature is in flux as we learn and develop. Our inner nature is "unadapting, unalterable" (*Social*, 25–26); "the subconscious is completely resistant to change in its circumstances, and remains unaltered by the outward economic modification of its environment."

Auden's essay on "Writing" and his conception of the subconscious social self is directly from Heard, with its prehistoric "co-consciousness" and subsequent individualism. *Auden*: "At sometime or other in human history," writes Auden, "man became self conscious, he began to feel, I am I, and You are Not I; we are shut inside ourselves and apart from each other." Society is "an individual thing, different from other things, but without meaning except in its connection with other things." Individuality superseded this sense of unity. By using language, individuals attempted to "bridge" the barrier between the individual and a larger whole. Auden describes language as "a tunnel under which the currents of feeling can pass unseen" ("Writing," 40–41). Language is a bridge of communication connecting our individual mind to a greater whole.

Auden's solution comes from Heard's theories on group meditation and *agape*. In "The Group Movement and The Middle Classes" (1934), Auden again co-opts Heard as he writes of "a group of very moderate size, probably not larger than twelve" in which it would be possible for an individual to "lose himself, for his death instincts to be neutralised in the same way as those of the separate cells of the metazoa neutralise each other in the body" (98).

Auden's poem "A Summer's Night" (1933), and his later commentary on the experience of the vision of *agape* in his introduction to *The Protestant Mystics*, equates to Heard's ideas concerning meditation. In "A Summer's Night," the speaker, sitting "equal with colleagues in a ring," finds himself possessed of a feeling of unity between them. The image of the ring appears in Heard's *Social Substance of Religion* in reference to early Christian *agape*. Heard believed that a "small group of about a dozen" had come together regularly and "formed an inward-looking group — perhaps a ring" (*Substance*, 213). Heard asserted that early Christians united in a common "psychic field" (*Substance*, 213), which reassured them of their spiritual connection. In Auden's introduction for *The Protestant Mystics* in 1963, he writes that in 1933, he "quite suddenly and unexpectedly" found himself "invaded by a power" which made it possible for him to know "what it means to love one's neighbour as oneself."

For the rest of Auden's career as a poet and also as a philosopher via his essays, the impetus of Heard's early influence that conditioned a search for consciousness in Auden would remain, steadfastly, the dominating concern of Auden's life and art. In the 1940s, Auden became a Christian existentialist deeply influenced by Heard and Jung. Heard was Auden's friend but Heard's best friend was Aldous Huxley.

Aldous Huxley's Time Must Have a Stop

The waning of the reputation of one of the most famous figures of the 20th century engendered an article by John Derbyshire in London's *New Criterion* of 21 February 2000 titled, "What Happened to Aldous Huxley?" Derbyshire wrote:

> Metaphysics is out of fashion.... Living as we do in such an un-metaphysical age, we are in a poor frame of mind to approach the writer [Huxley] who said the following thing, and who took it as a premise for his work through most of a long literary career.
> It is impossible to live without a metaphysic. The choice that is given us is not between some kind of metaphysic and no metaphysic; it is always between a good metaphysic and a bad metaphysic [Derbyshire, *online*].

As early as 1916 in a letter to his brother Julian, Huxley wrote: "I have come to agree with Thomas Aquinas that individuality in the animal kingdom if you like is nothing more than a question of mere matter. We are potentially at least, though the habit of matter has separated us, unanimous. One cannot escape mysticism; it positively thrusts itself, the only possibility, upon one" (*Letters*, 88). And in 1925: "I love the inner world as much or more than the outer. When the outer vexes me, I retire to the rational simplicities of the spirit" (*Along the Road* 110). The quest for choosing between a "good metaphysic and a bad metaphysic," and forming a way to live within the good metaphysic, is the fulcrum from which Huxley's entire body of fiction and non-fiction was launched. Even when he was at his most cynical and satirically sarcastic, this was a cry by an angry young man who depicted the worst so that one could try to imagine something better to take its place. He spent his entire life seeking the "something better" and knew it would be found in the world of the metaphysic over the physic. This itself from 1920 to 1963 was the major innovation of his work — only the presentations changed, as Huxley grew older, wiser — and less angry.

Huxley's novels of ideas are always about moral dilemmas that need to be sorted out. In the 1920s his characters wallow in the philosophy of meaninglessness with sarcasm as their defense veiling a prevalent despair. The other side of a cynical man is a fallen hero — or an aspiring hero. The characters secretly — or openly — seek a vehicle that can give meaning to a world that has realized that science, technology, and industry are not the answers. Huxley's protagonists evolve as either upward seekers of The Perennial Philosophy of mysticism, or they devolve downward into an even greater disaffected nihilism.

> *But thought's the slave of life, and life's time's fool,*
> *And time, that takes survey of all the world, Must have a stop*
> — Shakespeare, *Henry IV, Part I*

Huxley, despite his being called godless in the 1920s and 1930s, was far from being unspiritual. His cynical fiction was meant to display a world that was falling far short of the human potentiality that the mind, seeking, rather than rejecting an intuitive spirituality, could fulfill in a world where spirit would overcome materialism. Since much less has been written about Huxley's American writings after 1939 than his British writings before 1939, the full importance of Huxley's belief in the Perennial Philosophy and this philosophy's meaning has been given little coverage, which means that his American work cannot be fully understood and appreciated. One cannot do justice to Huxley without a proper account of his mystical beliefs.

When he came to America in 1939 with Gerald Heard, they both had been interested in the nature of evolving consciousness for many years. Heard and Huxley began attending the lectures at the Vedanta Society of Southern California. Vedanta, a mystical philosophy, is the basis for all subsequent mystical branches of the Hindu, Greek, Roman, Judaic, Islamic, and Christian religions. In 1945, Huxley anthologized the mystical writings of all religions in his book, *The Perennial Philosophy*, augmented with his brilliant commentary. This book would lead to a booming renewal of interest in Eastern and mystical philosophy that is still prominent with the 1960–1970s perhaps the zenith, with translations of the Vedas selling in the millions.

In the novel *Time Must Have a Stop* (1945) Huxley intends to introduce the Perennial Philosophy to readers and also to write of Uncle Eustace's dying in terms of the Tibetan Book of the Dead, aka the Bardo Thodol, a Mayahana Buddhist text that describes the transitional state between the death of one body and the spirit of that body having a rebirth in a new body.

A body is a suitcase that carries the spirit around; suitcases may wear down or change, but the spiritual contents remain. The fact that the youth Sebastian later loses an arm is meant to signify that while his body has changed; his spirit has grown and this is what measures his existence, not his body.

The first half of the novel sets the stage for the second half. Huxley as narrator very early indicates where he is heading in this passage on Sebastian, "he had read Nietzsche, and since then had learned to Love his Fate. *Amor fati*— but tempered with a healthy cynicism" (2). At seventeen, one can intellectualize *amor fati*, but its reality requires trials more severe than just teenage angst. Huxley introduces Nietzsche here but is also nodding at Nietzsche's mentor,

Schopenhauer, who was the first notable Western philosopher to be thoroughly guided by Vedanta philosophy. To love fate is to accept that one's finite corporeal existence and that existence's travails are secondary to one's infinite spiritual existence. Hence, immediately in the novel, Huxley, in an incidental way, foreshadows the very serious considerations of fate and spirituality that are forthcoming.

Readers first encounter Bruno Rontini in a conversation about him while he is not yet present. Eustace says of Bruno: "He's the last person to gossip about a man when his back is turned.... There's nothing that so effectively ruins a conversation as charitableness. After all, no one can be amusing about other people's virtues" (82). Bruno's good nature is here explained; he is, in fact, an exemplar of Vedanta's two simple rules of ethical conduct: do no harm and compassion for all. Two pages later Eustace reads aloud a passage from a book he just purchased:

> "Grace did not fail thee, but thou wast wanting to grace. God did not deprive thee of the operation of love, but thou didst deprive his love of thy co-operation. God would never have rejected thee, if thou hadst not rejected him." He turned back to the title page. "*Treatise of the Love of God* by St. Francois de Sales," he read. "Pity it isn't de Sade" [84].

Eustace's cynicism dots the text, which is counterpoint to his spiritual experience in the novel's second half.

The message that Eustace reads in de Sales is that one chooses to intuit God and seek upward transcendence; one, however, may, like de Sade, choose downward transcendence away from God. One rejects God; God rejects no one.

A character, Paul De Vries, an American from "New England" (home of Vedanta-inspired American transcendentalism) is fascinated by Einstein, (Huxley's reminder of the space-time possibilities that Einstein introduced), and seeks any evidence of an undifferentiated unity. He was hoping,

> that someday one might get a hunch, an illuminating intuition of the greater synthesis. For a synthesis there undoubtedly must be, a thought-bridge that would permit the mind to march discursively and logically from telepathy to the four-dimensional continuum.... There was the ultimate all-embracing field — the Brahma of Sankara [Vedanta] the One of Plotinus, the Ground of Eckhart and Boehme [German mystics] [92].

Huxley is giving readers an introduction to the Perennial Philosophy, which will be continued in Bruno's bookshop. A young man comes in and asks for a book on comparative religion. Bruno shows him the standard didactic selections, which the aspiring young philosopher buys. Bruno adds, "'if you ever get tired of this...' ... in their deep sockets the blue eyes twinkled with an almost mischievous light. '...This kind of learned frivolity ... remember, I've got a considerable stock of really serious books on the subject.... Scupoli, the Bhagavatam, the Tao Te Ching, the Theologica Germanica, the Graces of Interior

Prayer'" (102). Thus, Huxley suggest texts if readers are so inclined to learn more.

Bruno becomes a source for felicitous thoughts that also teach; often, these thoughts come as a *pas de deux* with the cynical Eustace, such as one on goodness:

> Eustace: ... if only people would realize that moral principles are like measles.... [that come and go].
> Bruno: One doesn't have to catch the infection of goodness, if one doesn't want to. The will is always free.... If only you could forgive the good [that refutes Eustace's cynicism]. Then you might allow yourself to be forgiven ... for being what you are. For being a human being. Yes, God can forgive you even that, if you really want it. Can forgive your separateness so completely that you can be made one with him" [105].

The verbal duets between Eustace and Bruno are discussions of oppositions that need to be reconciled. Bruno's importuning to Eustace that he drop his cynicism and seriously consider his spiritual future takes on great significance when later Eustace is dying. Throughout the novel, passages both serious and lighthearted speak of the nature of the Perennial Philosophy and names many of its advocates that are in Huxley's anthology, *The Perennial Philosophy*, which would be published the year after *Time Must Have a Stop*, as if the latter was meant to introduce the former, which, in fact, it was.

The second half of the novel mainly concerns Eustace's dying. Peter Bowering writes that it is divided into three parts:

> The Chikhai Bardo which describes the happenings immediately after death; then, the Chonyid Bardo which deals with karmic visions and hallucinations; and, finally, the Sidpa Bardo which is concerned with the events leading up to reincarnation. In the Chikhai Bardo the deceased is faced with the ... Dharma-Kaya, or the Clear Light of the Void. This is symbolic of the purest and highest state of spiritual being.... If, through a lack of spiritual insight, the dead person is unable to recognize the light as the manifestation of his own spiritual consciousness, karmic illusions begin to cloud his vision ... and he enters into the second Bardo. In the Chonyid Bardo he is subjected to what Evans-Wentz calls the, "solemn and mighty panorama" of "the consciousness-content of his personality." If the deceased is spiritually immature and unable to recognize the fantasy world confronting him as the product of his own consciousness he will pass into ... the Sipa Bardo [and] the person becomes aware that he no longer has a corporeal body and the desire for a new incarnation begins to dominate his consciousness.... As Jung points out ... "freed from all illusion of genesis and decay ... life in the Bardo brings no eternal rewards or punishments, but merely a descent into a new life which shall bear the individual nearer to his final goal [a final complete merging into spiritual consciousness].... This ... goal is what he himself brings to birth as the last and highest fruit of the labours and aspirations of earthly existence." This is the essential teaching of *Time Must Have a Stop* [*Novels of Aldous Huxley*, 167–68].

Eustace was, just as Bruno knew, "spiritually immature at the time of his death." Sebastian, years later and after learning mysticism from Uncle Bruno, is more advanced spiritually and further along in the path of evolving spiritual consciousness and union with the Divine Ground of all existence. In the epilog, Sebastian is looking through his notebook of thoughts and quotations concerning mystical spirituality. This notebook had its real counterpart as Huxley was accumulating material for *The Perennial Philosophy*. Sebastian reads from his notebooks and readers lean more about mysticism.

Sebastian also remembers taking care of Bruno when he was dying of throat cancer and gradually lost his speech. There is great irony here as Huxley would die of throat cancer eighteen years later. Sebastian remembers Bruno's suffering.

> But there had also been the spectacle of Bruno's joyful serenity, and even, at one remove, a kind of participation in the knowledge of which that joy was the natural and inevitable expression — the knowledge of a timeless and infinite presence; the intuition, direct and infallible, that apart from the desire to be separate there was no separation, but an essential identity [286].

The last pages of Sebastian's notebook concern how time must have a stop in the mystical sense of the "vast landscape." These ruminations are followed by the Minimum Working Hypothesis, which by this juncture of the reader's mystical education resonates with the full import and impact of this spiritual novel.

In 1954 when Maria Huxley was dying and had reached the pre-death state of unconsciousness, Huxley read to her from the Bardo.

Doris Lessing: The Golden Notebook

In 1982, Lesley Hazleton writes of Doris Lessing's conversion to Sufism (Islamic mysticism) with quotes from Lessing:

> As for those who mourn her abandonment of a political stance, accusing her of turning mystical instead: "I don't see it as an 'instead.' The popular picture of me at the moment is, 'Here is this very political woman, extremely active politically for nearly all of her life, and now she's become a mystic.' First, I have not been active politically most of my life. Since I've been in England, I've been writing. And my studying Sufism is very much in this world — the aim is to be 'in the world but not of it,' as the Sufis say.
>
> The Sufis believe Sufism to be the secret teaching within all religions. It is a mystic philosophy whose quest is to achieve universal harmony with the spirit of Absolute Being; but to do this, unlike most other mystic philosophies, Sufism maintains involvement with this world, because the Sufis see themselves, as Mrs. Lessing explains, as "the substance of that current which can develop man into a higher stage of evolution"— [*New York Times*, July 25, 1982, partners.nytimes.com/books/99/01/10/specials/lessing-space.html].

While Lessing is quite clear about her interest in Sufism, Sufism does not have the monopoly on "the secret teaching within all religions." It is one of the manifestations of mysticism and its message is very much akin to the others in seeking "the substance of that current which can develop man into a higher stage of evolution."

By 1982, Lessing had embraced Sufism. No doubt her art after 1982 is influenced by mysticism. Her most famous work, however, is *The Golden Notebook* (1962), pre-dating her interest in Sufism. Does this mean *The Golden Notebook* is not mystical? The answer is no on three counts: (1) A purpose of this study proposes that all art is mystical, that is, supernatural, as art is attempting to evoke a reflection of the immediate reality of life that is no longer immediate. The ineffable immediacy remains ineffable; it can never be duplicated, only imitated; (2) the artist's effort is a vehicle for some intimation of transcendence that tries to make a bridge from the effable to the ineffable, from writer to reader; (3) Lessing says above: "I had an inclination toward mysticism — not religion — even then." Consequently, her intuition was inclined to mysticism, even if she had not yet defined what form of mysticism this would be.

The Golden Notebook, no differently than any artistic effort, is Lessing's attempt to bridge the ineffable nature of her own consciousness within the universal consciousness. Her comprehensive autobiographical epic is like *To the Lighthouse* in that Woolf considered writing it to be a process of self-psychoanalysis and an expiation of emotions. *Notebook*'s daring (in 1962) includes its structure, frank language, sexual talk and the role of the woman as a participator in that sexual talk, that had previously been a male-dominated province. Prior to 1962, women were sexual objects as seen and described by men. Lessing gave women, and *a woman*, Anna Wulf, the new role of sexual subject. Part of Lessing's craft was to allow Anna — as Everywoman — to have an overt sexual identity and the ability to speak and think about sex subjectively as an "I" and not just be referred to objectively as a "she." In its time, *The Golden Notebook* artfully depicts the manners, aspirations, anxieties and particular problems of the era that Lessing lived in and describes. Also in its time, it was a daring narrative experiment, dealing with the complex amphibian nature of all individuals through a particular individual, Anna. The craft of Lessing's experiment entails that the multiple notebooks cover the central themes that evolve into a concluding whole. The whole is the sum of all previous parts and in that regard this is a psychological — and mystical — novel. The author constructs her parts in order to deconstruct Anna's life. Anna is a sometime Communist, very left writer in postwar London living with her small daughter, Janet.

Anna is dealing with writer's block, which is an extended metaphor of the various blocks in her life particularly and lives in general. The notebooks detail Anna from 1950 to 1957 with flashbacks of her experience in World War II Africa. A novel within the novel, *Free Women*, is layered over the notebooks and takes place in 1957, in which we see a disillusioned "Anna" who, dejected over a bad affair, gives herself and her time to Molly and her son Tommy, whose suicide attempt takes a toll on both Molly and Anna. The last section of *Free Women* has Anna recovering and going into social work. The title, *Free Women*, is itself a wry commentary as the women are not free. The idea of free women in this novel is only an unfulfilled wish.

The book's divided structure is designed by Lessing to depict the divisions within the whirlwind of society and how the whirlwind affects and fragments the mind. Lessing understands fragmentation but does not, however, ultimately let the divisiveness win the battle. In Lessing's 1972 preface of a new edition of *Notebook*, she writes: "Yet the essence of the book, the organisation of it, everything in it, says implicitly and explicitly, that we must not divide things off, must not compartmentalize" (iii). In a sense the divided structure is really anti-structure in a manner that refers to *The Waste Land*'s seeming fragmentation. Both show what the world is to the subjective person who looks at it in its fragments. The five different notebooks look at the whirlwind from different points of view that will eventually merge in the last chapter, "The Golden Notebook," of which Lessing writes in the 1972 preface: "In the inner *Golden Notebook*, which is written by both of them [Anna and Saul], you can no longer distinguish between what is Saul and what is Anna, and between them and the other people in the book" (iv). Lessing, by crafting her multiple interpretations, is not really writing about division, but a multiplicity of inclusion, which seems to reflect her interest in and inclination toward mysticism and the evolution of consciousness. That evolution, just like the structure of *Notebook*, asserts that the many drops of water that are individuals are really merged into a sea of consciousness. This role of consciousness is similar to Virginia Woolf's sense of consciousness in *To the Lighthouse*, and one sees *Lighthouse* as a prelude to *Notebook*. For Lessing, her reading of Woolf factored into how she chose to craft *Notebook*.

> Woolf's approach to autobiography, her concerns with selfhood and writing, and possibly even her own "madness," I suggest here, become Lessing's legacy. Certainly, as I have already mentioned, semantic and psychological echoes of Woolf exist in Lessing. By absorbing Woolf into her own work, for example through her fictive "self" Anna in *The Golden Notebook*, Lessing is confirming to some extent Woolf's belief that "we think back through our mothers if we are women" (Rubenstein, 16). At times it seems as though Lessing provides us with a paraphrase of Woolf's words or at least her sentiments. For example in her autobiographical "A Sketch of the Past" Woolf describes her ideal memoirs and says, "[w]hat I write today I should not write in a year's time" (*Moments*, 12). In a corresponding manner Lessing writes in *Under My Skin*, "I am trying to write this book honestly. But were I to write it aged eighty-five, how different would it be?" It is apparent then, that like Woolf, Lessing believes memory to be "a careless and lazy organ" (13) — [Scott, www.otago.ac.nz/Deep South/vol3no2/scott.html].

Woolf depicted the male-female dichotomy as an internalized psychological and emotional battle that was much more important than the external jousting in the antecedents of Austen, George Eliot, et al. Lessing follows suit. In the *Notebook* Anna thinks, that " if Marxism means anything, it means that a little novel about the emotions reflects 'what's real' since the emotions are a function and a product of a society." Woolf did the same.

One can also compare *Lighthouse* and *Notebook* as experiments in structure: *Lighthouse* has single days in between which is the "offstage" part two, where the summer house seems to have its own consciousness; *Notebook* has its five different notebooks. The notebooks depict Anna's life and include long flashbacks that illuminate her life as lived during World War II in Africa. The "novel" in *Notebook*, *Free Women*, takes place in 1957 and is an extension of Anna's life with its story of the trials and tribulations of an Anna surrogate. Lessing's craft here is to let Anna comment on herself in a "pseudo"-objective manner by making herself a character in Anna's novel. Lessing takes this method even further by having Saul write the last part of the last notebook, so that Anna is even more "objectivized" by a male. There is a one-male-fits all component heightened by Lessing, giving Anna's surrogate, Ella, a lover named Paul in the yellow book and a lover named Saul in the blue and gold books as if they are nearly one and the same. Lessing (Anna) has Paul be a psychiatrist as if to signify that Anna is being "objectivized" by a professional "objectivizer" who sanctions the male dominance over women through the authority of his position. In the blue book Anna herself and not a surrogate begins psychotherapy and it seems that Lessing has Anna foreshadow, or set up this choice by having previously engaged in it as Ella.

Lessing's choice of psychology in *Notebook* is Jungian, not Freudian, and there is enormous intention in that choice, one that brings the real Lessing and her interest in the metaphysical and mystical into *Notebook*. Her choice of Jung over Freud is interesting, given the otherwise sexual frankness this book achieved in 1962. Preferring Jung means choosing a more mystical sense of unity.

Another device Lessing uses in the notebooks is to bring in newspaper clippings as background for the events that surround Anna's life. Anna will collect the clippings compulsively as if to keep a record of her life that she is otherwise having difficulty maintaining of her own accord. The notebooks are structured in this fashion:

Black: Africa, with Anna dealing futilely with screen rights to her African novel, the clippings deal with violence in Africa.

Red: Communism, its rise and fall in Anna's perceptions, with clippings about McCarthy and the Rosenbergs.

Yellow: *The Shadow of a Third*, Anna's novel about Paul, the psychiatrist, with Ella, the Anna surrogate becoming disenchanted with Communism, which parallels her break with Paul. Here, *The Shadow of a Third*, as a novel within the novel, takes over for the clippings as the third voice (Ella) behind the second voice, (Anna), with Lessing as the first voice informing both.

Blue: psychotherapy and affairs that lead to the affair with Saul, clippings on H-bomb, Korean War,

Gold: Anna's breakdown into which Lessing brings in elements from the previous notebooks that become for Anna snapshot flashes of her past and its impact on the present. Saul "writes" the end of this section. With all of this diversity of self-interpretations, there is still a unity in that the parts are the whole of Anna's consciousness.

Another purpose of the clippings is to insert violence as a pervasive influence in this novel and life in general as per Lessing's vision. Violence is a backdrop to Anna's various notebooks. By juxtaposing seemingly unrelated events, this fragmented structure encourages readers to see the violence alluded to in the backdrop of the novel as intimately associated with the issues of race, sex, and class depicted in the foreground of the novel.

The Golden Notebook reveals that war exists in the midst of the mundane. There is a relationship between the psychic violence occurring in male-female relationships and the physical violence pervading the novel's backdrop. Lessing (Anna) writes: "We spend our lives fighting to get people very slightly less stupid than we are to accept truths that the great men have always known ... violence breeds violence. And we know it. But do the great masses of the world know it? No. It is our job to tell them" (431). This relates to the Gita's lesson of teaching by example.

Lessing is a "writer who espoused R.D. Laing's concept of mental breakdown as a breakthrough to a higher plane of reality" (Hazleton, *online*). This is the tearing down of old belief that precedes the building up of new belief. This theme finds expression in the novel by the divisions of the notebooks and with the different voices and points of view, all of which are surrogates for Lessing's voice. Anna (Lessing) deals with her inner self-divisions by reconstructing herself through a written analysis of her parts, each separately, although the final lesson by the end is that parts/whole are always unified once the parts are put back together. By integrating Anna's psyche in the social and political movements of her time, Lessing suggests that the individual is inevitably shaped by history. Anna (Lessing) is a creation of the culture in which she lives personally and politically. Her life is entangled with culturally endorsed ideas about romantic love, sex, family, friendship, and normalcy.

One can see why many women consider *The Golden Notebook* to be a founding novel of the women's movement. Yet, there is the ironically titled novel-within-the novel, *Free Women*, that seems to raise questions about the quality of that "freedom." Anna and Molly reflect women's struggles. Lessing has Anna suffer writer's block as a metaphor for the jammed synapses that constitute her life. Anna can no longer make sense of her life so she can't write either. Art is the reflection of life. Internal stress often freezes the psyche and the creative impulse within the psyche. Anna tries to write the truth but realizes it's not true — her "truth" is obfuscated by the external influences— and accommodations to these influences—that prevent a true internal independence. Lessing, through crafting her characters, explores the role of women in a still male-dominated world. Anna, like her friend Molly, is a divorced mother, raising a child on her own while struggling with other aspects of her life — professional, political, sexual. This allows Lessing to have readers evaluate Anna's relationship with her daughter, Janet, and to express how Lessing feels about herself as a mother. Through Richard and his criticism that Anna and Molly are "bad" mothers—responsible, for one thing, for Tommy's attempted suicide — Lessing gives voice to the complexities of mothering in the modern (and post-modern) world.

The entire novel exists as craft, a purposeful attempt, just as Woolf made a purposeful attempt, to do things differently and break away from tradition, a tradition much more formed by men than women, which itself gives Lessing cause to break from tradition. Lessing's main theme is the male-female dichotomy. Lessing uniquely crafts her book to give women the dominant voice and perspective in a way that resonated with female readers in 1962 who themselves were identifying with the fragmentation in their own lives. Lessing's craft gave those female readers the mirror in which they could identify themselves as not being isolated but part of a group all suffering equally. This is the role of art — to provide common identity and bridge the many islands that are individuals. Lessing succeeds in this. There is, in Anna as Lessing's surrogate, a height of self-reflexivity and self-identification. Lessing allows craft to become a spokesperson for Lessing and for other women.

Lessing's ambition is much like Don DeLillo in *Underworld* (to follow)— which is to present an encyclopedic view of an era. The male-female dichotomy (one of the foremost opposites needing to be reconciled) is evoked here in modern, post–World War II terms. Lessing's polemical side is closest to *Middlemarch*; yet, her voice also remembers Woolf, if not in Woolf's more elegant style. The structure is not linear, but circular, with the circles revolving around a center that goes back to Anna's consciousness, which is whole, even if it is she herself who feels fragmented. The whole remains; one must choose to reconstitute it. The parallels to Lessing's life become her craft as she is extrapolating Anna's events and emotions from her own events and emotions.

CHAPTER 5

Mystical Theory as Applied to 20th Century American Literature

Archibald MacLeish: The Dramatist as American Stoic — A Private Face in Public Places

> Private Places in Public Places
> Are Wiser and Nicer Than
> Public Faces in Private Places
>   W.H. Auden

> Art exists in the context of life; that art is an action on the scene of life; that art is a means of perceiving life; of ordering life; of making life intelligible; and thus also of changing it. Only in poetry does man appear, man as he really is in his sordidness and his nobility. Elsewhere in the University man is a clinical specimen, or an intellectual abstraction, or a member of a mathematical equation, or a fixed point in a final dogma. Only with [poets] is he himself... himself in all his unimaginable — unimaginable if literature had not perceived them — possibilities. — Archibald MacLeish

A strong component of this study has been the idea that duality is not really duality, but appears so as opposites needing to be reconciled along the path of evolving consciousness. For human consciousness the oppositions of Inner/Outer, Truly Weak/Truly Strong, and Public/Private remain paramount dichotomies that test human activity and determine whether one will find upward or downward transcendence. There had been an idea, up until this present era of media ubiquity, that an artist was compromised if one chose to both create art and also be in very public positions. This has been refuted numerous times in practice: Vachel Lindsay, Carl Sandburg, Wallace Stevens, Thornton Wilder, and particularly Archibald MacLeish. One can have a private face and keep that private face (meaning a sincere, maskless face) in private *and* public. MacLeish was the most public artist of his time.

Archibald MacLeish (1892–1982) "was a playwright, a lawyer, a teacher, a journalist as the first editor of *Fortune* magazine, a Librarian of Congress, an assistant secretary of state, and, above all, a poet. He wrote more than forty books of poems, plays, essays, and speeches; he won the Pulitzer Prize three times, received numerous other awards including the National Medal for Literature and the Presidential Medal of Freedom. He was called a fascist by communists and a communist by Senator Joseph McCarthy. Though Ezra Pound disdained his poetry, MacLeish was responsible, so much as anyone else, for Pound's release from long confinement in St. Elizabeth's [mental] Hospital." (Winnick xi). MacLeish's art began in the 1920s and 1930s and this turbulent era directly affected the themes and ideas, particularly in his verse plays, which MacLeish saw as vehicles to give his private views a public forum.

MacLeish was the editor of *Fortune* magazine in the 1930s while writing articles for it that exhorted corporate America to respond more compassionately to the Depression. He resigned from *Fortune* when he was pressured to be less of a critic of business. He entered government service in 1938 as assistant secretary of state and librarian of Congress under FDR. In the late 1940s and early 1950s he was a Harvard lecturer who wrote essays debunking McCarthyism. (MacLeish was also a prolific essayist on social issues in general.) His experience with the law, business, and government made him a pragmatist, and his art reflects this pragmatism with a starker, more stoic recognition of reality that began after his younger brother Kenneth was killed in World War I. His empathy increased in the1930s with his recognition of the rise of fascism in Europe and the suffering of the American people during the depression.

His early art was well-praised, but the more he engaged in public activism, moving smoothly from board room, to state room, to Harvard class room, the more he was sniped at by those who implied that "true" art could not emerge from such "compromised" activities. The vitriol (particularly from Edmund Wilson whose sniping seemed tinged with jealousy) was excessive at times, and even envious of a man who could move in these circles so fluidly. MacLeish was not introverted and his outspoken opinions invited vociferous responses.

During 1920, on a sabbatical in Paris, MacLeish, even before trying his hand at poetry, wrote his first verse play, *Nobodaddy*. This play and all the plays that followed were very much about how art can turn personal views into parables for a public forum, just as Tony Kushner does in the present.

Remembered principally as a poet — much of his poetry itself was meant to be declamatory as in his call for "Public Speech" in 1936 — MacLeish, nonetheless, won a Pulitzer Prize for drama with his Broadway play *J.B.* in 1957. In fact, there are very few twentieth century dramatists whose plays have been *heard* by as many people as MacLeish's verse radio plays, which were listened to from the late 1930s to 1976. His anti-fascist verse plays, *The Fall of the City*, 1937, and *Air Raid*, 1938, were the first verse plays ever broadcast in the United States (and the former was almost concurrent with England's first broadcast of a verse play by Louis MacNeice). MacLeish's dramatic vision, however, began taking shape in that very first play, *Nobodaddy*, written in 1920 (but not published until 1926), and although it had a limited printing and was never performed, *Nobodaddy* is still important as this play established themes that would persevere in the rest of this writer's art for the next sixty years. The prevalence of a writer's vision over a long period is an individual evolution of consciousness within the universal evolution of consciousness.

During *Nobodaddy*'s development, the American poet Conrad Aiken, also in Europe, influenced MacLeish. Aiken's own verse was greatly influenced by Freudian psychology. When *Nobodaddy* was published in 1926, MacLeish was not yet established as a poet of note and the play, which was a unique view of Adam and Eve and of Cain and Abel, received little attention. *Nobodaddy* (William Blake's name for God) was largely ignored, and the one extant review is noted by MacLeish biographer, Scott Donaldson: "the reviewer concluded that MacLeish had reworked the bible story with originality into a powerful psychological drama of man's aloneness in the universe" (166). The reviewer, Christopher Herter, a friend of MacLeish, had the benefit of some elucidation that may have helped him see the play's power. Feeling this "aloneness in the universe" had been MacLeish's reaction to his brother's death.

In MacLeish's introduction to *Nobodaddy*, he states:

> The literary interpretation of ancient legends as expression in metaphor of man's experience of nature is so common in our time that any other use of the material requires explanation. In the following poem [verse play] I have not treated the Hebrew legend of the Garden of Eden as a metaphor. I have not assumed that the legend as legend symbolizes the accident of human self-consciousness and the resultant human exclusion from nature, animal and inanimate. I have not taken the God of Genesis to be the mysterious universal will which man at that point in his history ceased to understand. I have not seen in Cain the beginning of the human effort to occupy a man-made, man-conscious, universe within or without the other. On the contrary, having to deal with the dramatic situation which the condition of self-consciousness in an indifferent universe seems to me to present, I have appropriated, for its dramatic values, the story of Eden [6–7].

MacLeish's appropriation of the Bible's primal stories as a source for present explanation refers to the Viconian essence of Poetic Wisdom or "first stories" that are reincarnated in every generation. MacLeish, in his thematic proclamation of dealing with "self-consciousness in an indifferent universe," also proclaimed his artistic role as an American stoic, pre-dating post–World War II Existentialists and staking out his territory for future art. MacLeish is not positing that the universe is, in fact, indifferent; rather, that this is the perception of humanity that cannot understand why there is suffering in the world except by seeing that indifference is the reason.

According to Donaldson, "in act I, Adam and Eve eat of the forbidden fruit, and so become aware of themselves as isolated and lonely creatures, severed from their oneness with animal nature. In act II, they flee from the garden, and discover the pain of alienation in a universe that does not care about human beings or their values. Act III takes place thirty-five years later, in the desert east of Eden. Drought has destroyed Cain's crops and threatens Abel's flocks. Yet, when Abel prays for permission to return to Eden and offers a sacrifice, Cain reacts with fury. 'If we bow,' he says, 'we'll never stand upright on earth again.' Abel may be willing to crawl before God, to sink back into oneness with nature of the Garden before consciousness [of the ego], but Cain is not" (165–66). And then Cain kills his brother and runs into a darkness from which man never fully emerges.

The idea of an "indifferent universe" in *Nobodaddy* is strictly a man-made construct predicated on the individual ego's belief that God should be somehow immanent and personal. In the pre-fall state, Adam was quite content to meld into a mute logic of "oneness" with nature. Nature represented a transcendent *God-as-an-intuitive feeling*, rather than a God that should respond to personal importuning that may consequently stir anger when the importuning is not directly answered. "Hell" is thinking that after eating the forbidden fruit, Adam would be superior to nature, and equal to the God who created nature. When no seeming benefits derive from this "knowledge," and when a drought follows the eating of the forbidden fruit, it seems to Eve that they are not just being ignored, but punished.

Adam, before his eating from the tree of knowledge, was faced with two choices, both of which were self-imagined (if not by a real Adam but by the Viconian storyteller that created him): Adam could succumb to the awe of nature and to his feelings of inferiority towards nature, or, by eating the fruit, assert his will to be god-like and superior to nature. Adam is urged to eat the forbidden fruit by his ego (and alter-ego) in the guise of the serpent — and also encouraged by Eve to do so as she does not fear what she does not understand (ignorance is bliss). They eat, and their guilt brings misery as they flee to the desert. A drought ensues; is this punishment or a coincidence? There is no answer, and their guilt endures for thirty-five years; Adam and Eve's grown sons, Cain and Abel, have assimilated this internal conflict by emulating it as witnessed in their parents. A psychological cycle is represented through metaphor and repeated ever after. The ebb and flow of this cycle is a continuous opposition that will be a perpetual test of human will that won't be reconciled any time soon.

Abel represents the "fallen" Adam and in his inherited guilt attempts reconciliation with the imagined "angry" god by killing a ram. This signifies the birth of ritual and religion. Cain is like the realist or rationalist Adam before the fall. Cain asserts his own will and resists Abel by seeking through reason to overcome superstition.

When man believes himself an integral, indivisible facet of nature, which *is* God, he is in paradise with no fear of corporeal death; when man resists nature and fears death, he is in misery and sees only nature's indifference to his imagination. Eden's harmony signifies man's acquiescent ignorance, and this ignorance is, indeed, bliss, but one where the assertive, self-proclaiming ego is not allowed to operate. The desert's disharmony — and the concomitant fear of being out of control — motivate man to try and take a form of Viconian control of his environment in some symbolic rite of his own devising; hence, Abel's bloodletting is the ego asserting itself through imaginative fantasy and attempting to appease "indifferent" nature and turn indifference into deference from nature. Cain cannot bear Abel's obsequious pleading to this god that has ignored them, and Cain rants at the thundering sky:

> Howl! Howl! Cough out your angry fires! Beat
> down
> The air with anger! I will stand here still.
> I am no breed of yours. I am the man,
> Cain....
>
> [to Abel who has implored his brother not to offend God]
>
> Because you fear must I fear too? Because you are a thing
> Of earth and water must I likewise be
> Water and earth? You are that root of me
> That ties itself far down in the old slime
> from which he [god] took us. But I will not have
> Roots in the earth. I am a man [63–65].

When Abel implores Cain not to anger God, Cain's anger at God has no tangible being to confront and Cain kills Abel instead. Cain challenges God to react to this murder:

> I have killed
> Your priest. I have profaned your sacrifice.
> I stand against you cursing you. Lift up,
> Lift up your hand and slay me....
> Where are you, god? Where are you god?
> Speak to me — [66].

Cain runs off into the darkness and metaphorically takes the future generations with him, as his dilemma or scenario has been repeated in every generation. Thus, in this early play, MacLeish poses man's eternal dilemma: should man act; how should he act; and will it matter in any consequence that represents some undefined metaphysical realm greater than himself if that realm seems voiceless? In effect, should man have faith in faith itself and act for the greater good even if that good is not manifest in tangible terms?

In 1935, fourteen years after *Nobodaddy*, MacLeish wrote his second play. Grover Smith, in his analysis of MacLeish, thought that *Nobodaddy*, "though excellent as a trial of philosophy," was not written to be staged, "thus the strength of his first stage play, *Panic*, 1935, is very impressive" (41). The "panic" referred to was the depression-era run on banks by the public because the public thought the banks might go bust. Smith continues:

The play is an admirable and curious hybrid. In sum, it is an Aristotelian tragedy with a special catastrophe, the withdrawal of the supporting characters' loyalty (the protagonist, a great man, suddenly ceases to be accepted as that); and this plot is superimposed on a proletarian drama conveyed by expressionistic techniques (*anonymous voices of the poor and unemployed in a time of financial crisis*). It is the unemployed who make the protagonist's fellow bankers lose confidence in him; and not what he does because of pride, but his vulnerability to the hatred of the mob because of who he is, that precipitates the "panic" causing his downfall [41–42].

MacLeish, having been editor of the business magazine, *Fortune*, had left that position because the magazine had not allowed him to be more aggressive in using it as a vehicle to help the unemployed. *Panic* allowed him to say what Fortune wouldn't. In a letter to *Fortune* owner, Henry Luce, MacLeish wrote: "For five years [since the crash of 1929] they [the capitalists power brokers] have been fearful, vacillating, bewildered and void. Their one hope has been to hang on. Their greatest fear has been the fear of falling off…. They are incapable of leadership. They are sterile. They sound empty when they are struck" (quoted in Donaldson, 239).

MacLeish, while blaming capitalists for a lack of imagination to meet the crisis of the Depression, nonetheless did not believe Marxism was an alternative solution either, and the play makes this case as well. Consequently, both sides of the boss-worker equation would find fault with MacLeish. Donaldson notes: "In *Panic*, therefore, he invented a protagonist, the powerful J.P McGafferty, who seems to have the capacity for leadership that [others] lacked. McGafferty takes a stand against the panic, and for a time reassures those who had been making a run on the banks" (239). But McGafferty's concern for his egoistic self-image skews his vision and he succumbs to vanity and fails.

When asked if the play held up as an example of Greek tragedy, MacLeish responded: "This is what it was supposed to be. *Oedipus* is obviously the model…. McGafferty was *it*, you know … and there were lots of examples [in real life]. They were going out of twenty-second floor windows all over Wall Street. So far as I know that's the only play which ever dealt with that problem" (*Reflections* 104). More precisely, the problem MacLeish was concerned with was the powerful McGafferty suddenly losing his power because both the universe and the public within that universe became indifferent to him. Not to be listened to was unbearable. The crowd, in fear, created a sense of panic until panic became inevitable. Of this, McGafferty said:

> Only the
> Trick time plays with us with his side-show mirrors
> Twisting the thing to come until it's vast:
> Larger than life: grotesque: inhuman: threatening — [80].

Fear of the unknown that may be waiting to create havoc supersedes rationality until the crowd panics, even without evidence that the fear has any basis. They cannot be persuaded otherwise.

Panic received largely positive reviews, but the financial realities of a Broadway that depression audiences couldn't afford, killed the play after only three performances. With this reality understood, MacLeish believed that radio should be the venue for his next plays, *The Fall of the City* and *Air Raid*.

The two plays were thematically similar to MacLeish's verse epic, *Conquistador*, 1932, which took the Pulitzer in poetry and had forecast the danger of fascism. The poem and the later plays reminded Americans of the importance of freedom and the insidious undercurrents that could work to take freedom away. These plays were parables about Europe and the events leading to the great tragedy of the Spanish Civil War in 1937, which watched Spain fall to Franco while much of the world stood by and refused to see. The bombing of Guernica and Hitler's inexorable terror were warnings and it seemed only the minority among artists and intellectuals could understand the threats posed to the near future.

The two radio plays, according to Phillip Gardner, "in their different ways used the vividness of what was happening elsewhere to suggest both the need for Americans to leap the gap of space with their concern, and the possibility that such things could happen here if the conscious efforts of democracy were relaxed. The monstrous inversion of human logic which Fascism meant for MacLeish is played with caustic wit in the mouth of the crowd in *The Fall of the City*: 'He's one man: we are but thousands'" (98).

According to Donaldson:

> At seven o'clock on the evening of 11 April 1937, Orson Welles' orotund voice delivered the first lines of MacLeish's verse play ... to a nationwide CBS radio audience. [In the days before television, this was substantial.] The setting was the city of Tenochtitlan, where legend had it, a woman had risen from the grave to warn of the coming of the conquering army. On the radio, neither the place nor time was specified. What MacLeish had in mind was a play-as-parable, conveying how easily people anywhere could be persuaded to accept what they construed to be their fate.

Welles, in the role of [radio] announcer, provides an eyewitness view of events in the great square where the citizens assemble. He sees the woman rise from the tomb and utter her dire prophecy:

> The city of masterless men
> Will take a master
> There will be shouting then:
> Blood after! [267]

MacLeish said later that *The Fall of the City* was about "the proneness of men to accept their own conqueror, accept the loss of their rights because it will in some way solve their problems or simplify their lives" (*Reflections* 107). This was what Germans and Italians had believed. It is a major theme for Isherwood and Auden in their play *The Ascent of F6*, also in 1937. The anonymous public would rather be passive than active. Modern propaganda purveyed through a compliant media can conquer without a shot if fear of the "other," an enemy more false than actual, is disseminated as the bogeyman of the mass that makes no effort to learn otherwise.

At the end of the play, the great denouement is that when the "conqueror" arrives, it turns out to be nothing but an empty helmet. Of this MacLeish said: "The end of the play, after the helmet has been found to be empty, does not refer to the conqueror. The conqueror is not the central figure. It's the people, crowding around and approaching him" (110). The announcer speaks:

> They don't see or they won't see.
> They are silent.
> The people invent their oppressors: they wish to believe in them.
> They wish to be free of their freedom: released from their liberty: [32]

Too many people do not want to make choices, fear making choices, and are too willing to let demagoguery choose for them. They are made to believe that if they are not for something that a seeming majority is for they will be subject to some amorphous form of a psychological and social ostracism. The urge to be identified as belonging to some group through an instinct for self-protective preservation is overwhelmingly a dominant strain of the passive majority. The activist artists and intellectuals are always the first targets of an emerging totalitarianism because they will be the first to see through the insidious propaganda. The public is turned against the artists and intellectuals; they are castigated, branded as elitists, blacklisted, and finally, killed. The dichotomy of "I am I; you are not I" is exponentially contagious so that this becomes "We are us; you are not us."

The response to the broadcast was immediate and positive, so much so that CBS wanted a sequel. This would be *Air Raid*, broadcast on Thursday, 27 October 1938. The play, written after the tragic aerial bombings of Guernica, Spain, reflected the new fascist warfare where cities and the civilians in them — men, women, and children — were killed indiscriminately. Once again, MacLeish wished to alert a national audience to the European tragedy and that the folly of war could reach anywhere — even the U.S.

For MacLeish, women are wise; men are not always as wise. A group of random female voices say:

> The wars!
> As though to make the wars were something wonderful!
> Talking of wars as though to die were something wonderful! [11]

The play is consumed with the fear of a coming air raid where no one can be safe. *Air Raid* was very well received. The review in *The Christian Century* said, "This not *an* air raid, but all air raids; the announcement, the incredulity, the expectation, the suspense, the diminishing margin of minutes — ten, six, three — the crescendo of sound, the piercing shriek, the single questing voice — silence" (quoted in Donaldson, 270).

MacLeish said in his foreword to *The Fall of the City*, "over the radio, verse is not an obstacle ... verse has no visual presence to compete with. Only the ear is engaged, and the ear is already half a poet" (x). The ear is listening to a reiteration of the first stories of the primal tribe.

In 1938, disturbed by *Time*'s conservative coverage of world events and its antipathy towards his pro–FDR/New Deal articles, MacLeish resigned from *Fortune* and was asked to be Librarian of Congress in 1939. There, he modernized the Library, sought greater recognition, and salaries for all librarians, and, as R.H. Winnick wrote, he "helped to redefine the profession by urging librarians to see that their proper place in the modern world was as champions to a cause: freedom of speech, freedom of thought, and, ultimately, human liberty" (xv).

In 1940, his controversial essay, *The Irresponsibles* asserted:

> History — if honest history continues to be written [compared to the rewritten history of totalitarianism] — will have one question to ask of our generation, people like ourselves. It will be asked of the books we have written, the carbon copies of our correspondence, the photographs of our faces, the minutes of our meetings in the famous rooms before the portraits of our spiritual begetters. The question will be this: Why did the scholars and the writers of our generation in this country, witnesses as they were to the destruction of writing and of scholarship in great areas of Europe and to the exile and the imprisonment and murder of men whose crime was scholarship and writing — witnesses also to the rise in their own country of the same destructive forces with the same impulses, the same motives, the same means — why did the scholars and writers of our generation in America fail to oppose those forces while they could — while there was still time and still place to oppose the enemies of scholarship and writing? [3–4].

In 1949, MacLeish went to Harvard as Boyleston Professor of Rhetoric and Oratory. Even as a teacher, MacLeish still could be aroused to public action, especially to confront injustice. In the late 1940s, early 1950s, this meant Joseph McCarthy. MacLeish did so in published letters to editors, essays, and satiric doggerel verse befitting McCarthy's ranting. McCarthy retaliated, Donaldson recorded, by accusing MacLeish of having "been affiliated with as vast a number of communist fronts as any other individual whom I have ever named" (426). MacLeish was honored. His anti–McCarthy stance culminated in his next play, which would, as he had done in *Nobodaddy*, reiterate an archetypal myth to metaphorize a modern dilemma. In turn, MacLeish's play, *The Trojan Horse*, of 1952 would be just as relevant in 2008.

The Trojan Horse was aired first by the BBC in January 1952, "but it wasn't written for them," MacLeish said. "It was written as a verse play for radio and the occasion ... was Senator [Joseph] McCarthy and his foul ways. Well they talk about people wrapping themselves in the flag. He really wrapped himself up in the wooden horse of patriotism" (*Reflections*, 191–92). Right after the BBC broadcast, *The Trojan Horse* was staged at The Poets' Theater of Cambridge, Massachusetts. "The play," Donaldson wrote, " is allegorical, directed at the enemies within" (428). The purpose, MacLeish later said in 1977, was to show how "an insignificant and unrespected member of the United States Senate launched an attack on the integrity of the American government [and] was supported by so large a body of American opinion that even his bravest and most admired opponents were silenced for a time.... Why had the Trojans taken the horse in, breaching their own walls to let it pass? Why had our deluded generation of Americans accepted McCarthy's enormous fabrication, made not of wood, but of lies?" (quoted in Donaldson 429).

In the play, a wise blind man "sees" what others do not:

> Bring that enormous image in
> To make patriots of us
> Sweating our public love by law
> And all of us will fear each other [22].

In MacLeish's political parables, going back to *Nobodaddy*, a principal theme is that when the public is indifferent to external forces, those forces can be manipulated to manipulate the public. Constituencies must be *aware*.

MacLeish's next play moved away from overt politics in the public arena to the politics of individual human relationships. In fact, for MacLeish (and any artist), the only real difference between public and private is in degree and the number of people involved. What applies to the one or the two applies to the many. In 1953, *This Music Crept by Me Upon the Waters* was also broadcast first by the BBC in June 1953, then presented at the Poets' Theater of Cambridge that fall. Placed in the Antilles among the affluent, a dinner party waits for a couple that are late. While they wait there is "small talk" within which there are much larger implications: "Happiness is difficult," a MacLeish surrogate states. "It takes a kind of courage" (14). For the author, this was the courage to resist the tug of the ego for "self-aggrandizement" which obfuscates purer feelings towards one's self and others.

MacLeish said of the play in 1985, it "is not simply an inward play about an inward subject, but it is on a much larger scale of significance than it seems to be.... It is a satiric and sardonic play ... about ... the experience of the confrontation with overwhelming stillness and beauty and the sense of *now*, now and forever" (*Reflections*, 194). The play's humor derives from the contrast of the *eternal now* with the characters' immediately mundane insecurities. If one could intuit the eternal now, one's perspective could judge petty predicaments for what they are in contrast to the vast landscape.

J.B.: A Play in Verse, 1957, is MacLeish's most well known drama as it was a hit on Broadway, premiering on 11 December 1958, and earning a Pulitzer Prize. In it, the themes that MacLeish first enunciated in *Nobodaddy* are present. MacLeish had not changed for his audiences, but his post–World War II audiences were more attuned to MacLeish's existential stoicism. Grover Smith wrote that, "*J.B.* [as in the biblical Job], is a King Lear who, divested of all illusions about a benevolent universe, is taught to endure and love" (44). J.B. does so with a contentment to be derived, not from importuning for special favors — as Abel had tried to do in *Nobodaddy* — but from a sense of an integral unicity or divinity with nature that is neither good nor evil but just *is*.

As a "play within a play," *J.B.* has a distant "announcer" offstage. Two clowns, Zuss and Nickles, first present a farce in a circus tent, then double as God and Satan as well as acting as a "chorus" announcing Job's trials. Smith says, "J.B. triumphs both over Zuss' [God's] humiliation of him and Nickles' [Satan's] temptation to hatred. Learning the truth about his God, he forgives him his injustice. With a love stronger than the unreasoning tyranny of heaven, he justifies that love by beginning to live again when his torment is finished" (44). MacLeish had been motivated to write this play when he visited bombed-out Europe after World War II. He asked himself about, "the question of belief in life," and, if one can, "believe in the justice of God in a world in which the innocent perish ... and brutal ... men foul all the lovely things" (quoted in Donaldson, 450). *J.B.* was well reviewed by poets and drama critics alike. *The New York Times* called it, "a remarkably compelling parable of our time" (quoted in Donaldson, 455). MacLeish waited ten years to do his next play, *Herakles,* another myth-inspired drama, and another story within a story.

In *Herakles,* a successful scientist of the present is a metaphorical Herakles laboring for mankind. His wife corresponds to Herakles' wife, Megara (who was played by Rosemary Harris in the play's only production at the University of Michigan at Ann Arbor in October of 1965). The scientist's son resents his father's success, which for him is a metaphorical death, and this is analogous to the sons Hercules accidentally killed after returning from the underworld. Myth and reality meet in Act II when the scientist's wife and Megara share the stage. The message is that myths began as realities that are aggrandized and then are ritualized by man's intuitive need for seeking universal and timeless meanings that transcend individual selves and integrate the finite one to the infinite many. Herakles as myth, and the scientist as a myth-in-the-making, act in the world for good, but confront hatred in others and egotism in themselves which embitter them. Selflessness is as difficult to achieve as happiness is. MacLeish said that just as Herakles was a myth that inadvertently destroyed, "This is also the myth of science for us" (*Reflections,* 214).

For MacLeish, science had become a tool to be manipulated for good or ill. The public — that faceless entity that can be easily seduced by the mass media, especially a media dominated by special interests — has nameless constituents who can hold opinions but absolve themselves of any responsibility for what the results of those opinions might entail: that is, fascist propaganda leading to persecution and murder. In the modern age of a universally — if not all astutely — educated public, media manipulation can promote almost anything — witness McCarthyism. "Sound bites" of limited, sometimes deliberately misleading — even false information — have replaced the full meals of greater information that one is too busy to digest. How can one truly act if one is uninformed or ill informed?

MacLeish would have agreed; his plays consistently concerned themselves with how man could or should act in what, to man, seemed an indifferent universe. (The indifference of many registered voters that stayed home in the 2000 U.S. Presidential election likely changed the course of history.) The other side of this coin is whether man, who is, for the most part, just as indifferent to the universe and all of its individual components, is really the perpetuator of a mistaken illusion of the universe's indifference which is actually his own self-imposed isolation inverted to place blame elsewhere. Man, as a *mass,* allows himself, by his apathy, to be swayed by whoever has the loudest and most strident voice because he has not involved himself, or only tangentially involved himself, in the collective process of living in society so he can make his own, non-dogmatized, informed decisions (as in Emerson's *Self-Reliance,* the American model for MacLeish's stoic philosophy).

In the 1960s MacLeish publicly argued against the Vietnam War, as did his lifelong friend, Thornton Wilder. This war, and the divisive furor it had inflamed in the American public, motivated MacLeish's next play. In 1971, MacLeish adapted his play, *Scratch,* from his friend, Stephen Vincent Benét's story, "The Devil and Daniel Webster." Whereas Benét had written a humorous folk tale about Webster, MacLeish tackled the historical Webster who, in 1857, was faced with the conflict of being against slavery, but wished to preserve the union by compromising his principles and not asking the South to end it. Webster would later realize that this was an untenable position. "It struck me," said MacLeish, "that maybe the famous trial [to get a man's soul back from the devil] before the jury of the dead and damned might be interesting to work on that way" (*Reflections,* 220). Written during the Nixon administration and considering the tribulations of that time, MacLeish intended *Scratch* as another political parable about whether one should act or not act, compromise or stand on principle. In the Foreword to *Scratch,* he wrote:

> The historic Webster demanded to be heard, for the historic Webster was the one man in that tragic time who had dared to face the contradiction. He understand, as even Emerson did not, that there is no choice between Liberty and Union in America — that what the American people had done when they established their self-governing state was to refuse to choose between the freedom of man and the government of men — what they had done indeed was precisely the opposite: *to choose both.* Webster had said so: "Liberty *and* union, now and forever, one and inseparable" [ix].

Scratch opened on Broadway in May of 1971. The play received mixed reviews, but the influential *New York Times* was one of the negative reviews and *Scratch* had a very short run. At the time, the play may have been too close to the events it was attempting to be a parable of to be fully appreciated, but its intentions and its conception are among MacLeish's best work and *Scratch* deserves to be reconsidered.

For America's Bicentennial, MacLeish was asked to write a verse play to be both broadcast on radio and staged for television in July of 1976. *The Great American Fourth of July Parade,* even as a celebration, warned that only apathy could prevent the U.S. from fulfilling its greatness. MacLeish was inspired by the letters of Thomas Jefferson to and from John Adams, particularly when Jefferson wrote (and says in the play): "The Mass of mankind has not been born with saddles on their backs for a favored few, booted and spurred, ready to ride them by the grace of God" (48). As biographer Donaldson wrote, for MacLeish, "Freedom was a process rather than a fulfillment, Archie said. What was important was the will to keep striving for it" (510). The process of the work is the goal, not the product of the work. The play, simple and straightforward, promotes these American ideas by having constituents of a parade-watching crowd comment on the meaning of the Fourth of July while the spirits of Jefferson and Adams comment on the comments.

MacLeish always believed, as did his friend Carl Sandburg, in *The People, Yes!* Yet neither believed this blindly. MacLeish, from *Nobodaddy* to *The Great American Fourth of July Parade,* questioned the role of man in his universe and the forces that can either diminish man or inspire him. A key for MacLeish, and consistently depicted in his plays, was the need for all men and women to be *aware* and to *act*—but with knowledge, not in the wake of false dogma. MacLeish influenced many personally and professionally. His legacy as a verse dramatist for radio, and his device of the "announcer," secures him a place that other dramatists have seen as a starting point. Archibald MacLeish was the artist as liberal humanist and patriot—but nobody's fool. He understood that the cause of freedom is an exacting discipline that sometimes requires stoic vigilance *and* sacrifice.

Finally, through all of his varied life, he was first and last, a poet of just causes.

A Short Note on J.D. Salinger, the Vedantist

In the 1950s Salinger sought out spiritual wisdom through Vedanta as established by his letters to the Vedanta Society of Southern California (in their archives), which referred him to Swami Nikhilananda of the New York Vedanta Society. (In 1950 the Swami signed and gave a copy of Huxley's essay collection *Themes and Variations* as a birthday present to Dr. Leopold Steiglitz, brother of Alfred, the art maven.)[1] In the early fifties Salinger studied Advaita Vedanta at the Ramakrishna Vivekananda Center in New York with Nikhilananda. The goal of Vedanta in its most basic teaching is that a person can learn to abnegate the willful ego and renounce attachment to the temptations of the material world. While an aspirant can live in the world and eschew temptation, it has also been a factor in mysticism that sometimes an individual may need to get away from the sources of temptation. Salinger dropped out of the opportunities for celebrity, preferring to focus on the inner rather than the outer. He continued to write, and his art reflected Vedanta. In *Franny and Zooey*, Buddy Glass (Salinger) lives in a private, rustic setting, as did Salinger. The novel argues that the artist can worry only about his own art, and not its reception. This is in the spirit of the Vedantic renunciation of attachment to the fruits of one's labor.

Holden Caulfield in *The Catcher in the Rye* is not dissimilar to Buddha, particularly in Hesse's *Siddhartha*. Both experience the material world and decide in their different ways that this world does not work for them. *Catcher* is a critique of self-indulgent middle to upper-middle class life in America. When this writer taught *Catcher*, he asked students to think of it as a mystery strewn with clues that are hints to Holden's life and psychological difficulties. In this case, seeming randomness is not really random, but only appears to be. A reader learns that these clues point to a whole that is Holden's unconscious. Holden seeks meaning outside of himself. Meaning isn't there; it's inside and the purpose of his seeing the psychoanalyst is to find the inside and give it meaning.

In "Teddy," from *Nine Stories*, there is a child who is moved by Vedanta philosophy, and Salinger uses this vehicle to describe Vedanta and meditation: "But I wouldn't have had to get incarnated in an American body if I hadn't met that lady. I mean it's very hard to meditate and live a spiritual life in America" (*Nine Stories* 287). Salinger is also speaking for himself:

"As I understand it ... you hold pretty firmly to the Vedantic theory of reincarnation" [*Nine Stories* 286].

"I was six when I first saw that everything was God.... My sister was only a very tiny child then, and she was drinking her milk, and all of a sudden I saw that *she* was God and the *milk* was God. I mean, all she was doing was pouring God into God, if you know what I mean" [288].

"So—this is my point—what you have to do is vomit up if you want to see things as they really are" [a tearing-down of old belief so that there can be a building-up of new belief] [291].

Logic's the first thing you have to get rid of [replace logic with intuition] [290].

Seymour Glass in the stories of *Franny and Zooey* also spreads Salinger's Eastern influences. Seymour at eleven reads Chinese poets. After Seymour killed himself, his brother, Buddy, says: "He was the only person I've ever habitually consorted with ... who more frequently than not tallied with the classical conception, as I saw it, of a mukta, a ringding enlightened man, a God-knower" ("Introduction," 202). Suicide, herein, is not the sin of Western religion but a possible act of freedom from a disappointing material reality. The name Glass itself is a reference to Emerson's transparent eyeball where a person's spirit looks out and also looks back in.

In 1961 John Updike reviewed *Franny and Zooey*. It must be noted that in 1961 Salinger was not yet the figure whose *Catcher in the Rye* became a staple of American education; nor had the 1960s explosion of interest in Eastern philosophy as yet taken hold. Updike does his best to put Salinger in a context but does not necessarily quite succeed. Updike is wary of an approach that narrates by dwelling on subjectively introverted and mundane observations that seem disparate, although he suspects that there is some kind of revelation going on; yet he cannot define that revelation.

Forty-four years later, introversion and subjectivity are frequent rather than rare. Updike does refer to Salinger's interest in "Buddhism" but does so without a serious relation of what Buddhism and Eastern philosophy mean to Salinger or what it might mean to understand Salinger's stories. More recent critical analysis of Salinger does incorporate this relation.[2]

In 2001, Janet Malcolm, in her essay, "Justice to J.D. Salinger," revisits the 1961 antipathy to *Franny and Zooey*: "When 'Franny' and Zooey" appeared in book form in 1961, a flood of pent-up resentment was released. The critical reception — by, among others, Alfred Kazin, Mary McCarthy, Joan Didion, and John Updike — was more like a public birching than an ordinary occasion of failure to please. "Zooey" had already been pronounced "an interminable, an appallingly bad story," by Maxwell Geismar and "a piece of shapeless self-indulgence" by George Steiner.... Today "Zooey ... is arguably Salinger's masterpiece. Rereading it and its companion piece "Franny" is no less rewarding than rereading *The Great Gatsby*. It remains brilliant and is in no essential sense dated. It is the contemporary criticism that has dated" (www.nybooks.com/articles/14272).

Gabriel García Márquez *and* One Hundred Years of Solitude: *Magic Realism as a Synonym for Mysticism*

Many years later, as he faced the firing squad, Colonel Aureliano Buendia was to remember that distant afternoon when his father took him to discover ice.

This sentence opens García Márquez's *One Hundred Years of Solitude*, which was published in 1967 to great critical and commercial success in Spanish, which was followed by translations (English in 1970) that also were a great success. Macondo, Colombia, was the fictional setting; however, the figurative "Macondo" became as much or more well known than actual Colombian towns or towns anywhere. García Márquez takes Colombian history as reference points, but not in total; rather, he sees certain events as important and uses them as a basis for the myths that history often becomes. The opening sentence has become famous and still serves to set the tone and the plan for the novel. The sentence is analogously metaphorical for many ideas that the words infer.

The sentence intimates three of the author's fictional strategies that will factor throughout *One Hundred Years of Solitude*: (1) in the sentence three different times are indicated, and this forecasts the ongoing movement of time in flux, moving forward and back while chronicling the history of Macondo and one of its families; (2) there is also in this sentence the violence and death that pervades the novel, and, (3) the mythical/mystical allusion to the discovery of ice signifies that myth and magic — "magic realism"— will be important factors. Within the narrative these themes are contained but as the sentence above shows, García Márquez used a straightforward prose technique that indicates these themes but does so between the lines rather than narrating them didactically; consequently, the novel has a fast, readable pace that is enjoyable for readers who want more action and prefer having the philosophy alluded to rather than explained.

García Márquez and other Latin America writers were influenced by Faulkner who previously had "played" with time in a manner that García Márquez expands upon. Indeed, the "firing squad" episode will not be realized until Chapter 7. Chapter 1 evokes an idyllic setting in the past; Chapter 2 moves to Sir Francis Drake's assault. Another García Márquez contribution is his interplay of realism and myth/magic and how these interrelate, with the myth and magic being as real to the characters in their psychological importance as the events in the characters' lives that are influenced by the myth and magic. In real life — that is, the author's life — people's psyches are intertwined with an external reality as well as their internal world of dreams and fantasy. García Márquez does not separate the two worlds in his novel just as they are not separated in the world outside his novel. The author's reflexivity near the end of the novel signifies that his own external reality and the novel's internal reality are also intertwined, and that myth, magic, and dreams are what unite the two worlds. A key impetus in the novel is the pig's tail (symbol for incest) that becomes both a catalyst and a curse.

"Magic Realism" does not conflate "magic" with "real" but uses the former to heighten realism by having the real become a sharp contrast and juxtaposition to the magic, thus emphasizing the impact of the real for the reader's attention. The magic is not, however, way "out there" and it is not too acute a fantasy; instead, it is always related to the pragmatic reality of the characters' lives. For example, Father Reyna uses magic to raise money, or Remedios ascends to heaven clutching her prized sheets. The magic, representing the psyche, counterpoints the real and dramatizes the real through this artful juxtaposition.

One Hundred Years of Solitude also deals with imperialism, empire-building, and piratical exploitation with the Spanish invaders first, then Drake, and later the banana company. Time is not linear like a river but rather like Wilder's "vast landscape" which, if one could stand back far enough, one could see all events and their interdependence simultaneously. Repetition plays a large part in terms of events and names that also signify a non-linear approach and convey the theme of history repeating itself for those who do not learn from the past.

García Márquez's thematic intention is to place history in a circular context that deals with initial causes and how these causes spawn events that are repetitions of previous events and previous causes. A very amusing use of circularity as a symbol is in the case of Jose Arcada's tattooed penis, which intertwines words in different languages. This fascinates women that pay him to use it. In this symbol there is a most intense blending of past and future as metaphor with the intertwined words (and also the intertwined text of the novel's mysterious ancient parchment as document) representing the past figuratively while the physical act of sexual intercourse integrates the past, present, and future literally, as it is from this intercourse that new life continues. Also representing repetition and circularity is Chapter 6, which begins by enumerating Colonel Aureliano Buendia's military career in satirical terms: his 32 rebellions fail; his 17 sons are all killed, almost all on the same night; he eludes 14 attempted murders and 73 ambushes. All of this turns Aureliano into a mythical figure with Quixote-esque attributes. Another symbolic circularity in *One Hundred Years of Solitude* is that the previous generations haunt the next as in Hawthorne's *The House of the Seven Gables*. The significant difference is that García Márquez is not figurative in his use of ghosts but literal, as the ghosts of the past are "real" to the characters in the novel. More circularity is signified when the author, García Márquez, and his wife, Mercedes, enter the novel as characters, which is the author's way of both haunting his own novel and also attaching his novel to an external reality. Circularity is ultimately rendered in the symbolic form of Melquiades' parchment and the denouement of its meaning as it is explained in the last chapter. The parchment and the novel are very much the same so that the parchment, written in the past, has chronicled the future even to the last sentence: "The first of the line is tied to a tree and the last is being eaten by ants" (301). Hence, fatalism is symbolized in the parchment and in the novel. The characters are fated to forget their history but the parchment and novel preserve it. The parchment has been protected by magic throughout the novel for it is the link that preserves the continuity of truth even when history might be distorted by faulty memory or as propaganda perpetrated by external forces to control a populace. (Such as when it is reported that a labor rally ended peacefully when in fact many were killed.) García Márquez heightens the message of the parchment's circularity by its being written predominantly in Sanskrit. Sanskrit is the language of the oldest recorded scriptures, the ancient Hindu Vedas such as the Bhagavad-Gita and the Upanishads. García Márquez goes as far back as he can go and across continents to link together the circle of time and place as continuous and contiguous—a vast landscape. Yet, the novel also says that the parchment was written in Melquiades' native tongue, but if this is Sanskrit then Melquiades has been around for over 2,000 years. The parchment also has hints of Augustus and the Lacedemonians to further signify an all-encompassing inclusiveness of time and space. The novel itself has biblical allusions that add to the timelessness.

Characterization in this novel supports the theme of circularity with the repeated names and events that occur in one family that really represents the repetitions of all peoples and events throughout the history of humanity. There are basic types in the family. For the men, Arcadio is mercurial and extroverted while Aureliano is more of an introverted thinker. Both men are archetypes but not fixed in a Jungian sense. In this novel they are aspects of a duality within each character that indicates that both the real people among readers and the novel's fictional characters cannot be clearly defined in absolutes, but will have — and in the case of fictional characters — should have certain prominent characteristics within which there are dualistic ambiguities. Men form the women in this novel but the women ultimately control their families and perpetuate the family's continuity. Still, this is a continuity without progress that is demonstrated in the repetition of names, showing how the family is stuck in a past that they do not learn from or evolve from. Only the parchment has recorded change; the characters do not. García Márquez's point of view is produced from his characters through antithesis: Don't do as they do, learn from their mistakes and omissions. Still, while the characters are recognizable types, just as in real life, they have realistic and identifiable nuances of individuality.

The plot is determined by two dominant factors: the repetition of the family names, and the repetition of events such as the finding of the Spanish ship and the suit of armor that signify conquest in the past by the Spanish that is then replicated by Drake and finally by capitalists. The setting of Macondo begins as a new Eden that tries to stave off the corruption of its idyllic isolation by outsiders. However, Macondo's cycles do not teach as the past is not remembered and only the immediacy of present circumstances is dealt with. García Márquez evokes Macondo so that the reader appreciates its virtues but also understands how its beauty and solitude contribute to the cycles that perpetuate through the family's generations. García Márquez uses actual history as landmarks or milestones but his history of Macondo is an amalgam and composite of the *tone* of Colombia's history rather than an accurate chronicle.

One Hundred Years of Solitude would seem to reflect the spirit of its time as it frames the examinations of existentialism in the years preceding it; it also fits in with the concurrent liberal trends of the 1960s. In the 1960s metaphysical concerns regained a surge of popularity, and this is reflected in the novel, particularly with the parchment's language being mainly in Sanskrit, the original language of the Vedic texts that in the 1960s sold in the millions around the world.

García Márquez's novel ends when Fernanda dies and the family ends as well. Yet, in the act of reading the parchment, which is also the novel, Aureliano/García Márquez provide the verbal artifact that lives forever. The ghosts of the novel are metaphors for the verbal artifact that the novel becomes; the ending intimates continuity beyond death that is mystical.

Don DeLillo: Underworld

> And to complicate matters there is the exploration of "under" as failure (as represented let's say by the losing Dodger, Ralph Branca) and success. It is possible to read any page to see references to unknowing, undoing and other words using this prefix.
> DeLillo is, in effect, posing philosophical questions about the nature of knowledge and ontology. Underworld suggests the notion of mystery, occult, and secret forces. But is there an underworld opposed to the "world"? What are the limits or boundaries of "under"? Is there any routine, known "world" which the "under" subverts? Perhaps the linkage of Branca and Thompson — the loser and the winner — recur throughout the novel to remind us that opposites are somehow always linked. High and low are relative — are, indeed, married. — Irving Malin

Don DeLillo's *Underworld* (1997) is a vision of the "vast landscape" as the zeitgeist of his time. His narrative propulsion comes from the reconciliation of opposites that are — just as they have always been — "married" in essence if not in appearance. DeLillo's description of 1950s and '60s comic Lenny Bruce's monologue is about how language is the synthesized outcome of much living, and thoughts about living, conveyed through a language that is metaphorical, symbolic, and analogous to much more than just the words that are spoken and heard. A single word ignites a torrent of words; a stream of consciousness represents a totality of consciousness.

> He did psychoanalysis, personal reminiscence, he did voices and accents, grandmotherly groans, scenes from prison movies, and he finally closed the show with a monologue that had a kind of abridged syntax, a thing without connectives, he was cooking free-form, closer to music than speech, doing a spoken jazz in which slang generates a matching argot, like musicians trading fours, the road band, the sideman's inner riff, and when the crowd dispersed they took this rap mosaic with them into strip joints and bars and late-night diners ... and it was Lenny's own hard bop, his speeches to the people that rode the broad Chicago night [586].

This description of a Lenny Bruce monologue as a free-form improvisation reflects DeLillo's approach to his novel. Shifts in context run throughout *Underworld* but there is an underlying sensibility and worldview within the structure of the whole novel. DeLillo deals with parts that always go back to the impetus of a centrifugal whole, an inspired impetus that is the hub from which the many spokes of DeLillo's wheel (or world) revolve and allow this vehicle, *Underworld*, to roll. Bruce was a comedian as social commentator. DeLillo is also a comedian as social commentator.

Much literary criticism says that DeLillo is a postmodernist writer, yet *Underworld* has a disrupted narration that is closer to modernism. Nonetheless behind the narration is a worldview like Bruce's riff that interconnects the novel's holistic themes despite the jars and jolts of shifting context and narration. In this, DeLillo operates similarly to Lessing's *The Golden Notebook*. One of DeLillo's themes is the post–World War II Cold War development of a pervasive paranoia generated by the Soviet Union that permeated American culture. DeLillo then sees the end of the cold war as one where the U.S. had both military power and capitalist consumerism while the U.S.S.R. had only the military power but without the consumerism to pay for it. Still, the paranoia did not end with the cold war but has lasted after it as a condition of the American psyche.

The novel reflects a rampant, near-rabid consumerism along with the dependence on advertising images in the manner of Horkheimer, and Adorno. The power that this represents is seen as a microcosm for American life in the modus operandi of "The Culture Industry." A correlation is made that the compulsion to purchase is fueled by the cold war paranoia that turned the consumer toys into sedatives and pacifiers, much like in Huxley's *Brave New World*. DeLillo, through the character Lundy, observes: "You need the leaders of both sides to keep the cold war going. It's the one constant thing. It's honest, it's dependable. Because when the tension and rivalry comes to an end, that's when your worst nightmares begin. All the power and intimidation of the state will seep out of your personal bloodstream" (170). Lundy's point is that the Cold War obscured the fact that bulldozer capitalism is a threat to world sanity and its onslaught cares nothing about humanity and the environment humanity lives in.

The novel's period is from the famous Bobby Thompson home run in 1951 to the fall of the Soviet Union forty years later. There is also an epilogue that signifies the new Internet world of 1997. The novel travels through Boston, New York, Wisconsin, Minnesota, the southwestern desert, Los Angeles, San Francisco, and the Soviet Union. There is waste everywhere — both military and a profligate consumer waste without accompanying civility, decency or good taste. This is DeLillo's prose account of *The Waste Land*, one that is both above world but more so is Underworld, with the different connotations of the word — a criminal underworld, business underworld, government underworld, racial underworld (as hidden prejudice). Moreover, DeLillo is not averse to cultural symbols such as Pluto, god of the underworld, Bruegel's *The Triumph of Death*, and a possible lost film of Eisenstein, *Untervwelt*, to signify the fear and paranoia of Cold War annihilation. Still it is the waste, including radioactive waste, that is burying the soul of humanity in an underworld of a potential oblivion of societal disconnection — perhaps ultimately symbolized in the novel by the homeless of New York City.

DeLillo juxtaposed narratives with different times and characters. The main connector of these different contexts is Nick Shay who is looking to connect past and present as he travels through the novel. A tension is developed with the flashbacks that reveal information much more mysteriously or unexpectedly than would a linear plot. In Part 1 (1992) we know Nick's end. Then we learn how he gets to the end. His crisis and search for self has its impetus in the knowledge that his wife, Miriam, is having an affair and in an article he reads about someone he once knew. His search tries to connect the dots from his childhood to his present and make sense of the lines in between. Nick is an Everyman for Everyreader to identify with. He is in the waste management business in order to drive one of the novel's major themes. He deflects his own angst and self-criticism by being a joker for co-workers and similar tactics. When he reads about Klara Sax, an artist who is presently working outdoors with giant scrap, we learn he had an affair with her forty years before. He looks for her, and this becomes his journey through a past that was once much more solid for him and that had a sense of community now missing. He grew up in the Italian-American section of the Bronx, and his psychology and vocabulary are infused with youthful ideas of a criminal underworld as well as a real tragedy, that of his being a teenager and shooting and killing a friend, which put him into the juvenile corrections system. The unraveling of this information is in reverse and we learn that the victim, George, was an older surrogate father figure who is not without foibles. He is a heroin addict and the shooting is not intentional, but may have been George's attempt at suicide by giving Nick the shotgun and saying, "It is empty, so why don't you pull the trigger." It isn't empty. Nick's musings about his "tough" past are, in fact, based on an accident.

George is a surrogate father figure and Klara is a surrogate mother (and Oedipal) figure. She is 34 and Nick 17 or so at the time of their affair, one that is a catalyst for Klara to leave her middle-class married life and become an artist. Nick kills the surrogate father and has sex with the surrogate mother. The main narratives concern the actors in the Nick-Klara affair. The subplots are satellites off the main plot. Matt Shay, Nick's younger brother is a chess whiz who forsakes chess for service in Vietnam and later works in an underground facility for developing nuclear weapons. His intellectuality is transferred from chess to death. Klara's subplot is that in 1974, after much artistic success, she is unable to produce new art for a period but then recovers and works again. During her affair with Nick, Klara's husband, Alfred, deludes himself into thinking that his marriage to Klara is fine. In Part 2 he is an old man taking care of his senile sister.

One must now shift to the all-important prologue that seems to signify an end of a certain type of community and innocence and the beginning of Cold War paranoia. The prologue also serves as the initiating conceit that provides the link that runs through the novel. This is the baseball that is the center of the prologue, as it is the ball hit by Giant Bobby Thompson for the "Shot Heard Round the World" on October 3, 1951. In the story's present, it is Nick who has the ball. In 1951 Nick was a Dodger fan, and as an impressionable boy the stunning loss is a huge disappointment that becomes a metaphoric symbol for the loss of community that also begins in 1951. A rivalry between baseball teams, however serious to fans, is really an extension of baseball as a game of fun for player and spectator. This innocent kind of rivalry is supplanted by a

Cold War rivalry that is not a game and not fun. This loss is further symbolized by a missing twelve hours in the ball's history, which has been traced by Lundy the memorabilia collector. Indeed, the ball's history is explored in sections that are spaced between parts 1 and 2, 3 and 4, 5 and 6. By 1992 both the Cold War and the game of baseball have changed. In 1992 Nick attends a Dodger-Giant game in Los Angeles. Both the Dodgers and Giants left for California in 1957, itself a rupture of innocence, as fan allegiance and loyalty meant nothing to the owners only interested in money. The message is that capitalist and market forces drive everything on both a local and global scale. Nick sits behind glass in a box, separated from the community of the crowd. The 1992 game is contrasted with the 1951 game. DeLillo chose the earlier game because of the date, which he links to another event: the Soviet Union's test of a nuclear weapon that truly signified the beginning of the Cold War. Yet, in the context of the novel, it is the game that Americans remember, not the U.S.S.R.'s nuke test. This represents a choice to remember innocence nostalgically and deny the memory of a more threatening reality. The nostalgia is represented in the prologue by the game itself plus the iconic and real figures, Russ Hodges, Leo ("Nice guys finish last") Durocher, Frank Sinatra, Jackie Gleason, Toots Shor, and J. Edgar Hoover — all representing the repressed 1950s, a decade that would be one of transition from the pre–Cold War era to the 1960s, a decade that gave vent to the steam of release built up during the 1950s. The Nick-Klara affair of 1952 symbolized Klara's secret release from repression in that decade, one that was expressed by her more publicly as an artist in the next decade. Sinatra and Gleason are the public figures who act out independence and a seeming rebelliousness that is actually rather benign but which the public enjoyed vicariously. Hoover is the behind-the-scenes malignant neo-fascist repressor motivated by a deep paranoia that is both his personally and a symbol of American angst. (And one must remember that he was the chief accomplice for the prince of paranoia, Joe McCarthy.) The prologue seems a lot of fun with the teasing banter between the principals but this fun is intruded on by an FBI agent quietly bringing Hoover the news of the Soviet Union's bomb test. Hence, the contrast of a game and fans enjoying the game with a very negative world-changing event sets the tone and mood for the rest of the novel. With the crowd cheering in joy after the home run, it is Hoover who glances at the page from *Life* magazine of Bruegel's *Triumph of Death* that starkly symbolizes the end of one era represented by the baseball game and the beginning of the Cold War era.

Race is another theme for DeLillo. Baseball brought Jackie Robinson to the major leagues and his emergence was a national symbol for a new era of acceptance, even if still not fully realized. It is African American adolescent Cotter Martin who gets the home run ball and it is Martin with whom DeLillo opens the novel. White, middle-aged Bill in the prologue befriends Cotter as both realize they have played hooky from school and work. When Cotter gets the ball. Bill tries to cajole it out of him until Cotter resists and Bill becomes vehement and chases him but doesn't catch him. Three more chapters on race appear in between larger divisions in the novel. They concern how Cotter's father takes the ball from him just as Bill wanted to, betraying his son's love for baseball purity with the father's efforts to sell the ball. The father's betrayal of his son is meant to correlate with Nick's father's disappearance. The ball is the link between the two fathers.

Media is yet another theme. Are events "true" until they are represented and recorded by print and electronic media? Do the media versions replicate or replace reality with newer, improved, myth-laden versions? The symbol for this theme is the announcer of the opening baseball game, Russ Hodges, who recalls and relates how he used to simulate baseball games from the facts printed on a newswire as if he were seeing it live. A great irony is that Ronald Reagan began his media career also simulating baseball games and then later simulated being a president while the country was run by the people who had propped him up into office. He was a creation, a symbol, "the great communicator." In reality, Reagan was a pitchman just as he had pitched Borax soap in TV commercials. Reagan evoked an American past that was more nostalgic myth than reality. The selling of politicians who are controlled by special interests is just another grand manipulation by the powers behind the powers that are the market forces of America, which are, by extension, the market forces of the world. The correlations of market and media symbols are clear in many of DeLillo's chapter titles that are borrowed from iconic American or world cultural symbols.

Enter the condom as a new marketing darling with its own mall store. In the past the condom had the simpler utilitarian functions of birth control and non-life threatening disease prevention. This is indeed nostalgic compared to the new era where condoms now must prevent AIDS. The idea is that marketing can take the fear and guilt away from any product and that since condom sales increased enormously with the advent of AIDS, Condoms are big money and there is no shame in how they are marketed.

Underworld has major themes that spin off into correlated tributaries that meander but never lose sight of a central proposition. There is a past and there is a present. The past has largely become invention through media that is expert in the invention of the real. The past influences the present, but which past is real — the remembered past or the created past? This is a key to Nick's quest. Where is the past and how will he find it amidst the transformations that can even persuade memory to believe more in the inventions, the myths, than to truly remember reality? (This is also a theme in George Orwell's 1938 novel *Coming Up for Air*.)

In the end, the paranoia of the Cold War may be preferred to the post–Cold War free-for-all where anything goes. Paranoia makes one asks questions and forms a pervasive layer of resistance to accepting all of the lies that market forces can create. This is a generalization that has too many shades of gray to be accepted in total. DeLillo does not expect his readers to do so. Certainly since this novel's publication 9/11/01 has given back to the U.S. the paranoia of the Cold War and then some.

Underworld is enormously ambitious and in its very ambitions there are pitfalls. The novel is didactic, a "novel of ideas." The plot is meant to move the ideas forward so that events and characters serve the ideas. Hence, characters are extensions of DeLillo's voice, and sometimes their independence, or their roundness, is sacrificed to dialog that is not realistic but more of a didactic DeLillo superimposing his voice and thoughts on to their speech in a way that is a disservice to both DeLillo and the characters. But this is only true for those readers who do not want didacticism in their fiction. For the most part, based on the book's largely positive reception and commercial appeal, there are many readers who like the ideas and overlook any twinges of non-realism that are eschewed for the sake of these ideas. These readers may not notice the false notes in some of the dialog that sounds more mechanized to serve an end that DeLillo has pre-designated. Indeed, the very length of this novel seems to be meant to say, "this is an epic" and will be treated with the reverence an epic deserves, including soapbox speeches that are supposed to be coming out as one-on-one conversations. There were too many moments when voices did not ring true and make one pause and think, "People don't talk like that."

Nonetheless, in its effort to pose opposites, in its conception of time as circular, not linear, in its concern with alienation, which by its presence signifies the absence of a unity that is desired by Nick and readers, *Underworld* seeks, like *The Waste Land*, to tear down all negative belief in order to prompt the reader to build up new and positive belief antithetically.

The Fragments of Heraclitus *and Guy Davenport's "The Death of Picasso"*

> What Kafka had to be so clear and simple about was that nothing is clear and simple. On his deathbed he said of a vase of flowers that they were like him: simultaneously alive and dead. All demarcations are shimmeringly blurred. Some powerful sets of opposites absolutely do not, as Heraclites said, cooperate. They fight. They tip over the balance of every certainty. We can, Kafka said, easily believe any truth and its negative at the same time.—Guy Davenport, *The Hunter Gracchus*
>
> We know much more than we can say.—Michael Polanyi
>
> The desire and pursuit of the whole is love.—Plato

If one knows that Guy Davenport has translated *The Fragments of Heraclitus* (which sound like the Upanishads), then one can look at Davenport's story, "The Death of Picasso," as being informed from this perspective. Certainly in the *Fragments* and "The Death of Picasso" both writers are advocating philosopher Polanyi's dictum that "we know much more than we can say." Moreover, both writers, in their attempts to say in words—and never quite evoking all that they know—are striving to bridge the ineffable within consciousness that seeks "the desire and pursuit of the whole..."

The artist and philosopher know that words are an inadequate depiction of the world of consciousness that exists between the words and between the lines: Heraclitus, Fragment 116, "The unseen design of things is more harmonious than the seen," and, "Not I but the world says: All is one" (heraclitus01.tripod.com/heraclitus.htm). There, in the interstices, is the ineffable, yet intuitively felt knowledge that is far more profound than the signifiers of words and sentences, which are only analogous symbols that stimulate many more images and thoughts over and beyond and within the words that can never quite measure up to the cognitive ends of which the words are the means. Davenport writes above, "All demarcations are shimmeringly blurred." The "demarcations" represent the interstices where the very real and truest understanding of what we know exists, however tacitly, as opposed to the explicit word-symbols chosen to try and say what we know. There is a distinction between knowledge and understanding. Heraclites agrees: "knowledge is not intelligence" (F6 heraclitus01.tripod.com/heraclitus.htm). Knowledge is the conscious attempt to represent what we know. Understanding and intelligence are the profounder intuitions or ends that we *know* but cannot *say* with the means of a language that can never directly imitate the ineffable but only attempt to be analogous to the ineffable. And Davenport said, a bit like Vico, "Philosophy is the husband of art: the civility they beget is not a hostage to fortune but fortune itself" (31). The difference between what is known and conveyed with language, and that which is intuitively understood between the lines, becomes an ongoing battle from which new understanding derives. Heraclites, Nietzsche, Huxley, Auden, Polanyi, and Derrida knew this and wrote about it; Davenport knows it and still writes about it.

Davenport says, "Some powerful sets of opposites absolutely do not, as Heraclites said, cooperate. They fight. They tip over the balance of every certainty" (24). In saying this, however, Davenport is not quite remembering Fragments 26 and 27:

> It must be seen clearly that war is the natural state of man. Justice is contention. Through contention all things come.
>
> When Homer said he wished war might disappear from the lives of gods and men, he forgot that without opposition all things would cease to exist [heraclitus01.tripod.com/heraclitus.htm].

If one sees this a bit differently in the sense of mystical philosophy and the concept of a Vedic Reconciliation of Opposites, then the "sets of opposites" are actually cooperating by *being* in conflict, which is the intended design of evolving consciousness. There is a continuous and contiguous dialectical opposition and from every moment to moment, *is*ness to *is*ness, *istgeist* to *istgeist*, there is — metaphorically — a perpetual and simultaneous ascension and widening of a rising circle of consciousness, with the ascension and widening fueled by the fission of opposites "rubbing" together. The ascension and widening are neither steady in pace nor symmetrical in growth. There are ebbs and flows and one might picture, not the widening of the circle ever outward, but sometimes taking an elliptical orbit that will occasionally cross over itself inwardly before curving back outwardly again. (Heraclitus writes in F6 that the world "Divides and rejoins, goes forward and backward," and in F109, "The beginning of the circle is also its end.") This fission is manifested in all disciplines encompassing science, philosophy and art. Science measures nature; philosophy and art especially, "metaphorize" nature. Heraclitus's fragments are explicit philosophy — that is, he does not disguise his intentions through allegory or parable. Davenport is both philosophy — his translation of Heraclitus — and art, "The Death of Picasso." Yet, art is also philosophy told tacitly as parables or allegory. Sometimes even the artist is unaware of his intentions, but artistic expression is always an outcome of thoughts, feelings, and emotions that live in the interstices waiting to emerge if they are allowed to.

In the hands of an artist, vulgar, profane and lowbrow language can connote the numinous, sacred, and highbrow, but the words themselves can never denote or be numinous, sacred, and highbrow because the *Awe*-sociations of these terms only exist subliminally between the words, never in them. The artist/poet attempts, by abstraction, to infer the reverential, ritualized awe of the tribe/group that lies in the unified consciousness. This awe existed before the words did.

> *Wholeness arises from distinct particulars; distinct particulars arise from wholeness.* — Heraclitus
>
> *Private faces in public places are wiser and nicer than public faces in private places.* — W.H. Auden

These quotations might seem to evoke a sense of duality; yet, they do not in actuality as they are comprised of words. Words represent the outcomes of thought, and these thoughts are much more tacit than explicit or as Polanyi said, "We know much more than we can say." Words used in art are an even more heightened expression of thoughts, feelings and emotions, and they represent a complex weave of 'distinct particulars" into a "wholeness" that gives the most truthful representation of an era's zeitgeist and of an individual's *Weltanschauung* of his zeitgeist. Of this, as Huxley said, "And yet it is only by poets that the life of any epoch can be synthesized. Encyclopedias and guides to knowledge cannot do it, for the good reason that they affect only the intellectual surface of a man's life. The lower layers, the core of his being, they leave untouched."

Guy Davenport also understands the interrelation of the core and surface. The "wholeness" of his *Weltanschauung* informs his "distinct particulars," which are "appearances" provoked by his (or any artist's) uniquely intuitive evocation of the whole that reflects the interstices in the writer's cognitive processes. Davenport's "The Death of Picasso" is an exemplary demonstration of an artist's whole signified through distinct particulars, of which there are many. Davenport reveals himself and does so in the manner Auden admires—he shows his private face in public places—which for Auden meant an individual who did not wear a mask in order to hide his true self, thoughts, feelings, and emotions. Davenport reveals himself in a diverse set of direct and indirect allusions that infer a wide range of ideas and implications, all of which are particulars of Davenport's whole.

The poet's degree of proficiency in making his aesthetic choices depends on the depth of his perception. Page after page in "The Death of Picasso" unfolds with pointed references that come from Davenport's erudition, which is a map to his world: Van Gogh and Gauguin (Are they emblematic of Davenport's two characters—a middle-aged man given charge of a sixteen-year-old former male prostitute?), Tartarin de Tarascon, Paulus and Barnabus, Butler's *Erewhon* (an opposite as faux utopia and "nowhere"), and this reference precedes "Manfred's *Progetto e Utopia* (is Davenport's island locale in the story implying a quest for Utopia) Parmenides (and all of the Greek interconnections this name invokes not the least of which are *Phaedrus* and Walter Pater), Corelli, Telemann, Bach, and two characters that "practiced Corelli on our Flutes" (two flutes played by very diverse personas that can set aside differences and harmonize), Thoreau ("had a flute") and Thoreau is a symbol of man's harmony with nature—: "We ... perish the instant we take our eyes off nature" (Davenport, 33)—that line follows and supports the harmony of the two flutes of the characters. (Are they characters, or are they autobiographical as are Doctor Tomas's Aschenback and Tadzio? Is Davenport's "open hand in David" a reference to the "open hand" in *Death in Venice*, and is David, Tadzio?) And all of these allusions are just on the first page and they are relatively straightforward.

Then, perhaps, there are more allusions that stretch the parameters a little further off the margins: "The letter is from Theo." (Auden introduced and edited a volume of Van Gogh's letters), "Maigret [the French detective of the mystery writer, Georges Simenon] is comfortable in a constant discomfort ... cosseted by food and pipe" (36)—this image could also fit Auden, whose favorite leisure reading was mysteries—Raspail's handbook (self-cures, another notion the early Auden believed in just as he echoed Homer Lane, Groddeck, D.H. Lawrence, and Gide that physical discomfort was a sign of inner turmoil, a turmoil of "public faces in private places,"), "I get a gape and stare and something like a bark" (37). Is Sander's bark like Victor's lark in the snow of Paris? Auden also believed that the early human beings in the tribe did not communicate with words but with more of an unconscious, semi-telepathy that signified a collective awe, astonishment, and love for existence (*agape*). Is this critic leaning too far over the bow of the *H.M.S. Auden*? Is he giving Davenport intentions that weren't intended? The answer is in Davenport's title.

In "The Death of Picasso," the death of Picasso is not a focal point but a catalyst for thought. Picasso evokes particulars in the whole of consciousness from which the author's stream of consciousness is triggered — just like in real life. The artist is an evocative provocateur. A writer's particulars that emerge from the whole of his *Weltanschauung* are read by a reader who analogizes the writer's particulars to his own unique whole and the particulars that comprise his whole — or his *Weltanschauung*. The two *Weltanschauungs* communicate through the interstices of the words and lines to find their commonalities. The reader also jumps off the spaces between words and lines to form unique impressions and new particulars based on the provocations engendered by the writer's evocations. In sum: It doesn't matter if Davenport intended to refer to Auden or not. This reader-as-critic asserts his unique right to have the whole of his consciousness hunted by the prods of Davenport's allusions. An artist's presentation is also unique, even if it is about seemingly "normal" everyday stuff. The artist makes the "ordinary" extraordinary. Or as Davenport writes: "Is it that ordinary becomes only known as the unusual?" (38), or, "Culture abhors a plenum and has its finest moments hunting on a lean day," or "Art is bad when it is poor in news, dull, and has no rich uncle to brag about" (39). Auden said that a poet must be a mixture of "spy and gossip, a bit of a reporting journalist."

Davenport considers how opposition becomes energy that inspires thought. He is also considering the opposition of his two disparate characters and the irony of the figurative primal scream — Sander's "bark"— versus his "teacher's" erudition. The teacher freely admits he is being taught by Sander's "private face" in both private and public places. The student becomes the teacher; the writer becomes teacher to the reader. A student may even be awed by the teacher into a state of *awe*-sociations via the triggering of amazement so that *Eros* (the spiritual love of an individual) graduates into *Agape* (the love of all existence in a mystical sense). Innocence *is* regenerative. Humans wish to regenerate awe-struck innocence through various paths to transcendence of either an upward transcendence through romantic love, religious devotion, and art, or downward transcendence (herd intoxication, fanaticism, nationalism, narcotics).

The "show and tell" of youth, where student becomes teacher, always remains within the actual child or the adult's inner child as does the-child-as-student and also the child- or adult-as-teacher. The relationship of the good listener and the good teller is a perpetuation of the teacher-student dichotomy, and the emotional reciprocity integral to this dichotomy's communication is dependent on both the teller-as-teacher and the listener-as-student's need for mutual approval. The teller wants to gain approval by giving news; the good listener wants to gain approval by being an attentive audience for which he expects the same attention when he becomes the teller of news. Then the teacher-pupil roles reverse (a technique emulated in psychoanalysis and acting classes). The bottom line is this: listening or reading is just as, or even more important, than telling or writing. As Auden said earlier: "We respond and obey before we can summon and command." Auden also said: "Since we are not born with instinctive modes of behavior, the teacher-pupil [teller-listener] relationship is of essential importance to our lives." Hence, as child or adult, telling or listening is a continuation of the teacher-student relationship. To revisit Huxley:

> Artists are eminently teachable and also eminently teachers. They receive from events much more than most men receive, and they can transmit what they received with particular penetrative force, which drives their communication deep into the reader's mind. One of our most ordinary reactions to a good piece of literary art is expressed in the formula: "This is what I have always felt and thought, but have never been able to put clearly into words, even for myself [Huxley].

Auden agreed, "The reaction one hopes for from a poem is that the reader will say, 'Of course, I've always known that, but I've never realized it before.' The identification of fantasy is always an attempt to avoid one's own suffering: the identification of art is the *sharing* in the suffering of another."

Tony Kushner: Activist Jewish Mystic

> Every living creature has a heart, and every heart a thread.
> And He of Holy Wisdom draws all the threads together.
> From the fiery threads is woven time, and thus new days are
>   made;
>
> Unto the heart is given, unto the spring is given.
> As the spring pours waters through the days, the heart of the
>   world looks on.
>
> And so the World continues, until the world is gone.
>   Tony Kushner from his adaptation of S. Ansky's *A Dybbuk*

> Kushner: *art can help change people, who then decide to change their own lives, change their neighborhood, their community, their society, the world. I don't think art alone changes people, but consciousness, the life of the mind, is a critical force for change and art helps the shaping of consciousness ... watching theater teaches people a way of looking at the world with a doubleness of vision that's immensely useful — transformative, even. The audience in the theater has to wrestle with the dialectical nature of illusion and reality, Art has a power, but it's an indirect power. Art suggests. When people are ready to receive such suggestion, it can and does translate into action —* [Higgins, *New York Times*. June 4, 2004, www.nytimes.com/archives].

In 2003, James Fisher published his book, *Tony Kushner: Living Past Hope*. His first criticism on Kushner was in 1999, in which he compared Kushner to Thornton Wilder in an essay titled, "Troubling the Waters: Visions of Apocalypse in Wilder's *The Skin of Our Teeth* and Kushner's *Angels in America*" (*Thornton Wilder: New Essays*, 1999). That earlier essay hinted at the later book's subtitle, *Living Past Hope*:

> In *Angels*, Kushner's apocalyptic harbinger is an angel and, in the final scene of *Perestroika*, the play's survivors meet at Central park's Bethesda Fountain — which features a statue of the biblical angel who "troubled the waters," the subject of one of Wilder's early "three-minute" plays, "The Angel That Troubled the Waters," 1928. Kushner uses this imagery at the end of *Perestroika* and throughout both plays he "troubles the waters" of American life in a way that permits revelation to his characters, just as Wilder's invalids hope for a cure to their ills and a new beginning. In "The Angel That Troubled the Waters," the angel asks the Healer, "Without your wound where would your power be?" [149].

The characters of both *Skin* and *Angels* grow strong from their suffering, just as the cripples in "The Angel That Troubled the Waters" are healed. Indeed, without his wound how could the healer truly understand the suffering of others? Hence, compassion and healing are partners. Wilder and Kushner are two dramatists that do not mind overtly displaying personal and socio-political agendas in their work. Wilder's may have been subtler, but he was no less emphatic. Kushner's anti–Reagan era, AIDS- and Gay-sympathetic play is not subtle at all about his didactic intentions.

Kushner's plays, however often they may depict pain and suffering, are ultimately all about the political and spiritual possibilities for hope and healing. Kushner gives critics the very beneficial service of providing numerous sources in which he explains himself. Kushner's own words reveal him as an articulate, erudite, and passionate spokesperson. "Since it's true that everything is political (though not exclusively so) it becomes meaningless to talk about political and nonpolitical theater, and more useful to speak of a theater that presents the world as it is, an interwoven web of the public and the private" (quoted in Fisher, 25).

The duality of "public/private" is the modus operandi of life and literature. If characters (and people) were exactly what they seemed, life would be saner, safer, and also a numbing bore. Kushner is not boring; he knows that oppositions, duality and ambiguity fuel the universe, and they provide the emotional and intellectual fire in his plays. And while he challenges audiences intellectually, Kushner never forgets that people wish to be entertained as well as enlightened.

While Kushner was born in New York City in 1956, he grew up as a Jew in Louisiana. In 1974 he returned to New York City to attend Columbia. Things changed quickly and sharply as he fell in love with the New York theater scene and embraced his gayness. Milestones for him were Richard Scheckner's production of Brecht's *Mother Courage and Her Children*, which Kushner thinks "is the greatest play ever written" (1), and Richard Foreman's version of *The Threepenny Opera*. Brecht became Kushner's model for political theater in terms of technique and social activism. "I believed that theater, really good theater, had the potential for radical intervention, for effectual analysis. The things that were exciting me about Marx, specifically dialectics, I discovered in Brecht, in a wonderful witty and provocative form. I became very, very excited about doing theater as a result of reading Brecht" (quoted in Fisher, 6). Ultimately, Brecht would lead Kushner to Walter Benjamin and to Raymond Williams, and these three would, along with Jewish Mysticism (Kabbalah), inform Kushner's views on political theater, his interpretation of historical forces, and a definition of socialism.

After reading Brecht, Kushner read Walter Benjamin's *Understanding Brecht*, and "Theses on the Philosophy of History." In Kushner's *A Bright Room Called Day*, a character says, "history repeats itself, first as tragedy, then as farce."

> Kushner ... shares Benjamin's belief that history (social, political, and personal) teaches profound lessons and he understands that the concepts of apocalypse and the afterlife are fraught with the same struggles, confusions, and pain encountered in real life. Kushner is inspired by Benjamin's assertion that, as [Kushner] describes it, one is "constantly looking back at the rubble of history. The most dangerous thing is to become set upon some notion of the future that isn't rooted in the bleakest, most terrifying idea of what's piled behind you" [Fisher, 7].

For Kushner, what was "piled behind" both A *Bright Room Called Day* and *Angels in America* was the 1980s of Reagan, neo-conservatism, anti–AIDS phobia and homophobia. Both plays use past history and tragedy to illustrate and teach in the present. *Bright Room*'s metaphor is Nazi Germany, and *Angels* uses Roy Cohn (who embodied the oxymoron of being a "gay homophobe"). Throughout Kushner's work Brecht provides the "how," Benjamin, the rationale, Raymond Williams, a future solution; mysticism forms his concept of social activism.

> The realm of socialism, Williams posits [in "Walking Backwards into the Future," 1985], is more than merely a place for "stranded utopians and sectarians...." In Williams' essays there is a belief that with socialism, the "power of private capital to shape or influence ... is replaced by active and often local social decision, in what is always in practice the real disposition of our lives," and there is "an immense and widespread longing for this kind of practical share in shaping our own lives. It has never yet been fully articulated politically and it is our strongest resource, if we can learn to deal honestly with it, for a socialist future." Williams envisions this future as one in which, "the public interest is not singular but is a complex and interactive network of *different* real interests. A sharing plan begins from this acknowledgement of *diversity*, and encourages the true social processes of open discussion, negotiation and agreement." Williams' concept of a socialist society significantly shapes Kushner's conception of America under Reagan. For Kushner, Reagan leads an abandonment

of the notion of a society concerned with the "longstanding problems of virtue and happiness...." A reformed society built on a progressive, compassionately humanist doctrine that draws its strength from the hard lessons of the past is central to both Williams' [and Benjamin's] theories and *Angels* [Fisher, 57].

In *Angels* Kushner uses Roy Cohn to symbolize the sum total of the Reagan era. Another character in *Angels* points to Cohn, who is dying of AIDS, and says, "I'll show you America. Terminal, crazy, and mean." Cohn represents Kushner's idea that if corruption and greed and badness exist in powerful members of a society, it will ultimately trickle down into each individual. While Kushner leans on Brecht, Benjamin, and Williams for an underlying philosophy behind his plays, it is Tennessee Williams's "spirit" and his homosexuality that became Kushner's inspiration for the tone of his plays. There are correlations between *Angels* and Williams's plays: classically epic emotions with dark and light poetic images of illusion and reality and the beautiful and the terrifying aspects of humanity. (Fisher also notes that besides Williams, Wilder, and O'Neill, Kushner is not too taken with other past American dramatists. Among contemporary Americans, he favors John Guare, who has also been inspired by Wilder.)

There are many more influences on Kushner: Marx, Trotsky, Christianity, Judaism, and Eastern versions of spirituality, German Classicism, the poets Rilke and Stanley Kunitz, recent contemporary theater — Richard Foreman, Harvey Fierstein, Charles Ludlam, Larry Kramer, Terence McNally, Paula Vogel (another Wilder fan), and Britons including Caryl Churchill and David Hare. Kushner's intellectual curiosity is wide and diverse and he brings this depth to his art and essays.

Kushner turned to Walter Benjamin's image of the Angel of History as the guiding metaphor. The very nature of a play with angels as a metaphor signifies mystical interest. Kushner's adaptation of S. Ansky's[3] *A Dybbuk* (1914), confirms this. A "dybbuk" is a Jewish soul that is restless, brooding, and homeless, and this soul attempts to enter the body of another person to try for a resolution. The male character, Chonen, a student of the Kabbala, is promised to Leah by his father, but Leah's father wants a more lucrative match, so he breaks the vow and she marries another. Chonen starves himself to death, a spiritually bereft death, and his soul wanders and comes to inhabit Leah. This type of possession is also featured in the Japanese Noh plays, and Yeats took the idea from the Noh and reprised it in his Celtic legend plays. Throughout history, the initial forms of religions derived from mystical antecedents that were not rigid. The mystical branches also keep their distance from dogma and religious orthodoxy. The dybbuk, Chonen, is exorcised from Leah. Nonetheless, when Leah dies, she and Chonen are reunited.

The significance of the play's subtitle, *Between Two Worlds*, is, in part, that the play works on dual levels: The character Solomon says, "Death resides in life, male in female, the spiritual in the female, religious doubt in devotion, evil in goodness, social well-being in private acts, Hasidism in modernity, the holy in the profane." This is a near–Upanishadic accounting of the Reconciliation of Opposites. By the character saying "in" for each pair, rather "to" or "versus" or "against," Kushner has enunciated the purest essence of how the opposites are working in tandem by design to fuel the fission of evolving consciousness. Kushner is an activist and speaks his mind concerning social, political, economic, and gay issues; he knows that each individual must change from within before he can truly act in the world.

Ansky's version and Kushner's end with this same verse:

Why did the soul,
Oh tell me this,
Tumble from Heaven
To the Great Abyss?
The most profound descents contain
Ascensions to the heights again ... [9, 106–7]

Chapter Notes

Introduction

1. *Philosophia Perennis*: The term *philosophia perennis* first appeared in the Renaissance although its intended meaning is much older. The term *philosophia perennis* is associated with the philosopher Leibniz, in whose writings it appears and whose thought aims at many characteristics essential to it; however, he himself found it in Augustinus Steuchius, a theologian of the sixteenth century who in 1540 published the *De philosophia perenni sive veterum philosophorum cum theologia christiana consensu libri X*, a work which quickly passed through several editions. The term has also been applied retroactively to the Scholastics. Steuch's work returns to a revealed absolute truth made known to man before his fall. Leibniz in the next century and in the later years of his life took the term for the philosophy he was developing. Leibniz had already known of Steuch, noting him and his work in his journals. In these journals Leibniz gives a brief sketch of the contributions of the major schools and also makes a reference to the East.

2. Even science, that kingdom of supposed empirical objectivity, is dependent on language in order to learn science and make new discoveries about science. Since scientists are using language to explain discoveries, and since language is a medium of subjective interpretation, science is not nearly so objective as might be assumed. Michael Polanyi, scientist and philosopher, makes this case in *Personal Knowledge* (an early salvo of post-modernism). All efforts to acquire knowledge are personal, meaning subjective, not objective. When Polanyi says that "we know more than we can say" (*Tacit Dimension*), he is asserting that language is merely the outcome or tip of a vast iceberg that contains knowledge held both consciously and unconsciously in the mind and memory from which we reflexively make correlations that can be enunciated or acted upon. The above introduction to which this note refers is a synthesized outcome of much reading, research, and life experience that knows much more than it can say.

We must conclude that the paradigmatic case of scientific knowledge, in which all faculties that are necessary for finding and holding scientific knowledge are fully developed, is the knowledge of approaching discovery.

To hold such knowledge is an act deeply committed to the conviction that there is something there to be discovered. It is personal, in the sense of involving the personality of him who holds it, and also in the sense of being, as a rule, solitary; but there is no trace in it of self-indulgence. The discoverer is filled with a compelling sense of responsibility for the pursuit of a hidden truth, which demands his services for revealing it. His act of knowing exercises a personal judgment in relating evidence to an external reality, an aspect of which he is seeking to apprehend [Polanyi, *Tacit Dimension*, 24–25].

3. Huxley discusses upward and downward transcendence in his book, *Grey Eminence*.

Chapter 1

1. While Vedanta's fundamentals are simple, the philosophy of Vedanta is no less com-

plex in detail than any other philosophy, East or West. There has been a Western tendency to see only the "dumbing-down" (as per Horkheimer and Adorno's "The Culture Industry") of Vedanta by pseudo-mystics who make it mind-candy for pop culture acquisition by the constituents of a "fix-it-quick," less-than-discerning public.

2. Adi Shankaracharya, "Shankara" (788–820). Shankara's philosophy is called Kevaladvaita, and is a guide to Vedanta. The Supreme Spirit or the Brahman is alone real and the individual self is only the Supreme Self and no other. Brahman is supreme intelligence, devoid of attributes, form, changes or limitations. It is self-luminous and all pervading and is without a second. The empirical world is unreal, an illusion born of ignorance. The spirit of an individual continues in reincarnation only as long as it retains attachment due to ignorance or Maya. If it casts off the veil of Maya through spiritual knowledge it will realize its identity with the Brahman (Ultimate Reality). Isherwood and Prabhavananda translated Shankara's seminal text, *The Crest Jewel of Discrimination*.

Chapter 3

1. Abhinavagupta lived in Kashmir in northern India at the end of the 10th century and beginning of the 11th century. He was a scholar and prolific writer, as well as a highly accomplished yogi. His commentary on the Bhagavad-Gita, known in Sanskrit as the *Gitartha Samgraha*, was one of the very earliest. In addition to his work on philosophy and spirituality, he wrote on dramaturgy, poetics, rhetoric and aesthetics. See Patrick Colm Hogan, "Toward a Cognitive Science of Poetics: Anandavardhana, Abhinavagupta, and the Theory of Literature," *College Literature* 23, 1 (February 1996): 164 (15 pages).

Bharata's *Natyashastra* (c. 600 B.C.) was a treatise on Indian art — music, dance, literature — from a Vedantist perspective.

Chapter 4

1. Purohit was born in India on October 12, 1882. As a child he became proficient in Marathi, English, and Sanskrit. He was well educated, obtaining a B.A. in philosophy at Calcutta University in 1903 and a law degree from Deccan College and Bombay University. Purohit never practiced as a lawyer. In 1930 he went to Europe where he met W.B. Yeats, who became a friend and helped arrange for the publication of Purohit's books. These included *The Autobiography of an Indian Monk* (1932), a translation of Hamsa Swami's *The Holy Mountain* (1934), a translation of the *Bhagavad-Gita Gita* (1935), a translation of *The Ten Principal Upanishads* (in collaboration with Yeats, 1937), and a translation of Gitanjali's *Aphorisms of Yoga* (1938).

2. Buddha teaches that desire and temptation are a terrible fire that will destroy the body, and more importantly, deny the spirit in that body its spiritual salvation. One must abnegate the willful ego and refuse materiality for its own sake. One can live in the material world while not being affected by it if the spirit remains pure.

3. In the early 1990s film *Mad Max beyond Thunderdome*, Max (Mel Gibson) faces a kangaroo court where the motto is "break a deal, face the wheel." The wheel has diverse punishments and it is spun to determine which will be meted out.

4. Johnson, PhD, Edwin Clark (Toby), Catholic monk turned activist, psychotherapist and spiritual writer, was born in 1945 in San Antonio TX. He entered religious life after high school, first as a Marianist and then as a Servite. After leaving seminary in 1970, he moved to San Francisco and lived in the Bay Area throughout the 1970s. While a student at the California Institute of Integral Studies, from which he received a master's in Comparative Religion and a doctorate in Counseling Psychology, Johnson was on staff at the Mann Ranch Seminars, a Jungian-oriented summer retreat program. There he befriended religion scholar Joseph Campbell and came to regard himself "an apostle of Campbell's vision to the gay community."

5. Paul Eros wrote a very fine essay on Auden and Heard: "A Prevision of Agape: Gerald Heard's Importance to Auden" in *W.H. Auden: A Legacy*, ed. David Garrett Izzo (West Cornwall, CT: Locust Hill Press, 2002).

Chapter 5

1. This copy is in the Izzo collection.
2. For example: Sophia Mokotoff wrote about Salinger and Vedanta in 2002: (//data.georgetown.edu/faculty/ejm/engl893/finals/slm24/sophiasalinger.htm), and there is "The

Holy Refusal": A Vedantic Interpretation of J.D. Salinger's Silence" by Dipti R. Pattanaik, from *MELUS* Summer, 1998. This essay concludes that "keeping in mind the limited scope and inability of literary criticism to ascertain a writer's inner life, we can decode Salinger's silence as loud protest against the current aggressive, competitive action-ethic of the West, its largely materialistic pursuits with great emphasis on social success which whips up vainglory and pride, its acquisitive spirit and penchant for sensual pleasures that money and hypocrisy can buy" (*www.find articles.com/cf_0/m2278/2_23/54543100/p1/ article.jhtml*).

3. Ansky was a pseudonym for Schloyme Zanul Rapporport (1863–1920), who was born in Russia.

Bibliography

Achebe, Chinua. "Dead Man's Path." *Ways of Reading*, 5th edition. Ed. David Bartholomae and Anthony Petroksky. New York: Bedford/St. Martin's, 1999.
Adorno, Theodore, and Max Horkheimer. "The Culture Industry: Enlightenment as Mass Deception." Online at www.marxists.org/reference/subject/philosophy/works/ge/adorno.htm.
_____. The Culture Industry: Selected Essays on Mass Culture. London: Routledge, 1991.
Æ. *Letters from Æ*. Ed. Alan Denson. London: Abelard-Shuman, 1961.
_____. *Selected Poems*. New York: Macmillan, 1935.
_____. *Song and Its Fountains*. London: Macmillan, 1932.
Aithal, S. Krishnamoorthy. "Indian Allusions in Ulysses." *Eire-Ireland*, 14.4 (Summer 1979): 141–44.
Althaus, Horst. *Hegel: An Intellectual Biography*. London: Blackwell Publishers, 2000.
Ando, Shoei. *Zen and American Transcendentalism*. Tokyo: Hokuseido Press, 1970.
Auden, W. H. "Adam as a Welshman." *New York Review of Books*, 1 (Feb. 1963).
_____. *The Age of Anxiety*. New York: Random House, 1947.
_____. *A Certain World: A Commonplace Book*. New York: Viking, 1970.
_____. *Collected Poems*. New York: Random House, 1976.
_____. "The Dyer's Hand." *The Anchor Review*. New York: Doubleday Anchor Books, 1957, 255–301.
_____. *The Dyer's Hand*. New York: Random House, 1962.
_____. *The English Auden*. Ed. Edward Mendelson, New York: Random House, 1977.
_____. *Forewords and Afterwords*. Ed. Edward Mendelson, New York: Random House, 1973.
_____. "The Group Movement and the Middle Classes." *Oxford and the Groups*. Ed. R.H.S. Crossman. Oxford: Blackwell, 1934.
_____. "In Defence of Gossip." *Listener*, 18 (1937): 1371–1372.
_____. "Interview with W.H. Auden." *Antaeus*. New York: Ecco Press, Spring 1972, 135–144.
_____. "Interview with W.H. Auden." *Writers at Work: Paris Review Interviews*, Fourth Series. New York: Viking, 1976.
_____. "Introduction." *Shakespeare: The Sonnets*. New York: Signet Classics, 1964.
_____. *Letter to Lord Byron in Collected Poems*. Ed. Edward Mendelson. New York: Random House, 1976.
_____. "The Magician from Mississippi," *Mid-Century*, No. 8 (1960): 3–9.
_____. "Mimesis & Allegory." *English Institute Essays*, New York: Columbia University Press, 1941, 1–19.

_____. "Nature, History, and Poetry." *Thought*, 25 (1950): 412–422.
_____. "New Year Letter." *Collected Poems*. New York: Random House, 1976.
_____. "A Novel by Goethe." *New York Times*, Oct. 18, 1964, Section 7, 2.
_____. *Poets of the English Language III*. New York: Viking Press, 1950.
_____. *The Prolific and the Devourer*. Hopewell, NJ: Ecco Press, 1993.
_____. "The Protestant Mystics." *Forewords and Afterwords*. London: Faber and Faber, 1973. 49–78.
_____. "The Real World." *The New Republic*. December 9, 1967, 25–27.
_____. "Review of Open House (Roethke)." *Saturday Review of Literature*, April 5, 1941, 30–31.
_____. "Robert Frost." *The Dyer's Hand*. New York: Random House, 1962, 337–53.
_____. "The Sea and the Mirror." *For the Time Being*, New York: Random House, 1944.
_____. *Secondary Worlds*. New York: Random House, 1968.
_____. "The Secret Agent." Ed. Edward Mendelson. *W. H. Auden: Collected Poems*. London: Faber and Faber, 1976. 41.
_____. *Shakespeare, The Sonnets*. New York: Signet Classics, 1964.
_____. "Squares and Oblongs." *Poets at Work*. New York: Harcourt, Brace, 1948.
_____. "A Summer's Night." *W. H. Auden: Collected Poems*. Ed. Edward Mendelson. London: Faber and Faber, 1976.
_____. "Today's Poet." *Mademoiselle*. April 1962, 187.
_____. "Walter de la Mare." *Forewords and Afterwords*. New York: Random House, 1976, 384–94.
_____. "Words and the Word." *Secondary Worlds*. New York: Random House, 1968, 117–44.
_____, ed. *The Living Thoughts of Kierkegaard*. Bloomington: Midland Books, 1963.
_____, with Christopher Isherwood. *The Ascent of F6*. New York: Random House, 1937.
Balk, Mary McArdle. "Yeats's "John Sherman": An Early Attempt to Reconcile Opposites." *Yeats Eliot Review* 6.i (1979): 45–50.
Bandyopadhyaya, Pranab. *Great Indian Saints*. Calcutta: United Writers, 1993.
Barrie, Jay Michael. "Introduction." *Training for the Life of the Spirit*, by Gerald Heard. New York: Rudolph Steiner Publications, 1975.
Bedford, Sybille. *Aldous Huxley*. London: Chatto & Windus, 1973.
Benton, Jill. *Naomi Mitchison: A Century of Experiment in Life and Letters*. London: Pandora, 1990.
Berg, James, and Christopher Freeman. *Conversations with Christopher Isherwood*. Jackson: Mississippi University Press, 2001.
_____, eds. *Isherwood Century*. Madison: University of Wisconsin, 2000.
The Bhagavad-Gita. Trans. Prabhavananda and Christopher Isherwood. Los Angeles: Marcel Rodd, 1944.
Blank, Martin, ed. *Critical Essays on Thornton Wilder*. New York: G.K. Hall, 1996.
Bloom, Harold. "Introduction." *Selected Writings of Walter Pater*. New York: Columbia University Press, 1974.
Bowering, Peter. *The Novels of Aldous Huxley*. London: University of London Press, 1968.
Brahma, N. K. *Philosophy of Hindu Sadhana*, London: Kegan Paul Trench, Trubner, 1932. Reprint. 1999.
Bridges, Hal. *American Mysticism*. New York: Harper & Row, 1970.
Buber, Martin. "Ueber Jakob Boehme," *Wiener Rundschau* V, 12 (June 15, 1901): 251–253. Translation: Bruce Janz & Eve Sommerfeld. Online at pegasus.cc.ucf.edu/~janzb/boehme/wienrund.htm.
_____. "Zur Geschichte des Individuations Problem (Nicolaus von Cusa und Jacob

Boehme)." Buber's Doctoral Dissertation for University of Vienna, 1904, currently in the Martin Buber Archives, Tel Aviv, Israel, 38, SR 16:63.
Bucknell, Katherine. "Auden's Writing Essay." *W. H. Auden: "The Map of All My Youth."* Ed. Katherine Bucknell and Nicholas Jenkins. Oxford: Clarendon Press, 1990.
Byer, James Edwin, "The Literary Criticism of W.H. Auden: Theory and Practice." Dissertation, Duke University, 1971, 79–84.
Callan, Edward. *Auden: A Carnival of Intellect.* Oxford: Oxford University Press, 1983.
Campbell, Joseph. *A Joseph Campbell Companion.* Ed. Diane K. Osborn. New York: HarperCollins. 1992,
_____. *Myths to Live By.* New York: Bantam, 1988.
_____, and Henry Morton Robinson. *A Skeleton Key to Finnegans Wake.* New York: Harcourt, Brace, 1944.
Carpenter, Humphrey. *W.H. Auden, A Biography.* New York: Houghton Mifflin, 1981.
Cather, Willa. *Death Comes for the Archbishop.* New York: Alfred A, Knopf, 1927.
Caudwell, Christopher. *Illusion and Reality.* London: Macmillan, 1937.
Clarke, J.J. *Oriental Enlightenment: The Encounter between Asian and Western Thought.* London: Routledge, 1997.
Connelly, Joseph F. "J. B. Yeats's Imaginative Forays into Writing: Memory, Moment and Creative Impulse." *Notes on Modern Irish Literature* 7, no. 1 (1995): 41–49.
Coomaraswamy, Ananda K. *The Dance of Shiva.* New York: Dover, 1985.
Cowley, Malcolm. *After the Genteel Tradition.* New York: Norton, 1936.
_____. "Time Abolished." *A Second Flowering.* New York: Viking, 1973, 114–29.
Davie, Donald. "T. S. Eliot: The End of an Era," *Twentieth Century* 159, no. 950 (April 1956): 350–62.
Davenport, Guy. "The Death of Picasso." *The Death of Picasso and Other Writings.* Washington, D.C.: Shoemaker & Hoard, 2003.
_____. *The Hunter Gracchus and Other Essays.* New York: Counterpoint Press, 1997.
DeLaura, David. *Hebrew and Hellene in Victorian England: Newman, Arnold, and Pater.* Austin: University of Texas Press, 1969.
DeLillo, Don. *Underworld.* New York: Scribner's, 1997.
Derbyshire, John. "Whatever Happened to Aldous Huxley." *New Criterion.* February, 2003.
Deussen, Paul. *Outline of the Vedanta System of Philosophy according to Shankara.* Trans. from French by J.H. Woods & C.B. Runkle. Cambridge, MA: Harvard University Press, 1927.
Dewey, Joseph, Steven G. Kellman, and Irving Malin, Eds. *Underworlds: Perspectives on Don DeLillo's "Underworld."* Newark: University of Delaware Press, 2002.
Doherty, Gerald. "The World That Shines and Sounds: W. B. Yeats and Daisetz Suzuki." *Irish Renaissance Annual* 4 (1983): 57–75.
Donaldson, Scott. *Archibald MacLeish: An American Life.* Boston: Houghton Mifflin, 1992.
Dunaway, David King. *Huxley in Hollywood.* New York: Harper & Row, 1989.
Durant, Will. *Story of Civilization: Our Oriental Heritage.* New York: Simon and Schuster, 1935.
Dwivedi, N. "The Indian Temper in Eliot's Poetry." *Banasthali Patrika*, 19 (1972): 48–53.
Eglinton, John. *A Memoir of Æ.* London: Macmillan, 1937.
Eliade, Mircea. *The Forge and the Crucible.* Harper & Row, 1962.
_____. *Shamanism: Archaic Techniques of Ecstasy.* Bollingen Series LXXVI. Princeton, NJ: Princeton University Press, 1972.
_____. *Yoga: Immortality and Freedom.* New York: Pantheon Books, 1958
Eliot, T.S. *After Strange Gods: A Primer of Modern Heresy.* London: Faber, 1933.
_____. "Burnt Norton." Online at www.allspirit.co.uk/norton.html.
_____. "Christianity and Communism," *The Listener*, 16 March 1932, 383.

_____. *Christianity and Culture*. New York: Harcourt, Brace, and World, 1949.
_____. "A Commentary." *Criterion*, 3, no. 11 (April 1925): 342.
_____. "East Coker." *Four Quartets*. New York: Harcourt, Brace, and World, 1943.
_____. "Foreword" to G. V. Desani's *Hali, A Play*. London: Saturn Press, 1950.
_____. "The Preacher as Artist." *The Athenaeum*, 28 November 1919, p. 1252.
_____. "Preface" to *Thoughts for Meditation; A Way to Recovery from Within*. Ed. N. Gangulee. Boston: Beacon Press, 1952.
_____. "Review of Study of Hindu Philosophy: Sri Ananda Acharya." *International Journal of Ethics*, 28, no. 3 (April 1918): 445–446. The author is given as "T. S. E."
_____. "'T. S. Eliot Answers Questions" [1949]. *T. S. Eliot: Homage from India*. Ed. P. Lal. Interview by Ranjee Shahani. Calcutta: Writers Workshop, 1965.
_____. *The Use of Poetry and the Use of Criticism*. London: Faber, 1933.
_____. *The Waste Land. A Facsimile and Transcript of the Original Drafts*. London: Faber and Faber, 1971.
_____. "The Waste Land." *The Norton Anthology of Modern Poetry*. Ed. Richard Ellmann and Robert O'Clair. New York: Norton, 1988.
Ellmann, Richard. *James Joyce*. Revised Ed. Oxford: Oxford University Press, 1983.
Emerson, Ralph Waldo. *The Complete Works of Ralph Waldo Emerson*. Concord Edition. 12 Vols. Boston and New York: Houghton Mifflin, 1903.
_____. *Journals of Ralph Waldo Emerson*. 10 Vols. Ed., Edward Waldo Emerson and Waldo Emerson Forbes. Boston: Houghton Mifflin, 1909–1914, 7:241–42 and 7:511.
_____. *The Letters of Ralph Waldo Emerson*. Ed. Ralph L. Rusk. 6 vols. New York and London: Columbia University Press, 1939.
Eros, Paul. "A Prevision of Agape: Gerald Heard's Importance to Auden." *W.H. Auden: A Legacy*. Ed. David Garrett Izzo. West Cornwall, CT: Locust Hill Press, 2002.
Feuerstein, Georg, Subhash Kak, and David Frawley. *In Search of the Cradle of Civilization: New Light on Ancient India*. Wheaton, IL: Quest Books, 1995,
Finney, Brian. *Christopher Isherwood: A Critical Biography*. London: Oxford University Press, 1976.
Fisher, James. *The Theater of Tony Kushner*. New York: Routledge, 2002.
Friedman, Barton R. "Yeatsian (Meta) Physics: The Resurrection and the Irrational." *Yeats: An Annual of Critical and Textual Studies*, 8 (1990): 144–165.
Fry, Roger. "To G. L. Dickinson," 27 November 1931, letter 675 of *The Letters of Roger Fry* Vol. 2. London: Chatto and Windus, 1972.
Gardner, Philip. "Verse Plays for Radio." *Proceedings of the Archibald MacLeish Symposium*. Ed. Bernard Drabeck, Helen Ellis, and Seymour Rudin. Lanham, MD: University Press of America, 1988, 96–104.
Garrett, Eileen. *Many Voices: The Autobiography of a Medium*. New York: Putnam, 1968.
Gautier, Francois. *Arise O' India!* New Delhi: Har-Anand Publication, 1997.
George Gessner, ed. *Anthology of American Poetry*. New York: Gramercy, 1994.
Ghosh, D.B. "The Concept of Karma in T. S. Eliot." *Jabalpur Journal of Comparative Literature*, 12 (1974): 14–21.
_____. "Karma as a Mode of Salvation in T. S. Eliot," *Jabalpur Journal of Comparative Literature*, 12 (1974): 125–135.
Gibbon, Monk. "Foreword." *Letters from Æ*. Ed. Alan Denson. London: Abulard Shuman, 1961, xii–xvi.
Gilbert, Stuart. *James Joyce's Ulysses: A Study*. New York: Vintage Books, 1955.
Gillespie, Diane, and Leslie Hankins, eds. *Virginia Woolf and the Arts: Selected Papers from the Sixth Annual Conference on Virginia Woolf*. Clemson University, June 13–16, 1996. New York: Pace University Press, 1997.
Gitanjali. *Aphorisms of Yoga*. Trans. Purohit Swamy. Introduction by W.B. Yeats. London: Faber and Faber, 1937.

Gitanjali (aka Patangali). *Song Offerings*. Trans. Rabindranath Tagore. Introduction by W. B. Yeats. New York and London: Macmillan, 1912.
Glasheen, Adaline. *Third Census of Finnegans Wake: An Index of the Characters and Their Roles*. Berkeley: University of California Press, 1977.
Gokhale, B.G. *India in the American Mind*. Bombay: Popular Prakashan, 1992.
Gough, Val. "'With Some Irony in Her Interrogation': Woolf's Ironic Mysticism." *Virginia Woolf and the Arts: Selected Papers from the Sixth Annual Conference on Virginia Woolf*, Clemson University, June 13–16, 1996. Ed. Diane F. Gillespie and Leslie K. Hankins. New York: Pace University Press, 1997, 85–90.
Grant, Sara. *Toward an Alternative Theology: Confessions of a Non-Dualist Christian*. South Bend, IN: University of Notre Dame Press, 2001.
Guenon, Rene. *Study of the Hindu Doctrines*. London: Luzac, 1945,
Halfbass, Wilhelm. *India and Europe*. Albany: State University of New York Press, 1988.
Harrison, Gilbert. *The Enthusiast: A Life of Thornton Wilder*. New York: Ticknor & Fields, 1983.
Harrison, Thomas J. *1910: The Emancipation of Dissonance*. Los Angeles: University of California Press, 1996. Online at www.italian.ucla.edu/faculty/harrison/Essays/1910_Introduction.htm.
Hazelton, Lesley. "Doris Lessing on Feminism, Communism and 'Space Fiction.'" *New York Times*, July 25, 1982. Online at //partners.nytimes.com/books/99/01/10/specials/lessing-space.html.
Heard, Gerald. *The Ascent of Humanity*. London: Jonathan Cape, 1929.
_____. *The Code of Christ*. New York: Harper & Bros., 1941.
_____. *The Creed of Christ* .New York: Harper & Bros., 1940. (This book and *The Code of Christ* are reinterpretations of the New Testament with the overview of Vedanta.)
_____. *The Emergence of Man*. London: Jonathan Cape, 1931.
_____. *The Five Ages of Man*. New York: Julian Press, 1963.
_____. "The History of Ideas, or How We Got Separate." *An Outline for Boys and Girls and Their Parents*. Ed. Naomi Mitchison. London: Gollancz, 1932, 417–59.
_____. "Men and Books." Rev. of *Ancient Art and Social Ritual* by Jane Harrison. *The Sacred Dance* by W. O. Osterley. *Time and Tide*, 26 October 1935: 1545–46.
_____. "Philosophia Perennis." *Vedanta for the Western World*. Ed. Christopher Isherwood. Los Angeles: Marcel Rodd, 1946.
_____. *A Preface to Prayer*. New York: Harper & Bros., 1944.
_____. "Religion and the Problems of Modern Society." *Time and Tide*, 30 January 1932, 115–116; 6 February 1932, 145–146; 13 February 1932, 168; 20 February 1932, 197–98.
_____. "Rev. of *Exploring the Stratosphere*." *Times Literary Supplement*, 27 June 1936, 547.
_____. "Rev. of *Science Front, 1936*." *Times Literary Supplement*, 15 May 1937, 382–83.
_____. "The Significance of the New Pacifism." *The New Pacifism* Ed. Gerald K. Hibbert. London: Allenson, 1936, 13–22.
_____. *The Social Substance of Religion*. London: Allen and Unwin, 1931.
_____. *The Source of Civilization*. London: Jonathan Cape, 1935.
_____. *Training for the Life of the Spirit*. New York: Rudolph Steiner Publications, 1975.
Hegel, G.F. "Introduction." On the Philosophy of Religions. Online at www.marxists.org/reference/archive/hegel/works/re/parta.htm.
_____. *Lectures on the Philosophy of Religions*. Trans. E. B. Speirs and J. B. Sanderson. Distributed for the Thoemmes Continuum. 1895 Edition. 3 Volumes. 1895, 1999.
Higgins, Chester. "10 Questions for Tony Kushner." *New York Times*. June 4, 2004, www.nytimes.com/archives.
Hinduism Today, 59 (April-May-June 2004). Online at www.hinduismtoday.com.
Hoffman, Daniel. *An Armada of Thirty Whales*. New Haven: Yale University Press, 1954.

Hogan, Paul Colm. "Toward a Cognitive Science of Poetics: Anandavardhana, Abhinavagupta, and the Theory of Literature." *College Literature*, 23, no. 1 (February 1996): 164 (15 pages).
Hornby, Nick. "Rock of Ages," *New York Times*. Online at www.nytimes.com/2004/05/21/opinion/21HORN.html.
Hoult, Powis. *A Dictionary of Some Theosophical Terms*. London: Theosophical Publishing Society, 1910.
The Thirteen Principal Upanishads. Trans. R. E. Hume. London: Oxford University Press, 1934.
Huxley, Aldous. *After Many a Summer Dies the Swan*. New York: Harper's, 1939.
———. *Aldous Huxley: Between the Wars*. Chicago: Ivan R. Dee, 1994.
———. *Along The Road*. London: Chatto & Windus, 1925.
———. *Ape and Essence*. New York: Harper & Bros., 1948.
———. "Art." *The Human Situation*. New York: Harper & Row, 1977.
———. *Beyond the Mexique Bay*. London: Chatto & Windus, 1934.
———. *Brave New World*. London: Chatto & Windus, 1932.
———. *The Burning Wheel*. London: Blackwell, 1916.
———. *Crome Yellow*. London: Chatto & Windus, 1921.
———. *The Devils of Loudon*. New York: Harper, 1952.
———. *Do What You Will*. London: Chatto & Windus, 1929.
———. *Ends and Means*. New York: Harper & Bros., 1937.
———. *Essays New and Old*. New York: George H. Doran, 1927.
———. *Eyeless in Gaza*. London: Chatto & Windus, 1936.
———. *Grey Eminence*. New York: Harper & Bros., 1941.
———. *The Human Situation*. New York: Harper & Row, 1977.
———. "Introduction." *The Bhagavad-Gita*. Trans. Isherwood-Prabhavananda. Los Angeles: Marcel Rodd, 1944, 5–18.
———. " Introduction." Krishnamurti. *The First and Last Freedom*. New York: Harper's, 1954.
———. *Island*. New York: Harper & Row, 1962.
———. "Knowledge and Understanding." *Adonis and the Alphabet*. New York: Harpers, 1956.
———. *Letters of Aldous Huxley*. London: Chatto & Windus, 1969.
———. *Literature and Science*. New York: Harper & Row, 1963.
———. "Man and Religion." *The Human Situation*. New York: Harper & Row, 1959.
———. *Music at Night*. London: Chatto & Windus, 1931.
———. *The Olive Tree*. London: Chatto & Windus, 1936.
———. "On Language." *The MIT Lectures, Tiburon (CA): Big Sur Tapes*. 1972.
———. *On the Margin*. London: Chatto & Windus, 1923.
———. "One and Many." *Do What You Will*. London: Chatto & Windus, 1929.
———. *The Perennial Philosophy*. New York: Harper, 1945.
———. *Point Counter Point*. London: Chatto & Windus, 1928.
———."The Subject Matter of Poetry." *On The Margin*. London: Chatto & Windus, 1923, 26–38.
———. *Texts and Pretexts*. London: Chatto & Windus, 1932.
———. *Themes and Variations*. New York: Harper & Bros., 1950.
———. *Time Must Have a Stop*. New York: Harpers, 1944.
———. *Tomorrow and Tomorrow and Tomorrow*. New York: Harper's, 1956.
———. "Tragedy and the Whole Truth." *Music at Night*. London: Chatto & Windus, 1931, 3–18.
———. *Vulgarity in Literature*. London: Chatto & Windus, 1931.
———. *Words and Their Meanings*. Los Angeles: Ward Ritchie Press, 1940.

──. *Writers at Work: The Paris Review Interviews, Second Series*. New York: Viking, 1965.
Huxley, Laura. *A Personal View of Aldous Huxley: This Timeless Moment*. New York: Farrar, Strauss, Giroux, 1968.
Hynes, Samuel. *The Auden Generation*. Princeton: Princeton University Press, 1976.
Jameson, Frederick. *Marxism and Form: Twentieth-Century Dialectical Theories of Literature*. Princeton, NJ: Princeton University Press, 1972.
Isherwood, Christopher. *An Approach to Vedanta*. Hollywood: Vedanta Press, 1963.
──. "The Art of Fiction: Christopher Isherwood." Interview with W.I. Scobie. *Writers at Work: The Paris Review Interviews, Fourth Series*. Ed. George Plimpton. New York: Viking, 1974.
──. "Christopher Isherwood." *Writers at Work: The Paris Review Interviews, Fourth Series*. Ed. George Plimpton. New York: Viking, 1974.
──. *Diaries: 1939–1960*. Ed. Katherine Bucknell. San Francisco: Harper, 1996.
──. *Exhumations*. New York: Simon and Schuster, 1966.
──. *How to Know God: The Yogi Aphorisms of Patanjali*. Trans. with commentary Isherwood-Swami Prabhavananda. New York: Harper, 1953.
──. *The Intimate Journals of Charles Baudelaire*. Trans. Hollywood: Marcel Rodd, 1947.
──. *Down There on a Visit*. New York: Simon and Schuster, 1961.
──. *Lions and Shadows*. London: Hogarth Press, 1938.
──. *A Meeting by the River*. New York: Simon and Schuster, 1967.
──. *Prater Violet*. New York: Random House, 1945.
──. *Ramakrishna and His Disciples*. New York: Simon and Schuster, 1965.
──. *Shankara's Crest Jewel of Discrimination*. Trans. with Swami Prabhavananda Hollywood: Vedanta Press, 1947.
──. *A Single Man*. New York: Simon and Schuster, 1964.
──. *The Song of God: Bhagavad-Gita*. Trans. with Swami Prabhavananda. Hollywood, Marcel Rodd, 1944.
──. "Virginia Woolf." *Exhumations*. New York: Simon and Schuster, 1966.
──. *The Wishing Tree: Writings on Mystical Religion*. San Francisco: Harper's, 1987.
──, ed. *Vedanta for Modern Man*. New York: Harper, 1951.
──, ed. *Vedanta for the Western World*. New York: Marcel Rodd, 1945.
──, and W.H. Auden. *The Ascent of F6*. New York: Random House, 1937.
Ito, Eishiro. "Mediterranean Joyce Meditates on Buddha." *Language and Culture* (Center for Language and Culture Education and Research, Iwate Prefectural University), no. 5 (January 2003): 53–64.
Jackson, Carl T., *The Oriental Religions and American Thought: Nineteenth-Century Explorations*. Westport, CT: Greenwood Press, 1981.
──. *Vedanta for the West*. Bloomington: Indiana University Press, 1994.
Jaffe, Aniela. *Was Jung a Mystic? (and Other Essays)*. Einsiedeln, Switzerland: Daimon Verlag, 1989.
Jain, Sushil. "Indian Elements in the Poetry of W. B. Yeats with Special Reference to Yeats' Relationship with Chatterjee and Tagore." *Comparative Literature Studies*, 7 (1970): 82–96.
Jaurretche, Colleen. *The Sensual Philosophy: Joyce and the Aesthetics of Mysticism*. Madison: University of Wisconsin, 1997.
Jensen, Ejner. "The Antinomical Vision of W. B. Yeats." *Xavier Review*, 3 (1964): 127–45.
Joad, C.E.M. *Counter Attacks from the East*. London: G. Allen & Unwin, 1933.
Johnson, Edwin Clark (Toby). *The Myth of the Great Secret*. New York: Morrow, 1982.
Joyce, James. *The Critical Writings of James Joyce*. Ed. Ellsworth Mason & Richard Ellmann. Ithaca, NY: Cornell University Press, 1990.

_____. *A Portrait of the Artist as a Young Man*. London: Penguin.
_____. *Stephen Hero*. New York: A New Directions Book, 1963.
_____. *Ulysses*. London: The Bodley Head, 1986.
_____. *Ulysses Annotated*. Ed. Don Gifford and Robert J. Seidman. 2nd Ed. Berkeley: University of California Press, 1988.
Jung, C.G. *Psychological Types*. New York: Routledge, 1971.
Kain, Richard M., and James H. O'Brien. *George Russell (Æ)*. Lewisburg, PA: Bucknell University Press, 1976.
Kane, Julie. "Varieties of Mystical Experience in the Writings of Virginia Woolf." *Twentieth Century Literature*, 41, no. 4: 328–49.
Kenner, Hugh. *The Invisible Poet: T S. Eliot*. New York: Harcourt, Brace and World, 1959, 289–323. Published first (1949) in *Hudson Review* as "Eliot's Moral Dialectic."
Kierkegaard, Søren. *The Living Thoughts of Kierkegaard*. Ed. by W. H. Auden. Bloomington: Midland Books, 1963.
_____. [Various selections] in *The Viking Book of Aphorisms*. New York: Viking, 1962.
Knapp. Stephen. *Proof of Vedic Culture's Global Existence*. Detroit: World Relief Network, 1998, introduction, vii.
Kulkarni, H.B. *Moby Dick: A Hindu Avatar, a Study of Hindu Myth and Thought in Moby-Dick*. Orem: Utah State University Press, 1970.
Kuner, M.C. *Thornton Wilder: The Bright and the Dark*. New York: Crowell, 1972.
Lannoy, Richard. *The Speaking Tree: A Study of Indian Culture and Society*. London: Oxford University Press, 1971.
Lao Tzu. *The Way of Life*. Trans. Witter Bynner. New York: John Day, 1944.
Lavine, T. Z. *From Socrates to Sartre: The Philosophic Quest*. New York: Bantam, 1984.
Leavis, F.R. "Four Quartets." *The Living Principle*. *"English" as a Discipline of Thought*. New York: Oxford University Press, 1975, p. 159.
Lenoski, Daniel. "W. B. Yeats: God and Imagination." *English Studies in Canada*, 6 (1980): 84–93.
Lessing, Doris. *The Golden Notebook*. New York: Harper Perennial, 1999.
_____. "Sketches from Bohemia." *The Guardian*, Saturday June 14, 2003. Online at books.guardian.co.uk/review/story/0,12084,976709,00.html,
_____. *Under My Skin: Volume One of My Autobiography, to 1949*. Hammersmith, London: HarperCollins, 1994.
Lita, Ana. "'Seeing' Human Goodness: Iris Murdoch On Moral Virtue." *Minerva — An Internet Journal of Philosophy*, 7 (2003). Online at www.ul.ie/~philos/vol7/murdoch.html.
London, D.P. *India and World Civilization*. London: Macmillan, 1993.
London, J.J. *Oriental Enlightenment: The Encounter between Asian and Western Thought*. New York: Routledge, 1997.
Londraville, Richard. "The Dramatic Function of Yeats's Dreaming Back." *Yeats: An Annual of Critical and Textual Studies*, 7 (1989): 99–124.
M. *Gospel of Ramakrishna*. Foreword by Christopher Isherwood. New York: Vedanta Society, 1947.
MacLeish, Archibald. *Air Raid*. New York: Harcourt, Brace, 1938.
_____. *Conquistador*. Boston: Houghton Mifflin, 1932.
_____. "Expatriates in Paris." *Riders on the Earth*. Boston: Houghton Mifflin, 1978, 89–93.
_____. *The Fall of the City*. New York: Farrar & Rinehart, 1937.
_____. "Foreword." *The Fall of the City*. New York: Farrar & Rinehart, 1937.
_____. "Foreword." *Nobodaddy*. Cambridge, MA: Dunster House, 1926.
_____. "Foreword." *Scratch*. Boston: Houghton Mifflin, 1971.

_____. *The Great American Fourth of July Parade*. Pittsburgh: University of Pittsburgh Press, 1975.
_____. *Herakles*. Boston: Houghton Mifflin, 1967.
_____. *The Irresponsibles*. New York: Duell, Sloan and Pearce, 1940.
_____. "The Isolation of the American Artist." *A Continuing Journey*. Boston: Houghton Mifflin, 1967, 176–87.
_____. *J.B.* Boston: Houghton Mifflin, 1957.
_____. *The Letters of Archibald MacLeish*. Ed. R.H. Winnick. Boston: Houghton Mifflin, 1990.
_____. *Reflections*. Eds. Bernard Drabeck and Helen E. Ellis. Foreword by Richard Wilbur. Amherst: University of Massachusetts Press, 1986.
MacNeice, Louis. *The Poetry of W. B. Yeats*. London: Faber and Faber, 1941.
Malcolm, Janet. "Justice to J.D. Salinger." *New York Review of Books*, 48, no. 10, June 21, 2001. Online at www.nybooks.com/articles/14272.
Malin, Irving. "Underworld." *The Review of Contemporary Fiction*, 27, no. 3. Online at www.centerforbookculture.org/review/bookreviews/97_3/reviews_97_3.html.
Mann, Neil. "*A Vision*: Ideas of God and Man." *Yeats Annual*, 8 (1991): 157–75.
Martin, W. R. "A Note on Pater's *The Renaissance* and Some Later Yeats Poems." *Canadian Journal of Irish Studies* 15.1 (1989): 20–22.
Meihuizen, Nicholas. "Yeats, Jung and the Integration of Archetypes." *Theoria: A Journal of Studies in the Arts, Humanities and Social Sciences*, 80 (1992): 101–16.
Matthews, T.S. *Great Tom*. New York: Harper & Row, 1974.
Maugham, William Somerset. *The Razor's Edge*. New York: Doubleday, 1944.
McDermont, Robert A. "Introduction," *The Spirit of Modern India*. Ed. Robert A McDermont and V. S. Naravane. New York: Thomas Y. Crowell, 1974, 6–7.
McDiarmid, Lucy. "W. H. Auden's 'In the Year of My Youth...'" *Review of English Studies. New Series*, 29, no. 115 (1978): 267–312.
McNelly Kearns, Cleo. *T.S. Eliot and Indic Traditions. A Study in Poetry and Belief*. Cambridge: Cambridge University Press, 1987.
Mendelson, Edward. *Early Auden*. London: Faber and Faber, 1981.
_____. *Later Auden*. London: Faber and Faber, 1999.
Menon, Sumitra. Lecture given to the Santa Barbara Vedanta Society, Feb. 24, 1991, on "J.D. Salinger and Vedanta." Society archives.
Menuhin, Yehudi. *Unfinished Journey*. New York: Knopf, 1977.
Miller, Henry. *The Air-Conditioned Nightmare*. New York: New Directions, 1945.
_____. Letter of Henry Miller to Ursula Bond, June 16, 1962, archives of the Vedanta Society of Southern California.
Minow-Pinsky, Makiko. "'How then does light return to the world after the eclipse of the sun? Miraculously, frailty': A Psychoanalytic Interpretation of Woolf's Mysticism." *Virginia Woolf and the Arts*. New York: Pace University Press, 1997.
Moeller, Carol J. "Moral Attention: Toward a Liberationist Ethics of Everyday Life." Online at www.soar.moravian.edu/props/AlmMoe98prop.html.
Mohanty, Satya P. "Can Our Values Be Objective?" *Aesthetics in a Multicultural Age*. Ed. Emory Elliott, Lou Freitas Caton, and Jeffrey Rhyne. London: Oxford University Press, 2002, 32–60.
_____. *Literary Theory and the Claims of History: Postmodernism, Objectivity, Multicultural Politic*. Ithaca, NY: Cornell University Press, 1997.
Monroe, Harriet. "H.D." *Poets and Their Art*. New York: Macmillan, 1932.
Mookerji, Radha Kumud. *Ancient Indian Education*. Delhi: Motilal Banarsidass, 1969.
Moore, George. *Hail and Farewell: Vale*. London: William Heinemann, 1914.
Moore, Madeline. *The Short Season between Two Silences: The Mystical and the Political in the Novels of Virginia Woolf*. Winchester, MA: Allen and Unwin, 1984.

Morgan, Ted. *Maugham*. New York: Simon and Schuster, 1980.
Morris, Theresa. SUNY New Paltz, presentation at the SUNY Oneonta Philosophy Conference on March 31, 2000. Online at //organizations.oneonta.edu/philosc/abstracts 01.html.
Murdoch, Iris. *Existentialists and Mystics: Writings on Philosophy and Literature*. London: Penguin, 1998.
_____. "Interview." Online at ParisReview.com, www.theparisreview.org/viewinterview.php/prmMID/2313
_____. *Metaphysics as a Guide to Morals*. London: Penguin Press, 1998.
_____. *The Sovereignty of Good*. London: Routledge and Kegan Paul, 1970.
Murshid, K. S. "A Note on T. S. Eliot's Debt to the East." *Venture* 5, no. I (June 1968): 43–50.
Nageswara, G. "The Upanishads and The Waste Land." *Literary Studies* (Ed. K.P.K. Menon), 2 (1972): 75–91.
Nehru, J. *The Discovery of India*. London: Oxford University Press, 1995.
Nicholson, Harold. *Diaries and Letters, 1930–1939*. Ed. Nigel Nicolson. London: Collins, 1966.
Nietzsche, Friedrich. *On the Genealogy of Morality*. Indianapolis, IN: Hackett Publishing, 1998.
Norton Anthology of Modern Poetry. 2nd. Ed. Richard Ellmann and Robert O'Clair. New York: Norton, 1988.
Nussbaum, Martha C. "The Window: Knowledge of Other Minds in Virginia Woolf's To the Lighthouse." *New Literary History*, 26, no. 4 (fall 1995): 731–53.
Olcott, Henry S. *The Buddhist Catechism*. 36th Ed. London: Theosophical Society, 1903.
Olney, James. *The Rhizome and the Flower: The Perennial Philosophy — Yeats and Jung*. Berkeley: University of California Press, 1980.
_____. "Sex and the Dead: Daimones of Yeats and Jung." *Studies in the Literary Imagination* (Atlanta: Georgia State University), 14, no. 1 (Spring 1981): 43–60.
O'Reilly, David. "Faith" (*Philadelphia Inquirer* Section), Sunday, June 18, 2000, 1, 6.
Palkhivala, Nani A. *India's Priceless Heritage*. Bombay: Bharatiya Vidya Bhavan, 1980.
Pandit, Sri. *Upanishads*. www.vedah.com/org2/literature/pdf_docs/Upanishads.pdf
Patri, Umesh. *Hindu Scriptures and American Transcendentalists*. New Delhi, India: Intellectual Pub. House, 1987.
Paz, Octavio. *Light of India*. New York: Harcourt, Brace, 1997.
Perl, Jeffrey, and Andrew P. Tuck. "The Hidden Advantage of Tradition: On the Significance of T. S. Eliot's Indic Studies." *Philosophy East and West*, 35 (April 1985): 116–31.
Piazza, Paul. *Christopher Isherwood: Myth and Anti-Myth*. New York: Columbia University Press, 1978.
Polanyi, Michael. *Knowing and Being*. Ed. with an introduction by Marjorie Grene. Chicago: University of Chicago Press, 1969.
_____. *Personal Knowledge. Towards a Post Critical Philosophy*. London: Routledge, 1958. Reprint. 1998.
_____. *The Study of Man*. Chicago: University of Chicago Press, 1964.
_____. *The Tacit Dimension*, New York: Anchor Books, 1967.
_____, and Prosch, Harry. *Meaning*. Chicago: University of Chicago Press, 1975.
Prabuddhaprana, Pravrajika. *Tantine: The Life of Josephine MacLeod*. Dakshineswar, Calcutta: Sri Sarada Math, 1990.
Pratt, Mary Louise. "Arts of the Contact Zone." *Ways of Reading*. 5th ed. Ed. David Bartholomae and Anthony Petroksk. New York: Bedford/St. Martin's, 1999. Online at web.nwe.ufl.edu/~stripp/2504/pratt.html.

Pyarelal, P. *Thoreau, Tolstoy, and Gandhi.* New Delhi: Oxford University Press, 1948.
Raju, P.T "The Principle of Four-Cornered Negation in Indian Philosophy." *The Review of Metaphysics,* June 1954. Online at www.aarweb.org/syllabus/syllabi/g/gier/307/dialectic.htm.
Ramaswami, Dewan Bahadur. *Indian Culture and the Modern Age.* Sastri, India: Annamalai University, 1981.
Rayapati, J.P. Rao. *Early American Interest in Vedanta.* New York: Asia Publishing House, 1973.
_____. "T. S. Eliot's Use of the Upanishads." *Aryan Path,* 38, no. 6 (June 1967): 266–71.
Rich, Adrienne. *A Change of World.* New Haven: Yale University Press, 1951.
Rubenstein, Roberta. "Fixing the Past: Yearning and Nostalgia in Woolf and Lessing." *Woolf and Lessing: Breaking the Mold.* Ed. Ruth Saxton and Jean Tobin. New York: St Martin's Press, 1994, 16.
Salinger, J.D. *Franny and Zooey.* New York: Little, Brown, 1991.
Sastri, Nilakanta, and G. Srinivasachari. *Advanced History of India.* Bombay: Allied Publishers, 1970.
Sawyer, Dana. *Aldous Huxley: A Biography.* New York: Crossroads Publishing, 2002.
_____. "'What Kind of a Mystic Was Aldous Huxley Anyway?' A Brief Appraisal of His Mysticism." *Aldous Huxley Annual,* 2 (2002): 207–18.
Schrödinger, E. C. *Science Theory and Man.* New York: Dover, 1957.
Schwerdt, Lisa. *Isherwood's Fiction.* London: Macmillan, 1989.
Scott, Lynda. "Similarities between Virginia Woolf and Doris Lessing." *Deep South,* 3, no. 2 (Winter 1997). Online at www.otago.ac.nz/DeepSouth/vol3no2/scott.html.
Seiden, M. *William Butler Yeats: The Poet as Mythmaker 1865–1939.* East Lansing: Michigan State University Press, 1962.
Sena, Vinod. "W. B. Yeats and the Indian Way of Wisdom." *New Quest* 62 (1969): 76–79.
Shrivastava, S.N.L. *Sankara and Bradley: A Comparative and Critical Study.* Delhi: Motilal Banarsidass, 1968.
Singhal, D.P. *India and World Civilization.* London: Macmillan, 1993.
Smith, Huston. *The Religions of Man.* New York: Harper & Row, 1964).
_____. *The World's Religions.* San Francisco: Harper, 1999.
Sormon, Guy. *The Genius of India.* London: Macmillan, 2001.
Spender, Stephen. *The Destructive Element.* London: Jonathan Cape, 1937.
_____. *Journals.* Franklin, PA: Franklin Press, 1985.
_____. *Letters to Christopher.* Ed. Lee Bartlett. Santa Barbara, CA: Black Sparrow Press, 1980.
_____. *Poems.* New York: Random House, 1934.
_____. *T. S. Eliot.* New York: Viking, 1976.
_____. *The Thirties and After.* New York: Random House, 1978.
_____. *World within World.* London: Hamish Hamilton, 1951.
Sri, P.S. "The Influence of Vedanta on the Mature Poetry of Yeats." *Swansea Review,* (1994): 493–510.
_____. *T.S. Eliot, Vedanta and Buddhism.* Vancouver: University of British Columbia, 1985.
_____. "Yeats and Mohini Chatterjee." *Yeats Annual,* 11 (1995): 61–76.
Srivastava, Narsingh. "The Ideas of the Bhagavad-Gita in Four Quartets of T. S. Eliot." *Comparative Literature,* 19, no. 2 (spring 1977): 97–108.
Strong, L. A. G. "'Æ'—a Practical Mystic." *Listener,* 53 (10 March 1955) 427–28.
Subhas, Sarkar. "The Impact of Indian Philosophy on T. S. Eliot." *Modern Review,* 761 (May 1970): 366–68.

Summerfield, Henry. *That Myriad Minded Man: A Biography of G.W. Russell "Æ" 1867–1935*. Gerrards Cross, UK: Colin Smythe, 1975.
Summers, Claude. *Christopher Isherwood*. New York: Unger, 1980.
Taylor, Edmund. *Richer by Asia*. London: Secker and Warburg, 1948.
Thoreau, H. D. *Journal*, 1:55. The Journal is published as vols. 7–20 in *The Writings of Henry David Thoreau*, ed. Bradford Torrey and Francis H. Allen, 20 vols. 1906. Reprint. New York: AMS Press, 1968).
_____. *The Writings of Henry D. Thoreau — Walden*. Princeton, NJ: Princeton University Press, 1989.
Toynbee, Arnold. *One World and India*. New Delhi: Indian Council for Cultural Relations, 1960.
Torwesten, Hans. *Vedanta — Heart of Hinduism*. New York: Grove, 1991.
Traversi, Derek. *T. S. Eliot: The Longer Poems*. New York: Harcourt Brace Jovanovich, 1976.
Upanishads. Trans. by Shree Purohit Swami and W. B. Yeats. London: Faber and Faber, 1937.
Upanishads. Trans. by Swami Prabhavananda and Frederick Manchester. New York: New American Library, 1957.
Updike, John. "Anxious Days for the Glass Family." *New York Times*. September 17, 1961. Online at partners.nytimes.com/books/ 98/09/13/specials/salinger-franny01.html.
Vedanta for the Western World. Ed. Christopher Isherwood. Los Angeles: Marcel Rodd, 1949.
Vico, Giambattista. *The New Science*. 3rd Ed. New York: Penguin, 1999.
Walsh, Thomas. *Contemporary Authors: New Revised Series*. 147 vols. Detroit: Gale Research, 1990. Vols. 28, 93.
Watts, Alan. *The Legacy of Asia and Western Man*. London: John Murry, 1940.
_____. Introduction. *Spiritual Practices of India*. Ed. Frederic Spiegelberg. Westport, CT: Greenwood Press, 1951.
Weiss, Jeffrey. "Spiderman's Theme Appears in Many Faiths." *Raleigh News and Observer*. Friday, July 9, 2004, 5E, syndicated from *Dallas Morning News*.
Wilde, Alan. *Christopher Isherwood*. New York: Twayne, 1971.
Wilder, Thornton. *The Eighth Day*. New York: Harper & Row, 1967.
Williams, Charles. *The Descent of the Dove*. New York: Meridian Books, 1956.
Wilson, Lois. *Lois Remembers*. New York: Al-Anon Family Group Headquarters, 1979.
Woodroffe, John. *Is India Civilized — Essays on Indian Culture*. London: Penguin, 1991.
Woolf, Virginia. *The Diary of Virginia Woolf*. Vol. IV. Ed. Anne Oliver Bell. London: Hogarth Press, 1982. Diary entry of 1 February 1932.
_____. *Moments of Being — Unpublished Autobiographical Writings*. Ed. Jeanne Schulkind. New York: Harcourt Brace Jovanovich, 1976.
_____. *To the Lighthouse*. New York: Harvest, 1989.
Wyatt, C.S. "Existentialism and Hegel." Online at www.tameri.com/csw/exist/hegel.asp.
Yeats, W.B. *Autobiographies*. London: Macmillan, 1955.
_____. *Essays and Introductions*. London and New York: Macmillan, 1961.
_____. "Introduction." Gitanjali (aka Patangili), *Song Offerings*. Trans. by Rabindranath Tagore. New York and London: Macmillan, 1912, 1913.
_____. "Upanishads." State University of New York at Stony Brook University Libraries. West Campus — William Butler Yeats Microfilmed Manuscripts and Correspondence Collection.
_____. *A Vision*. 1937. Reprint. London: Macmillan, 1962.
_____. *A Vision: An Explanation of Life Founded upon the Writings of Giraldus and upon Certain Doctrines Attributed to Kusta Ben Luka*. London: T. Werner Laurie, 1925.
Yutang, Lin. *The Wisdom of China and India*. New York: Modern Library, 1955.

Zaehner, R.C. *The Bhagavad-Gita with a Commentary on the Original Sources.* New York: Oxford University Press, 1973.
____. *Concordant Discord.* Oxford: Clarendon, 1970.
Zimmer, Heinrich. *The Philosophies of India.* New York: Pantheon, 1951.

Index

Achebe, Chinua 88–91; "Dead Man's Path" 88–91
"Adonis and the Alphabet" 43, 53
Æ [AE] (George Russell) 93, 98–103, 107, 108, 115; "Dusk" 102; "The Hour of Twilight" 100; *A Song and Its Fountains* 102–103
After Strange Gods 104
Agape (vision of) 10, 66, 116
The Age of Anxiety 102
Ah-effect 48
Aiken, Conrad 32, 131
Air Raid 130, 135
Along the Road 118
Alyn, Kirk 1–2
The Angel That Troubled the Waters 57, 158–59
Angels in America 159
Ansky, S. 157; *A Dybbuk* 157
Antigone 73–75
Appearance and Reality 104
Aquinas, Thomas 118
Aristotle 18
An Armada of Thirty Whales 47
"Art" 34, 40, 56
"Art of the Contact Zone" 88–91
The Ascent of F6 (with Isherwood) 135
The Ascent of F6 (with W.H. Auden) 135
The Ascent of Humanity 116
Auden, W.H. 23–62, 97, 99, 102, 110, 115–118, 154; *The Age of Anxiety* 102; *The Ascent of F6* (with Isherwood) 135; *A Change of World* 58; "The Dyer's Hand," *Anchor Review* 58; *The Dyer's Hand* 59; "The Good Life" 26; "The Group Movement and the Middle Classes" 117; "The Guilty Vicarage" 33; "In a Time of War" 84; "In the Year of My Youth" 115, 117; "Interview with W.H. Auden" 32; "A Novel by Goethe" 31; "An Outline for Writing" 56; "Introduction" *An Armada of Thirty Whales* 47; "Introduction" *The Living Thoughts of Kierkegaard* 77; "Introduction" *Shakespeare: The Sonnets* 49, 54; "Letter to Lord Byron" 77; "Making, Knowing, and Judging" 44, 58; "Nature, History, and Poetry" 37; "The Protestant Mystics" 50, 54–55, 117; "Psychology and Art Today" 57; "Review of Open House" 34; "Robert Frost" 59; "The Secret Agent" 116–117; "A Summer Night" 117; "Today's Poet" 40; "The Virgin and the Dynamo" 44; "Walter de la Mere" 26, 41; "The World of the Sagas" 40; "Writing," *A Certain World* 29
Awe-sociations 23–61

Beckett, Samuel 25, 78
Benét, Stephen Vincent 140; "The Devil and Daniel Webster" 140
Benjamin, Walter 160
Besant, Annie 14
Bhagavad-Gita 8, 11, 15, 16, 18, 20, 42, 56, 66, 71, 87, 97, 98, 104, 109
Blake, William 131
Blavatsky, Helena 13–21, 93; *Secret Doctrine* 14
Bradley, F.H. 104; *Appearance and Reality* 104
Brahman 16, 164; Sat, Chit, Ananda 16
Brave New World 30, 148
Brecht, Bertolt 160; *Mother Courage* 160; *Threepenny Opera* 159
A Bright Room Called Day 159
Bruce, Lenny 147
Bruegel 148; *The Triumph of Death* 148
Buddha/Buddhism 106, 108, 143, 164
Buddhist Catechism 108
Burnt Norton 83, 104

Campbell, Joseph 109
The Catcher in the Rye 142
Caudwell, Christopher (Christopher St-John-Sprigg) 84, 104; *Illusion and Reality* 84, 104
Cave 21
A Change of World 58

Chatterjee, Mohini 93, 95, 98; *Man: Fragments of Forgotten History* 95
Churchill, Caryl 160
Cohn, Roy 159–160
Combinatoire 20, 83–84, 89
Coming Up for War 151
Conrad, Joseph 105; *Lord Jim* 105
Crest Jewel of Discrimination 15, 164
"The Culture Industry" 76–80, 148, 164

Dame Kind (vision of) 54
Davenport, Guy 152–157; "The Death of Picasso" 152–157
"Dead Man's Path" 88–91
"The Death of Picasso" 152–157
DeLillo Don 113, 127, 147–152; *Underworld* 113, 127, 147–152
Derbyshire, John 118; "What Happened to Aldous Huxley?" 118
The Destructive Element 105
"The Devil and Daniel Webster" 140
Dialectics 18–19, 63
Diaries 115
"Do What You Will" 30
Donaldson, Scott 131
Doors of Perception 15
Dowden, Edward 100
"The Dry Salvages" 104
"Dusk" 102
A Dybbuk 157, 159
"The Dyer's Hand," *Anchor Review* 58
"The Dyer's Hand," *The Dyer's Hand* 59

Eckhart, Meister 35, 101
Eden 28, 33, 35, 39, 46, 50
Edison, Thomas 15
"Education of an Amphibian" 43
The Eighth Day 36, 109
Eliot, T.S. 8, 32, 37, 83, 104–106; *After Strange Gods* 104; *Burnt Norton* 83, 104; "The Dry Salvages" 104; "The Fire Sermon" 106–107; "The Interpretation of Primitive Ritual" 104; "Review of (in *The Egoist*) Brahmadarsanam *or Intuition of the Absolute*" (Acharya) 104; *The Waste Land* 104–106, 124, 148, 152; "What the Thunder Said" 105
The Emergence of Man 27
Emerson, R.W. 6, 8, 17, 20–21, 45–46
Empson, William 109; Oversoul 17
Eros, Vision of 49–50
Essays and Introductions 96
Existentialists... 85, 86

The Fall of the City 130, 135, 136–137
Faulkner, William 144
Fierstein, Harvey 160
Finnegans Wake 108
"The Fire Sermon" 106–107
The First and Last Freedom 39, 46, 102
"Foreheads Villainous Low" 78

Foreman, Richard 160
Forster, E.M. 109, 112–113; *Howards End* 109
Fragments 57
Franny and Zooey 142
Freud, Sigmund 125

García Márquez, Gabriel 113, 143–146; Magic Realism 144–146; *One Hundred Years of Solitude* 113, 143–146
Genealogy of Morals 39, 69–74
Gibbon, Monk 100
Gitanjali/Patangali 15; Yogi Aphorisms 21
God-Awe Correlative 42, 44, 47, 48, 52, 58, 60
Goethe, Johann Wolfgang von 79; *Weltschmerz* 79; *Werther* 79
The Golden Notebook 122–127, 147
"The Good Life" 26
Gospel of Ramakrishna 109
The Great American Fourth of July Parade 141
Grey Eminence 163
"The Group Movement and the Middle Classes" 117
Guare, John 160
"The Guilty Vicarage" 33

Halley's Comet 5–6
Hare, David 160
Harrison, Thomas J. 5
Hawthorne, Nathaniel 145; *The House of the Seven Gables* 145
Hazleton, Lesley 122
Heard, Gerald 20, 24, 26–28, 38, 40, 64, 97, 99, 115–118, 119; *The Ascent of Humanity* 116; *The Emergence of Man* 27; "The History of Ideas or How We Got Separate" 116; *The Social Substance of Religion* 116
Hegel, Georg Wilhelm Friedrich 3, 6, 18–19, 20, 63, 89, 104; Dialectics 18–19, 63; *Philosophy of History* 104
Heraclites 104, 152–157; *Fragments* 57
Herakles 40
Hesse, Herman 142; *Siddhartha* 142
"The History of Ideas or How We Got Separate" 116
Hogarth Press 112
"'The Holy Refusal': A Vedantic Interpretation of J.D. Salinger's Silence" 164–165
Horkheimer and Adorno 76–80, 148, 164; "The Culture Industry" 76–80, 148, 164
Hornby, Nick 33
"The Hour of Twilight" 100
The House of the Seven Gables 145
Howards End 109
Huxley, Aldous 1, 5, 8, 10, 15, 20, 23–62, 76–80, 99, 102, 115–122, 149; "Adonis and the Alphabet" 43, 53; *Along the Road* 118; "Art" 34, 40, 56; *Brave New World* 30, 148; "Do What You Will" 30; *Doors of Perception* 15; "Education of an Amphibian 43; "Foreheads Villainous Low" 78; *Grey Eminence* 163; *Island* 15; "Knowledge and

Understanding" 39, 45, 46, 70; *Literature and Science* 43–44, 57; "Man and Religion" 24, 54; Minimum Working Hypothesis 11, 67; "Pascal" 42; "Seven Meditations" 38; *Texts and Pretexts* 25, 34, 41, 50–52, 53, 56; *Themes and Variations* 141; *Time Must Have a Stop* 118–122; "Tragedy and the Whole Truth" 31; Upward/downward transcendence 10; "Vulgarity in Literature" 51, 52; "Writers and Readers" 77
Huxley, Julian 118
Huxley, Maria 122

Illusion and Reality 84, 104
"In a Time of War" 84
"In the Year of My Youth" 115, 117
"The Interpretation of Primitive Ritual" 104
"Interview..." 85
"Interview with W.H. Auden" 32
The Irresponsibles 137
Isherwood, Christopher 1, 20, 57, 99, 110, 112; *The Ascent of F6* (with W.H. Auden) 135
Island 15
Istgeist /Isness 9, 24, 42, 44, 58, 70–74, 82

Jameson, Fredric 3, 6, 8, 20, 80–84, 89; *Combinatoire* 20, 83–84, 89; "Magical Narratives" 80; *Marxism and Form* 80
Jaurretche, Colleen 107
JB 138–139
Johnson, Toby 109, 164; *The Myth of the Great Secret* 109
Joyce, James 45, 68–69, 107–108; *Finnegans Wake* 108; *Portrait of the Artist as a Young Man* 45, 68–69, 107; "Review of *Soul of a People*" by H. Fielding Hall 108; *Stephen Hero* 108; *Ulysses* 108
Jung, Carl 3, 24, 97, 118, 124
"Justice to J.D. Salinger" 143

Kaballah 159
Kabir 101
Kane, Julie 110; "Varieties of Mystical Experiences in the Writings of Virginia Woolf" 110
Kant, Immanuel 8
Kearns, Mckelly 106
Kierkegaard, Søren 97
Knikhilananda, Swami 109, 141; *Gospel of Ramakrishna* 109
"Knowledge and Understanding" 39, 45, 46, 70
Kramer, Larry 160
Krishnamurti, Jiddu 14, 21, 39, 45, 46, 102; *The First and Last Freedom* 39, 46, 102
Kushner, Tony 130, 157–161; *Angels in America* 159; *A Bright Room Called Day* 159; *A Dybbuk* 159; *Perestroika* 159

Laing, R.D. 126

Lavine, T.Z. 19
Leibniz, Gottfried 163
Lessing, Doris 110, 122–127, 147; *The Golden Notebook* 122–127, 147; Sufism 122; *Under My Skin* 124
"Letter to Lord Byron" 77
Lindsay, Vachel 129
Lita, Ana 87; "'Seeing' Human Goodness: Iris Murdoch on Moral Virtue" 87
Literature and Science 43–44, 57
The Living Thoughts of Kierkegaard 77
Lord Jim 105
Ludlam, Charles 160

MacLeish, Archibald 107, 129–141; *Air Raid* 130, 135; *The Fall of the City* 130, 135, 136–137; *The Great American Fourth of July Parade* 141; *Herakles* 40; *The Irresponsibles* 137; *JB* 138–139; *This Music Crept by Me Upon the Waters* 138; *Nobodaddy* 130; *Public Speech* 130; *Scratch* 140–141; *The Trojan Horse* 137
MacNeice, Louis 93, 130
Magic Realism 144–146
"Magical Narratives" 80
"Making, Knowing, and Judging" 44, 58
Malcolm, Janet 143; "Justice to J.D. Salinger" 143
"Man and Religion" 24, 54
Man: Fragments of Forgotten History 95
Marxism and Form 80
Maya 16
McCarthy, Joseph 130, 137
McNally, Terence 160
Melville, Herman 25, 69
Metaphysics as a Guide to Morals 64, 85–90
Minimum Working Hypothesis 10–11, 67, 122
Mitchison, Naomi 115; *Outline for Boys and Girls and Their Parents* 116
Mohanty, Satya 10, 67, 69
Molokoff, Sophia 164–165
Moore, George 99
Moore, Madeline 111; *The Short Season Between Silences: The Mystical and Political in the Writings of Virginia Woolf* 111
Morris, Theresa 50
Mother Courage 160
Murdoch, Iris 50, 64, 85–90; *Existentialists...* 85, 86; "Interview..." 85; *Metaphysics as a Guide to Morals* 64, 85–90; *Sovereignty...* 86
Mute logic 64, 69
The Myth of the Great Secret 109

Nama-Rupa 43
"Nature, History, and Poetry" 37
Neti, neti 18, 96, 111
New Science 10, 23, 40, 64–68, 107
Nicholas of Cusa 18
Nicolson, Harold 115; *Diaries* 115
Nietzsche, Friedrich 8, 39, 45, 64, 69–74, 81,

105, 119; *Genealogy of Morals* 39, 69–74; *Ressentiment* 70–74, 81
Nine Stories 142
No-mind 45, 48, 83, 106
Nobodaddy 130
"A Novel by Goethe" 31

Olcott, Henry: *Buddhist Catechism* 108
One Hundred Years of Solitude 113, 143–146
"Open House" 34
Orwell, George 151; *Coming Up for War* 151
Outline for Boys and Girls and Their Parents 116
"An Outline for Writing" 56
Oversoul 17

"Pascal" 42
Pattainaik, Dipti 165; "'The Holy Refusal': A Vedantic Interpretation of J.D. Salinger's Silence" 164–165
The People, Yes 141
Perestroika 159
Personal Knowledge 47, 163
Phaedrus 20
Philosophy of History 104
Plato 16, 20, 50, 152; Cave 21; *Phaedrus* 20
Polanyi, Michael 8, 47, 61, 74, 152, 163; *Personal Knowledge* 47, 163; *The Tacit Dimension* 74, 163
Poma, Guaman 88
Portrait of the Artist as a Young Man 45, 68–69, 107
Pound, Ezra 130
Prabhavananda, Swami 20
Pratt, Mary Louise 88–91; "Art of the Contact Zone" 88–91
"The Protestant Mystics" 50, 54–55, 117
"Psychology and Art Today" 57
Public Speech 130

Raju, P.T. 18
Reagan, Ronald 159
Ressentiment 70–74, 81
"Review of (in *The Egoist*) Brahmadarsanam or Intuition of the Absolute" (Acharya) 104
"Review of *Soul of a People*" by H. Fielding Hall 108
Richards, I.A. 105
Rickey, Branch 107
Rig Veda 97
The Rising 26
"Robert Frost" 59
"A Room of One's Own" 113
Rushdie, Salmon 63

Salinger, J.D. 141; *The Catcher in the Rye* 142; *Franny and Zooey* 142; *Nine Stories* 142; "Teddy" 142
Sandburg, Carl 129, 141; *The People, Yes* 141
Sartre, Jean-Paul 19
Sat, chit, and ananda 16
Schopenhauer, Arthur 20, 64, 88, 96, 120

Schulkind, Jeanne 110; *Virginia Woolf—Moments of Being—Unpublished Autobiographical Writings* 110
Scratch 140–141
"The Secret Agent" 116–117
Secret Doctrine 14
"'Seeing' Human Goodness: Iris Murdoch on Moral Virtue" 87
"Seven Meditations" 38
Shakespeare, William 36, 85, 107, 119; *The Tempest* 107
Shakespeare: The Sonnets 49, 54
Shankara 8, 11, 15, 18, 164; *Crest Jewel of Discrimination* 15, 164
Shaw, G.B. 15
The Short Season Between Silences: The Mystical and Political in the Writings of Virginia Woolf 111
Shree Purohit Swami 95–96
Siddhartha 142
The Skin of Our Teeth 109
The Social Substance of Religion 116
A Song and Its Fountains 102–103
Sovereignty... 86
Spender, Stephen 105, 106; *The Destructive Element* 105; *T.S. Eliot* 106
Springsteen, Bruce 26; *The Rising* 26
Stephen Hero 108
Stephens, James 99
Stevens, Wallace 129
Stravinsky, Igor 25, 78
Sufism 122
"A Summer Night" 117

The Tacit Dimension 74, 163
Tagore, Rabindranath 94
Tat twam asi (Thou Art That/That Art Thou) 37, 65
"Teddy" 142
The Tempest 107
Texts and Pretexts 25, 34, 41, 50–52, 53, 56
Themes and Variations 141
Theosophy 6, 13–21, 93
This Music Crept by Me Upon the Waters 138
Thou Art That/That Art Thou (*tat twam asi*) 37, 65, 96
Threepenny Opera 159
Tibetan Book of the Dead (aka Bardo Thodal) 119, 121
Tillich, Paul 86, 97
Time Must Have a Stop 118–122
To the Lighthouse 109–115, 123
"Today's Poet" 40
The Tower 94
"Tragedy and the Whole Truth" 31
The Triumph of Death 148
The Trojan Horse 137
T.S. Eliot 106

Ulysses 108
Under My Skin 124

Underworld 113, 127, 147–152
Updike, John 143
Upward/downward transcendence 10

"Varieties of Mystical Experiences in the Writings of Virginia Woolf" 110
Verbal artifact 24
Vico, Giambattista 7, 8, 10, 23, 40, 45, 63, 64–68, 74, 81, 96, 107, 153; Mute Logic 64, 69; *New Science* 10, 23, 40, 64–68, 107
"The Virgin and the Dynamo" 44
Virginia Woolf — Moments of Being — Unpublished Autobiographical Writings 110
A Vision 93–98
Vogel, Paula 160
"Vulgarity in Literature" 51, 52

"Walter de la Mere" 26, 41
The Waste Land 104–106, 124, 148, 152
Webster, Daniel 140
Weil, Simone 50
Weltschmerz 79
Werther 79
"What Happened to Aldous Huxley?" 118
"What the Thunder Said" 105
"When I Heard the Learned Astronomer" 48
Whitman, Walt 48, 56; "When I Heard the Learned Astronomer" 48

Wilde, Oscar 15
Wilder, Thornton 9, 36, 57, 129, 158; *The Angel That Troubled the Waters* 158–159; *The Eighth Day* 36, 109; "Foreword," *The Angel That Troubled the Waters* 57; *The Skin of Our Teeth* 109
Williams, Raymond 159
Williams, Tennessee 160
Wilson, Edmund 130
The Winding Stair 94
Wombland 45
Woolf, Virginia 5, 84, 109–115, 124; Hogarth Press 112; "A Room of One's Own" 113; *To the Lighthouse* 109–115, 123
"The World of the Sagas" 40
Wright, Frank Lloyd 15
"Writers and Readers" 77
"Writing," *A Certain World* 29

Yeats, W.B. 13, 61, 93–98, 115; *Essays and Introductions* 96; *The Tower* 94; *A Vision* 93–98; *The Winding Stair* 94
Yogi Aphorisms 21

Zeitgeist 3, 24, 44, 80, 154
Zen Koan 45–48

www.ingramcontent.com/pod-product-compliance
Lightning Source LLC
Chambersburg PA
CBHW032103300426
44116CB00007B/869